A LUCKY BOY FROM BUFFALO

A LUCKY BOY
FROM BUFFALO

June, 2014

To Danny & Will —
 Listen up — your future is
bright.

All the best,
Patrick Blewett

PATRICK BLEWETT

ISBN: 978-0-615-87763-1

Printed in the United States of America

Editor: Janet Martin
Cover and Jacket Design: Linda Berry
Book Design: Lisa Allen
Printer: Sheridan Books, Inc.

*To my daughters, Michelle and Joanna,
and my grandchildren, Tyler, Joelle, and Bridget*

Acknowledgments

As this was my first experience writing a book, I quickly realized I would need all the help I could get. Fortunately, my long-time friend Tom Hudson had been writing books for several years so I turned to him for assistance. He graciously provided me with the names of his team, and their help has been invaluable.

I'd like to thank my editor Janet Martin for her knowledge and encouragement for me to stick with it. At first I wondered if I needed an editor but then I determined that if I self-edited the book, I'd naturally agree with everything I had written. That would have been a mistake. Janet has brought a high level of professionalism and dedication that has enhanced the quality of the book tremendously.

I'm also thankful to Lisa Allen, whose responsibility was the page layout and a second edit. She took my manuscript and transformed it into a book with pages that are pleasing to the eye, making the book attractive and welcoming.

Linda Berry designed the book cover, taking basic ideas and concepts and making them come to life. Her creativity in designing the cover invites one to come inside the book for a visit. Who says you can't judge a book by its cover?

John Beall from Sheridan Press provided me with technical assistance, explaining the process that takes the finished manuscript and converts it to an actual book. It's been a learning process for me, and John has been an excellent instructor.

Lastly, I'd like to thank my wife for enduring me throughout the better part of a year from start to finish. She spent many lonely nights while I worked in my office writing, and her selflessness is appreciated.

Contents

Introduction

Several years ago I decided that it might be interesting to write a memoir detailing various aspects of my life. After several false starts, I finally got serious about writing the book in the fall of 2012 and finished in the summer of 2013. My intent wasn't to publish a book for general consumption but to structure a narrative in concise form as a gift to my children, grandchildren, other relatives, and friends. However, my one condition is that our grandchildren not be allowed to read the book until they are at least eighteen years old.

For most of my life, I've been a today or tomorrow person and rarely a yesterday man. As such, it took deep digging into my memory for details, particularly as they related to my childhood. At times I would sit at the computer and laugh out loud; while at others, I'd become melancholy. My life has been a roller coaster ride and never dull. After having rollicking fun resulting in a disappointing high school record, I joined the U.S. Army for four years just two months after turning seventeen. I credit that experience with steering me in the right direction. Then too, I've had the good fortune to meet business people who had confidence in me and provided opportunities. Those kinds of people I tried not to disappoint, and the opportunities I tried hard not to squander. True, I've had successes and failures; but even in failure, I looked ahead with confidence that everything would work out. And it did.

The very best part of my life has been the last forty-four years married to my wife, Terry. She has been my inspiration—providing insight, love, and caring when I most needed it. She's always been by my side, my anchor in calm and turbulent seas, and my very best friend.

My first sixty-five years have been a fun ride. I invite you to hop aboard and share the journey with me.

Chapter 1

The Early Years
1947 to 1958

Buffalo, New York—often referred to as The Queen City, The Nickel City, and The City of Light—was the eighth largest city in the United States in 1900, and now, in 2013, is ranked number seventy-two. It is a city whose fortunes have risen and fallen, where the population swelled from 352,000 in 1900 to 580,000 in 1950 and declined to 261,000 in 2012.

It's a place in history where William McKinley, the twenty-fifth president of the United States, was assassinated and Theodore Roosevelt was sworn into office; where Grover Cleveland was sheriff and mayor before becoming governor of New York and the twenty-second and twenty-forth president; where Millard Fillmore co-founded the University of Buffalo and Buffalo General Hospital before he became our thirteenth president. It's where Chief Justice John Roberts was born.

Buffalo is located in western New York. It lies on the eastern shore of Lake Erie and is positioned at the head of the Niagara River across from Fort Erie, Ontario. Pierce Arrow luxury automobiles were manufactured in Buffalo, and during the 1900s, the city became a major railroad hub. In the early twentieth century, local mills benefited from hydroelectric power generated by the Niagara River. In fact, the city at one time featured the largest grain-milling center in the country as well as one of the largest steel mills. Buffalo earned the nickname City of Light because it boasted the first widely spread system of electric streetlights in the United States.

Buffalo: all this and more. Buffalo is the place where I was born.

I came into the world on a bitter wintry day with ominous dark clouds swirling in the sky, a fiercely sharp wind, and the

4

strong scent of snow in the air. While I'm not certain about the weather, it was November, and it was Buffalo, so I'm probably right. The year was 1947. The date was the 18th.

My parents named me Patrick since my older brother carried on the name of Timothy. He was Timothy III, and it would have been too confusing to have Timothy Jr., Timothy III, and Timothy IV in one household. Five years later my sister came along and she was named Patrice. Two Tims and two Pats created enough confusion.

My family lived on a small street off Englewood Avenue, three blocks from Main Street and four blocks from Kenmore Avenue in north Buffalo. Evadene was an attractive street with eight small houses separated by driveways. Large elm trees planted in front of each house provided a beautiful leafy canopy over the street. All but one of the houses was constructed of wood with clapboard exteriors and one-car garages in the rear.

My maternal grandmother, Alice Rast, owned our home at 26 Evadene. It was a modest dwelling, consisting of two bedrooms and one bathroom, a small kitchen, a dining room, and a living room on the first floor. There was also a sun porch, which was later made part of the living room by tearing out the wall, removing the individual exterior windows, and replacing them with a picture window. Before Patrice was born, we rented out the spare bedroom downstairs to a University of Buffalo student from New York named Mike Montemurno. My parents occupied the other first floor bedroom. Once Patrice came along in 1952, Mike moved out and Patrice moved into what was his bedroom. Upstairs the attic framing was finished with plaster walls, and my brother and I occupied a small bedroom measuring approximately ten by ten feet with a straight wall extending from the floor approximately three or four feet in height and a sloped wall following the roofline. Across the hall from our bedroom was an apartment, which was rented to provide the family with additional income. The tenant was Mrs. Weeks, a kindly older woman who, together with her Mexican Chihuahua and later my cat (Tiger), resided there for many years. The apartment had sloped ceilings with one main room, a kitchen, and a bathroom. Between our bedroom and the apartment was a small closet with room for my brother and me to hang our clothes.

Our world seemed all-inclusive—a safe and comfortable cocoon sheltered from danger and surrounded by good neighbors prepared to help if needed. Since the houses were close together and there was no air conditioning, in the warmer months when we ate dinner in the dining room, the Vitellos next door would also be dining about eight feet away, so everyone knew everything about everybody. Of course in the winter there was much more privacy. From an economic, ethnic, and religious point of view, everyone was the same.

I attended kindergarten at Public School Number 83, about two blocks from our house, and grades one through seven at St. Joseph's School, which was three blocks away. Mr. Sellers, the neighborhood grocer, was a block down the street; next door to him was the drycleaner, Mr. Garber; and the University of Buffalo could be reached in a ten-minute walk. If you headed in the other direction, you'd find Held's Bakery (the best rye bread in the world) and Federal Meat Market. The IGA was located across the street.

All kinds of services came right to our door: The milkman delivered to our milk box by the back door; the coal man delivered through a window into the coal bin in the basement; Oscar the German baker drove the streets with his leather purse on his side; the Dairy Queen was three blocks away; and even the Rag Man would peruse the streets from time to time yelling, "Got any rags?" Everything we needed was within walking distance.

One Christmas, Santa gave us children a basketball hoop, which my father promptly erected above the garage door. My brother and I played one-on-one for hours almost every day, with the "court" being the small concrete entry pad to the garage. The boundaries were the garage door, the back of the house, and the lawn (or snow) defining the ten-by-fifteen-foot court. In addition to the one-on-ones, we would often add two or three other players to each side, resulting in a lot of flying elbows and knees and banging into either the garage door or the rear of the house.

Another popular sport was Ping-Pong. One year Santa delivered a Ping-Pong table that we set up in the basement. My brother and I played often and had many neighborhood friends for doubles matches. The "slam" shot was a particular favorite and one that we continuously worked to improve.

Winters in Buffalo

Living in Buffalo across the Niagara River from Ontario, Canada, provided the perfect location to be introduced to the sport of ice hockey. Although Buffalo had an American Hockey

League team, the Bisons, I never attended a game. However, I played street hockey as often as possible on the "rink" on Evadene. When I say "on Evadene," I mean *on* Evadene. The snow plows were pretty good about clearing the streets in the city (even the small side streets), and we'd shovel the biggest mounds of remaining ice and snow to somewhat smooth it out and make the street playable for hockey. Street hockey is an interesting sport. We'd walk off the length, which resembled the length of a real ice hockey rink. Street curbs measured the width, which made for a long and narrow rink. Two mounds of ice at each end defined the goals. We all had our hockey sticks that were heavily shellacked and taped just like the pros. We gathered in front of my house and beat the hell out of the puck trying to get to the goal without ricocheting off the errant parked car encased in snow from the plows.

My most treasured Christmas gift was a pair of ice skates. I was about seven when they appeared under the tree. What a great present! I promptly laced them up on the front porch and walked to the street with ankles bent inward rather like a web-footed duck trying to make it to the rink (about twenty-five feet away). In later years my mother would burst into laughter as she recalled my trying to get down the driveway. An even funnier sight was watching me attempt to skate in the street with the various ruts and bumps of ice. Nonetheless, my ankles withstood the test, and it was an exciting experience to own my very own skates.

When not playing hockey, the neighborhood kids engaged in snowball fights. As there was no shortage of snow, the fights could rage on for hours. Each side picked its players, packed the balls, and threw them as rapidly as possible. Ice balls were particularly exciting, and if you received an incoming one in the head or face, it was something you remembered for a long time. In spite of the aggressive nature of this sport, I don't recall any injuries more serious than a bloody nose, a split lip, or a black-and-blue mark on the face. However, in the summertime, the stakes were higher and the risk of injury greater when we substituted rocks for snowballs. One side would gather in the backyard two doors away, the other team would congregate in my yard, and the rocks would start flying. The worst injury I sustained was a cut on the back of my head requiring two stitches. Shortly thereafter, I gave up the summer version of snowball fights.

During winters in Buffalo, there seemed to be no end to the snow. I suppose when you are only a few feet tall the amount of snow seems especially high, but when I looked out my bedroom window and saw the snow piled up to the top of the streetlight across the street, that confirmed that there *really was* a lot of snow. Of course, the plows helped with the height of the mounds, but nonetheless, this was real snow country. Aside from the snow providing a winter playground for kids, it also provided economic opportunity to me as I went from door to door offering my services to shovel walks and driveways. Business was very good indeed. I had some regular customers who depended on me to provide clearing services, and I shoveled for others from time to time. I have vivid memories of being out at night shoveling with the snow still falling, admiring the beauty of it and enjoying the serenity of the night. I believe I was about seven years old at the time.

Building snow forts was another wonderful pastime. This involved rolling snow into large balls (much like the type used to build a snowman) and stacking them to resemble an igloo. With the snow blocks in place, we hooked up the garden hose and sprayed them until they iced up. We congregated inside the forts and pretended we were in caves. The forts knocked out the wind, and they were actually warm ("warm" being a relative term).

The sport we called "poggying" was an interesting and exhilarating pastime. Although I'm somewhat dismayed that this sport never made it to Olympic status, it was surely an Olympic sport to us. Simply put, the sport of poggying consisted of standing next to a stop sign waiting for an approaching car. Once the car stopped, or at least slowed down, we'd run behind, grab onto the bumper, crouch down, and hang on for dear life. Most drivers seemed annoyed by our hanging onto their bumper, but others gunned it to see how far we could hang on. Either way it was fun. One especially memorable experience was the day Oscar the baker was parked on Evadene delivering baked goods to a neighbor. Out of Oscar's sight, Denny Mason and I ran behind his delivery truck and had a firm grip on the rear bumper. I recall he had recently had the truck painted pale yellow with red bumpers. Oscar finished his business, got into his truck, and took off as we were left sitting in the street with his red bumper in hand. The stunt did not go over well with Oscar.

About this time, television was invented, and it wasn't long before we owned one. It was an RCA Victor model with a small round screen housed in an upright wooden cabinet. The images were in black and white since color television hadn't yet been invented, and we received two channels (2 and 4). *The Howdy Doody Show* came on around 4 p.m., followed by *The Mickey Mouse Club*, which I particularly enjoyed as I had a crush on Darlene. Darlene was one of the Mouseketeers on the show, and I regularly shifted my affections between her and another girl named Cathy. Other favorite shows were *Captain Kangaroo* with Mr. Green Jeans and Buffalo Bob, who actually grew up in Buffalo. The show times were scheduled about the time the streetlights came on, which was our cue to return home. We were happy to come in from the cold to experience those televised events. Even after we had television, however, we continued to sit in the kitchen and listen to our beloved radio shows. *The Lone Ranger* was my favorite.

You may ask, "Who was that masked man?" just as many did on the show. The Lone Ranger was a fictional character, but he seemed larger-than-life to all who listened. He was an ex-Texas Ranger who, along with Tonto, his trusted Indian companion, led the fight for law and order in the American West. I can still hear the trademark sound of "Hi-Yo, Silver! Away!" and the thundering sound of Silver's hoofs as the Lone Ranger rode his white stallion to rescue those in distress. Tonto referred to the Lone Ranger as "Ke-mo-sah-bee," which meant "trusted friend," enhancing his role of a real American Indian. These phrases, along with the mystique of a man wearing a mask who used silver bullets and the exciting William Tell overture at the beginning of each show, made me feel like I was right there with them on the trail.

Each Christmas afternoon and evening we spent at my Grammy and Poppy's (my paternal grandparents) house, where all the relatives gathered from near and far for a big Christmas dinner. My grandparents set up long tables the length of the dining and living rooms, and thirty to forty people attended each year. My grandmother had an oven in the kitchen and a spare in the basement. Since my grandfather had worked for the gas company, he understood the inner workings and ran a separate gas line for a second oven downstairs. Grammy cooked two large turkeys to perfection and served them with mounds of mashed potatoes, stuffing, cranberries, breads, cakes, pies, and all the trimmings. My grandmother hired a woman each year to help with serving the food and with the cleanup. Her name was Robbie, and she lived near Canisius College. Actually, everyone helped with the cleanup, but Robbie was tremendously helpful and a delightful lady. My cousin, Les Lesniak, a lively character full of mischief, made the transformation from IBM executive to Santa Claus and provided abundant gifts and amusement for all.

School Days

I attended St. Joseph's Elementary School on Main Street three blocks from our house. The original brick building facing Main Street had a two-story addition behind it. Almost the entire area around the school was blacktopped with very little grass or plantings except for a grassy backyard. Inside, the classrooms were located on both levels. Adjacent to the school was the church, the rectory, and the convent housing the nuns. Along the right property line, a high chain link fence covered by enormous poplar trees separated the school from our neighbors, the Cantalician Center, which was a school for the mentally handicapped. On the left was the sprawling campus of the University of Buffalo.

I started in first grade and had a wonderful experience, although my grades were never noteworthy—mostly Bs and Cs, with an A thrown in every once in a while. Monsignor Albert Rung was the pastor of St. Joseph's Church, which was next door to the rectory and the school. I recall him as a strict, gruff old German. After he was named Vicar General of the Buffalo Diocese, he seemed even more dour, obstinate, and strict. I tried to steer clear of the good Monsignor as much as possible, but once I became an altar boy, avoiding him was nearly impossible. Associate priests were Father Connelly and Father Wetter. As strict and foreboding as Monsignor Rung was, Fathers Connelly and Wetter were friendly with outgoing personalities. They were involved with the neighborhood kids and were pleasant to be around. From time to time, they drove a group of us to Andersons Custard on Sheraton Drive for a treat. Both were generous with their time and money.

During these years I had the good fortune to meet Don Schugar, the basketball coach. I played on St. Joe's team for several years but was only a so-so player. My brother, who was two years older than I, was much better at the hoops. Like Fathers Connelly and Wetter, Mr. Schugar was a great guy, but he was a demanding coach who made us run drills over and over again until the plays were second nature to us. He also liked to win, and he instilled a strong desire in each player to do his best to attain victory. I remember him taking a few of us fishing a couple of times. Mr. Schugar was an exceptional role model for young boys growing up at St. Joe's. He taught us the importance of teamwork and the discipline that competitive sports provide. Furthermore, he was always available to help us in any way he could.

My third-grade teacher, Sister Pancratia, was an older nun, a bit portly with a gracious smile and a warm personality. I was quite fond of her and secured a regular volunteer job at the convent waxing and buffing the hallway and chapel floors. I particularly liked the idea of spending Saturday mornings working in the convent and became proficient with the big electric floor buffer. In return, I was given a generous lunch and kind words from the nuns. Another nun who left an impression on me was Sister Teresa, who was a tall, younger person with a welcoming smile. She often rolled up her sleeves and played baseball with us on the playground. It was quite a sight to see her at bat with the full nun garb, but she ingratiated herself with us all, and we bonded easily.

St. Joseph's Day, on March 19 each year, was a great event for me. All the students paraded around the statue of St. Joseph in the driveway of the school. Even better, the May Day procession involved altar boys who carried a large statue of Mary, followed by Monsignor Rung and the other priests and all the other students. I recall that a few girls selected from that year's First Communion class placed a crown of flowers on Mary's statue at the end of the ceremony.

My friends were also my classmates since we all walked to school. Vincent Gregg, also called Stubby Gregg, Denny Mason, Gary Staubitz, Norm Paulinni, Mike and Chucky Foran, and Johnny and Danny Phelan, who lived in the brick house on the corner of Evadene and Englewood, were regular guys whom I hung around with much of the time.

My experiences of being an altar boy and helping in the convent made me entertain thoughts of becoming a priest. My exposure to religion was for the most part positive, and becoming a priest seemed like a good idea. I thought about it from time to time but never discussed my thoughts with others. It was just something I would figure out over time. I remember the day I made my First Communion in May 1955. It was a beautiful and deeply religious day for me, and I still have the picture of all the boys and girls on the steps in front of St. Joe's. Of course, smack dab in the middle of all the kids stood Monsignor Rung. Sometimes I wonder if I would have been a good priest, but, of course, now I'll never know.

Summertime

Summers provided wonderful, exciting, and formative events during my youth. My paternal grandfather was retired from Iroquois Gas Company, where he had worked for many years. There was an amusement park in Canada named Crystal Beach, and once a year on "Iroquois Gas Day," Poppy would receive tickets from the gas company and pass them on to the grandchildren. We headed downtown to board the SS *Canandiana* (a passenger ferry typically referred to as The Crystal Beach Boat). The boat was about 200 feet long; it had brass railings and beautiful mahogany trim. After boarding, the first thing we did was to run to an area of the boat to look into a cutout in the main deck and view the engines at work. Then we lined the rails waving at boats passing by until we arrived at our destination, the Crystal Beach Amusement Park in Canada.

The boat ride was a great experience surpassed only by the park rides. The scariest was the Comet, which was a gigantic wooden roller coaster. The Fun House, Magic Carpet, and Bumper Cars were also great fun, but the Comet left indelible— even terrifying—memories.

Adventures at the Lake Shore

I have many happy memories of my boyhood summers at the Lake Shore. Actually, the township was named Derby, located several miles from Lake Erie, but we all referred to it as the Lake Shore. Before I was born, my dad's parents built Target Hot Dog Stand on the corner of Route 5 and a dirt road. At the end of the road, they also built a small wood cabin measuring about ten by ten feet, which contained a bed and a chair. Behind their cabin stood an outhouse and three small wooden outbuildings. Two were used for storage and one was my Uncle Hank's residence.

About one hundred feet from there, our summer home was perched on cinder block piers, its sides covered with tarpaper. The home contained one medium-sized room with a wood stove and two small bedrooms. The outhouse was out back; however, we did have running water inside the house. As a very young boy, we spent a month or so at the cottage to help with the hot dog stand. Actually, I was too young to help, but I do recall eating there and generally hanging around.

Across the road from the Target was the Woodbine Tavern, which was owned by my grandmother's sister, Jewel. It was built on cement piers, had a long wooden bar, several Formica tables with red plastic cushioned chairs, and a great shuffleboard-type bowling game. It was the only bar within miles, and the locals took full advantage of the food and especially the beer and liquor served there. There was also a horseshoe pit behind the restaurant that regularly saw action and a few cabins Aunt Jewel rented—often just for the night for those who overimbibed. Interestingly, not only did Aunt Jewel work there with her husband, but also her ex-husband! All seemed harmonious.

Uncle Hank, my grandmother's brother was somewhat of a recluse, but he was always kind to me. I don't believe he ever worked a day in his life, but he did have a penchant for drinking, and he did it well. The small residence behind my grandparents' cabin was his home for many years. Occasionally, he would decide to travel to the town of Tonawanda where he grew up. He would set out pulling a little red wagon, and along the trip he would pick up nuts, bolts, and bits of metal. It was a twenty-eight–mile journey, so he found places to stay along the way. The story I am told is when he finally arrived in Tonawanda, he would head to the local junk dealer, sell the metal bits, and then find a bar or two. It's my understanding that at times, the local jail served as his hotel. My grandmother always watched out for him, and my grandfather helped out as best he could.

My grandparents sold the land where the hot dog stand was located when I was about six and moved the building to join their small cabin, creating a living area, kitchen, and another bedroom. They had running water and—lo and behold—a toilet and a bathtub! They did not own a refrigerator, but they did have an icebox located just outside the kitchen door. My grandmother washed laundry by boiling a very large pot of water on the stove. She shaved flakes from a large bar of soap into the water and stirred the clothes with a sawed-off broom handle. There was a wringer outside affixed to a table, and once the clothes were washed and wrung out, they were hung on a clothesline to dry.

After a few years of summers at the shore, my family stopped going to our little cottage. But happily, I still continued to travel to the shore with my grandparents to spend a few weeks there. Eventually, Poppy developed cataracts, prompting Grammy to learn how to drive in her seventies. What adventures we had! We loaded up every square inch of the Plymouth with everything they needed from their house in Buffalo (including the parakeet), and off we'd go with Grammy driving, Poppy riding shotgun, and me wedged in the back seat with the bird cage. We'd drive across the Skyway, past the steel mills in South Buffalo, finally reaching their cottage at the Lake Shore.

There I felt like Huckleberry Finn. Behind the cabin there were woods teaming with large hardwood trees. Looking up, I felt that the trees almost reached the sky. Their closeness blocked any direct sunlight. The ground beneath them was covered in a blanket of dried leaves that made a crunching sound with every step. The only wildlife I ever saw was chipmunks and squirrels, although I imagined there were much more dangerous animals prowling the woods. I would get lost at times but always found my way back. I felt secure in the woods with my hunting knife attached to my belt. It had a bone handle with a Solingen steel blade of about six inches. I still have that knife.

One day, Poppy climbed his extension ladder and nailed a two-by-four board between two trees positioned about four feet apart. He affixed two eyebolts and chains at the top and a small board on the bottom and created a wonderful swing that got daily use. I enjoyed swinging in the swing and working around the cabin, and I enjoyed target practice with my gun. I guess I was about eight when I received a Daisy BB gun, which I carried regularly in the woods shooting at various targets.

Poppy taught me how to drain the radiator of their car and add antifreeze and how to start the car and drive it back and forth a few feet in the drive, which was no easy feat for a small boy trying to reach the clutch and gas pedal. Ultimately, at the age of about ten, I drove the car around the block on the dirt roads with Grammy and Poppy aboard. That was a thrill for a ten year old!

Poppy also taught me how to paint, and we painted the exterior of the new combined house as well as some interior woodwork. I was (and still am) a slow, but meticulous, painter. I learned how to use various tools. Hammers and saws were relatively easy. The crosscut saw took some practice. A crosscut saw is about six feet long with large teeth and a handle on one end and a regular saw handgrip on the other. It's used to cut large trees. One day after several tutorials, Poppy and I took on a dead tree about two feet in diameter. It was clear to land without hitting anything, but I can tell you, it was a big day for me when it came roaring down. Another exciting tool I liked to operate was the sickle to cut high grass. The sickle is very sharp, very efficient, and it's a tool that I learned to use with extreme caution.

During the summers when I was between nine and eleven years of age, I found several areas that I liked to fish. One of these was Eagle Bay. While my grandparents' home was not actually on the lake, it was nearby. On sunny mornings Grammy would drive me there. I rented an aluminum boat with a small outboard motor, loaded in my tackle and bait, cranked up the boat engine, and took off across the water. My usual catch was blue or yellow pike. Sometimes I'd hitchhike home if the fish weren't biting, but usually we would agree on a pickup time and Grammy would meet me. One danger of fishing in this spot was that it had a rocky bottom and anchors often got stuck. That situation necessitated my paying an additional "lost anchor" fee. As careful as I tried to be, I had to contribute to the lost anchor revenue at the marina several times each summer.

My fishing claim to fame occurred at Eagle Bay. One afternoon as I brought the boat in toward the dock, the owner saw my large catch of fish, and he took my picture with his camera. About a week later in the *Buffalo Evening News* there was a snapshot of me holding the multitude of fish I had caught.

In addition to Eagle Bay, I enjoyed another fishing spot—18-Mile Creek—about five miles from our cabin. I often hitchhiked or walked. Sometimes some kind soul picked me up. There was a diner along the way that was owned by a fellow named Vic Duino, a friend of my father. If I was walking, I'd often stop there on the way to or returning from the creek since he had a beautiful German shepherd dog that I got paid to wash and groom. Once at the creek, I faced a challenge: I had to slide down a big hill from the road to the creek, which was relatively easy. But to get back up the hill, I had to walk along the creek bed about fifteen minutes to get to a more level climbing spot. Fishing in 18-Mile Creek was more a pastime than a success, but I liked going there.

A third favorite fishing spot was on the Niagara River at the foot of Ferry Street a few blocks from my grandparents' house on the west side of Buffalo. The water current at this location ran about twelve miles per hour and provided a very different fishing experience from that of lakes and creeks. In order to fish in the river, I had to buy heavy sinkers, since the type I used in the lake or creek would be swiftly pulled by the river current. I often caught Sheep Head there, which is of the carp species. Sheep Head were not to my liking, so I always sold them for a dollar each to my fellow fisherman rather than bring them home.

There were other activities that made summers at Lake Shore special. At corn roasts—always popular—the corn ears (still in their husks) were soaked in water for hours. While the corn soaked, we'd build a booming wood fire. Then we rested the ears over the coals, turning them occasionally. Once we peeled away the burnt husks, the end result was a pile of delicious, tender, golden brown corn on the cob. Even now I can still taste it.

Once a year the fair came to Derby, pitching its tents at the firehouse on Route 5 just ten minutes from the cabin. The fair had the usual array of rides and refreshment stands and was always a good time. While the rides weren't the caliber of Crystal Beach, I did enjoy the Ferris wheel—especially when I was at the top and it stopped.

Summers at Home

When back on Evadene, I turned to other summer events. I spent many hours at Public School 83, where I attended kindergarten. There the City of Buffalo hired summer counselors to coordinate activities for neighborhood youth. I was particularly interested in basketball, baseball, and stickball. Of the three, I was best at baseball and stickball. My brother and I spent hours throwing pop flies back and forth. He was Mickey Mantle, and I was Willie Mays.

One of my favorite events was opening day for the AAA Minor League Buffalo Bisons baseball team. I remember it was always on a school day, but we were given the afternoon off. My favorite player was a huge man named Luke Easter, who was a left-hand batter (like me) but a right-hand thrower. His appearance was larger-than-life, and his physique more football like than that of a baseball player. He played first base and frequently hit booming homeruns. Every time he'd come to the plate the stadium would come alive with everyone yelling "Luke" but dragging it out to "Luuuuke," which sounded like boos to the untrained ear. I was about ten years old at the time. I'd take the bus with a few friends my age to Best Street and walk several blocks to the ballpark. It wasn't in a particularly good part of town, but we never had any problems, and it was a day full of excitement.

Summer also brought opportunities to earn money. Periodically I would set up a Kool-Aid stand in front of our house and sell cups for a few cents each. Considering we lived on a side street with eight houses and there was rarely through traffic, this was not an enriching enterprise. But it was fun, and I had a few sales and made a very small profit (I think).

In addition to my home-based beverage business, occasionally I would pull a wagon around the neighborhood to ask if anyone had bottles to add to the supply from our house. Pop bottles and beer bottles fetched a two-cent refund when returned to shops. I'd take them to our neighborhood store, Sellers, cash them out, and spend the proceeds on penny candy, licorice, and stick pretzels. Another source of income came from newspapers. As with the bottles, I'd go door to door collecting old newspapers. Once I had a large heap and tied them into manageable bundles, my father would drive me to a place that weighed them and paid me accordingly. Such was the life of a small-town summertime entrepreneur.

My Parents

In my early years I remember my parents as fun-loving people who were very social. We regularly attended family parties, usually at my Uncle Ed and Aunt Charlotte's house, which was about a ten-minute drive from ours. These get-togethers were always fun, with an ongoing poker game in the dining room, a horseshoe game out back, and dart throwing in the basement. There was an upright piano in the living room that often saw action while relatives sang familiar old-time songs. The house was filled with laughter.

I think my mother and father had a good marriage in the beginning, but for whatever reasons, it deteriorated over the years. Looking back, I realize that both my parents worked hard to raise my brother, sister, and me, and many of the ideals I have today are the result of their efforts.

My Father

My father, Timothy Edward Blewett, Jr., was born in 1915 at the family home located at 907 Prospect Street on the west side of Buffalo. He was named after his father, and he was called Ted. One of five children, he had two sisters (Anne and Charlotte) and two brothers (Robert and Richard). Sadly, my earliest memories of my father were visiting him at a tuberculosis sanitarium in Mount Morris, New York. I had not yet started elementary school, but I can remember him sitting in a wheelchair on a grassy knoll and quietly talking to everyone. He was in the sanitarium for a lengthy period of time. Apparently, my mother had also contracted TB in prior years but she had been cured. Eventually, my father also got well and came home.

Dad was a handsome man with jet-black hair, who ordinarily was clean-shaven but occasionally sported a neatly trimmed mustache. He was slender and about six feet tall. He was a good dresser and insisted on always having very shiny shoes, which I attended to on a regular basis. He smoked Lucky Strike cigarettes. Smoking was very socially acceptable then, and Dad did his fair share of it. He also enjoyed his beer. Genesee was his favorite, but he was pretty flexible about brands. I don't recall ever seeing him drink any other alcoholic beverage.

When I was very young, he worked at Dunlop Tire Company, where he apparently had been for several years. He subsequently left Dunlop and went to work for Tetley Tea.

I remember that part of his arrangement was that he got to drive a company car, a gray station wagon.

I loved my father deeply and always wanted to be with him. He would drive to Grammy's house often, and I'd go with him. We would stop there for lunch or maybe dinner and my grandmother would whip up something delicious. My father frequently stopped by one of his favorite bars in the evening to drink beer. Sometimes he would take me inside with him. Other times, he left me in the back seat of the '47 Chevy while he went in alone. In the winter, he left the engine running with the heater on. Sometimes he'd be gone for long periods of time, but I loved him so much that I didn't mind. Generally, he and I were alone on these field trips. I don't recall my brother ever being with us on the bar runs. I do recall Dad asking me not to discuss these events with my mother.

Dad could be a strict disciplinarian. My brother and I fought constantly—real fistfights. One day Dad bought each of us a pair of boxing gloves, took us in the basement, and insisted we "box" until we couldn't box any more. Tim kicked my ass. Next Dad bought a punching bag and told me if I wanted to win that I needed to practice daily, which I did for about a month. The next bout with Tim brought the same result—so much for the punching bag.

Once Dad bought me a mixed German shepherd puppy that we named Duke. He was a medium-sized dog, full of vim and vigor. When my mother came home, she and Dad got in a big fight, and the next thing I knew, Duke and I were in the Chevy with Dad on our way to Grammy's house. My father convinced

Poppy and Grammy to keep the dog for "a while." That wound up being many, many years, but Duke's presence provided just one more reason to spend time there.

My Mother

My mother, Helen Mary Winkler, was born on August 2, 1918, in Buffalo. She was an attractive woman who started out a brunette and wound up a blond. Either way, she was a head turner. She was about five foot three and had a nice figure and a warm smile. When she was young, her parents went through a nasty divorce and she was sent to live with her Aunt Mae. While I don't know the details and never asked because I was afraid to learn them, I do know that my mother later reconnected with her mother, and they became close. However, this youthful experience saddened my mother her entire life.

For many years my mother was a secretary at Canisius College in the athletic department, working for a fellow named Joe Curran. As part of her employment, she was given tickets to the Canisius College basketball games held at Memorial Auditorium ("The Aud") downtown. My mother, my brother Tim, and I would take the Number 8 Main Street bus and frequently attend games. I don't recall my father ever attending. I used to enjoy the games immensely and began to collect autographs of all the players on the Canisius team and most of the big name players on the opponent's teams. After the games, I'd wait outside the locker rooms. When the players would emerge, I'd politely ask for their autograph. Never once did a player refuse.

One of my favorite autograph stories happened when I was waiting outside the Dayton Flyers dressing room for Bill Uhl. Uhl was a good player, but what made him stand out in a crowd was his height. He was seven feet tall. He came out and stood on my foot while autographing my book. I was so excited about getting his autograph, I didn't say a word. I suspect he knew he was standing on my foot and was doing it as a joke. I didn't mind since I was successful in what I had set out to do.

On the occasions we couldn't attend the games, my mother, brother, and I would listen to the plays on the radio, and I kept score in my official basketball scorebook. Chuck Healey, the announcer, always did a fine job building the excitement of the game and sharing the rapture when Canisius won.

For one or two summers I was the batboy for the Canisius College baseball team. It played at Delaware Park, and I'd ride my bike to and from the games. I had a uniform and performed the usual duties of a batboy. My compensation for each game was a new baseball. I loved it and had several baseballs at the end of the season.

Canisius College was about a twenty-minute bus ride. My mother walked three blocks to board the Number 8 Main Street bus she rode to the campus and back. While both parents were at work, Mary Jane Lawson, who lived across the street, babysat us. She was friendly and very nice, keeping an eye on us but allowing us to still have fun. I normally cleaned the house and did the dishes on a daily basis so my mother wouldn't have to do it when she got home. I recall often giving her a foot rub to warm up and soothe her tired feet in the evening.

During the time Mother worked at Canisius, my brother and I battled, chased, and fought one another constantly. My sister took it upon herself to be the "house cop." She either called my mother at work to report what we were doing or she recorded the details so she could rat on us later. The words, "Mom, they're doing it again!" still ring in my ears.

My mother left Canisius and took another secretarial job at the University of Buffalo in the guidance office. As a result, we left behind the free tickets to the basketball games. In their place, my mother decided it was time for my brother and me to learn how to swim. My earliest experience didn't work out so well; hence, I remember it clearly.

My father took my brother and me out in a boat and tossed us overboard into a lake. I thought I was going to drown. He pulled me out, but it scared the hell out of me. As I recall, Tim had a similar experience. After that fiasco, Mom enrolled us in a swimming class at the indoor pool at the university. It was in the winter and the pool was located at the far end of the campus. For several Saturdays Tim and I would walk to the pool, change, and take our lessons. This went on for two seasons with limited success. I still can't swim, although I think Tim can make it a short distance.

Swimming was just one of many activities that consumed our days. There was also bowling and roller-skating, bike riding, boxcar building, and catching snakes. Yes, snakes, and that I'll describe a little later.

Meanwhile, my first bowling experience was at Central Park Lanes, which was located in a building on Main Street in the

Central Park area of Buffalo. Strangely enough, it was on the second floor. I don't recall what business was on the ground floor, but with the racket on the floor above, I'm certain it wasn't a library. Both my brother and I would go there to bowl or just to watch. There were about eight lanes and once in a while we'd pick up some money by being pinsetters. This was before automated pinsetters were invented, and it was an exciting time to crouch in a little cubby next to the pins. Strikes were particularly nerve-wracking since the pins flew all around us. I was never hit once. Lucky I guess. Afterward, my brother and I would rent shoes and have fun spending our earnings by bowling a few games.

Also in Central Park there was a roller rink where we rented skates on Saturday mornings. Like bowling, it was a good time. Then, too, I had a deep affinity for my bike. I remember when I first learned to ride without the training wheels. My balance was OK, but I had difficulty figuring out how to push back on the petals to stop. The method I developed for stopping was to slow down as much as possible by coasting and aim the front tire into a tree. It worked, and eventually I figured out how to stop without the collision. I would regularly wash my bike and take it to the ESSO station on the corner of Englewood and Kenmore to make sure the tires were properly inflated. I spray-painted it with a sort of Pepsi-Cola red, and it was flashy even though it didn't have fenders.

One summer boxcar racing was all the rage. I built my own boxcar using long bolts to secure the two-by-four axles and the wheels. I controlled the steering with pieces of clothesline attached to the axles. It was an interesting contraption, but its glitter lasted only a few weeks.

The railroad tracks were four blocks from our house. Regularly I headed in that direction to catch pollywogs and snakes in the standing water. As the tracks were elevated at the base of the hills, there were often pools of standing water, which provided a perfect habitat for these critters. For a cage to keep my snakes, I took a cigar box, cut off the top, and affixed screening in its place. After several untimely snake deaths, however, I decided to keep them only a day or two, and then release them. That method seemed to work out much better for me (and the snakes). All in all, I remember this time in my life as that of a normal kid living in the city with a nice family, friends, and lots of good times.

When I turned nine, however, things changed. I realized there was strife between my mother and father. There were some rather loud arguments that I would listen to from my brother's and my bedroom by leaning against the furnace vent. All was not well. My father would stay out longer and longer, drink more and more, and argue louder and louder. Grammy took up for him, and that caused bitterness between her and my mother. Likewise, my mother's mother took her side and that only added to an already tense situation.

About a year later I remember my father packing up and leaving us. He had lost his job at Tetley Tea and had briefly held several sales type jobs with none lasting very long. The story both my mother and father told us was that he was going to Florida to find work, and once he landed a job, we would join him. At the time I believed it mostly because I wanted to believe it. So off he went in a 1950 Ford that once belonged to his parents. We didn't have a car, which really didn't matter since my mother didn't have a license, and even if she did, we couldn't afford one.

Shortly afterward, Mom started seeing other men. The first I recall was a fellow named Bennie, who I nicknamed Bongo Bennie. I suppose he was a nice enough guy but he wasn't my father, and suddenly I realized maybe my father wasn't going to send for us. The second person to appear was a fellow Mom met at the Dellwood Ballroom named Jack Zack, who owned a small shoe store downtown. We started seeing Jack around more and more, and they went out together often. I didn't like this arrangement one bit and was animated about it often enough to border on outright disrespect. I went out of my way to be difficult and make sure Jack and my mother were aware of my distaste for this arrangement.

By this time I was between eleven and twelve years old and determined to change my environment. I spent as much time as possible at Grammy and Poppy's house on Prospect Avenue, which was easy to get to. I'd walk three blocks to Main Street, catch the Number 8 Main Street bus downtown to Sheldon Square, and transfer to the Number 13 Niagara Street bus, getting off a couple of blocks from their house. The Sheldon Square stop between routes housed the Palace Burlesque, which posted pinups of the current stars and the upcoming talent. Viewing the pinups provided entertainment during my trip.

My father's parents were very kind and loving people, and I enjoyed every minute I spent with them. At home I was becoming belligerent and difficult to handle and repeatedly asked my mother if I could move in with Grammy and Poppy. I kept trying to explain how unhappy I was. I think my grandparents were willing, but my Uncle Dick intervened. After discussing it with my mother, it was agreed that I could move in with Uncle Dick and my Aunt Jean. The day before I finished seventh grade at St. Joe's, I packed all my belongings. The following day Uncle Dick picked me up after school. A new phase of my life was about to begin.

Chapter 2

The Adolescent Years
1959 to 1964

My aunt, uncle, and their baby daughter Jane lived in the hamlet of Snyder, which is part of the suburb of Amherst. The address was 430 Darwin Drive, located on the corner of Darwin and Wehrle Drive, which had a steady flow of traffic. It was an attractive split-level style home on a large lot with an eat-in kitchen, dining room, and living room on the first floor. The second floor had two bedrooms and a bathroom. The third floor, which was originally an attic, had been refurbished into a large master bedroom and an office. An additional nicety was a breezeway between the house and two-car garage, which was a great spot to have dinner in the summer. I was assigned the bedroom at the top of the stairs, and Jane's room was down the hall on the opposite side of the bathroom. It was a nice corner room with windows facing two sides. This was the first time I had my own bedroom, and although it felt odd, I liked it.

My Uncle Dick was an attorney, and his firm was located downtown. The firm was originally named Cohen & Lombardo, but later additional lawyers were made partners and the new firm was called Cohen, Lombardo, Maisel, Blewett, and Fisher. The firm moved a couple of times due to buildings being renovated or demolished, but the earliest building I recall was the Edwards Building on the corner of Pearl and Edwards Street. Occasionally I would visit my uncle at his office. Of those times I have two vivid recollections. First, his desk was always covered with about twelve inches of papers and files. Actually, the desk, the credenza, and every other flat surface (including a large portion of the floor) were always covered by about twelve inches of paper and documents. My second recollection was the newsstand in the building lobby attended to by a blind man. I watched with great curiosity as people would purchase a paper or cigarettes and produce various denominations of bills. The man always gave back the correct change. How a blind person could discern various denominations of bills still remains a mystery to me.

Uncle Dick served in the U.S. Army during World War II and was injured in France when he stepped on a landmine. Doctors wanted to amputate his foot but he refused and instead went through more than two years of treatment in various army hospitals. The end result was he retained his foot. He had a specially made heavier right shoe, and he walked with a slight limp. He had attended Canisius College before the war and finished college there upon his return to Buffalo. He went on to the law school at the University of Buffalo, where he obtained his Juris Doctor (JD) degree. His first (and only) job as an attorney was with Cohen & Lombardo.

Aunt Jean was a registered nurse by education, but she was a housewife by the time I came on the scene. She was an excellent cook who always wanted to try new things, and, as far as I can recall, loved every type of food. She was a loving person but had a bit of a cold exterior that was not easy to warm up to. After some time I realized she had a very big heart but simply had difficulty showing her emotions. I later learned that she had grown up in a family whose wealth was derived from real estate investments. During the Great Depression, they lost virtually everything. As a result, Aunt Jean was frugal, and to those first meeting her, somewhat withdrawn. Once you knew her personality, you realized she had an excellent sense of humor and was quite pleasant.

Jane was just a baby and occupied much of Aunt Jean's time. As a matter of routine during the week, Uncle Dick would rise around seven in the morning and we would all have breakfast in the kitchen. I recall soft-boiled eggs being a favorite. My uncle left for work around 8 a.m., and he returned around 7 p.m. He would head upstairs to change out of his suit, and when he came back downstairs he would mix drinks for Aunt Jean and himself. It was usually a highball, an old fashioned, a martini, or a Manhattan, and every once and a while, a whiskey sour. The two of them would prepare a snack for all of us, ranging from clams with cocktail sauce, cheese and crackers, stuffed celery, or some other delectable item. This little party would last until after 8 p.m., when it was time to start getting dinner on the table. We normally ate around 8:30 p.m. or so each night.

As I had moved in with my aunt and uncle in June, school was out and I didn't know anyone. There weren't any children living next door or across the street. I assume I met some kids that summer, but I really don't recall any. I did meet some neighbors and made some money cutting lawns using Uncle Dick's power lawnmower, which was a new experience. On Evadene we had a very small patch of grass in the front and the back, and I cut that lawn using a reel blade manual push mower.

I was enrolled in Christ the King Elementary School on Main Street about a mile from the house for eighth grade. On the first day I met several other kids, and within a week I felt quite relaxed in my new school. Both the school and church were more modern than St. Joe's.

That fall my uncle received a telephone call from a person in Florida saying my father was very sick. The caller said my father had asked him to phone his brother Dick. Uncle Dick immediately left for Florida and was gone for a few days. He returned with my father, who was gaunt and looked terrible. He was sent to Buffalo State Hospital. Not only did he have severe physical problems, but also he was disoriented and didn't recognize some people. I visited him there only a few times. On November 14, 1960, two days prior to his forty-fifth birthday and four days before my thirteenth, my father died.

The funeral was held at Knapp Funeral Home on Leroy Avenue in Buffalo. All family funerals were held there since Doris Knapp was a relative. Wakes in Buffalo usually go on for three days, with visiting hours lasting most of the afternoon and ending around 9 p.m. This one was no exception. I remember many people coming to the funeral home, including my father's very good friends the Dempseys, our whole extended family—the Tirones, Durados, and Trippis from Prospect Avenue where he grew up—and others. My father's parents (Grammy and Poppy) were devastated. Parents don't expect to bury their children. My father's death was an extraordinarily sad time. My mother, whom I hadn't spoken to since I left home, was there, but I wouldn't talk to her. The burial was at Mt. Olivet Cemetery in Kenmore.

A month or two after my father's death, Uncle Dick asked to meet with me. I realized the conversation was not going to be pleasant. He told me my mother was going to marry Jack Zack, the man she had been seeing. I could understand getting remarried, but I could not understand why she was marrying so shortly after my father's death. I now know that my parents had, in fact, been separated, and if Dad hadn't gone to Florida, they would have probably divorced, but the idea of my mother marrying again was very difficult for me to accept at the time.

My life seemed quite different. Although I hadn't been with my father for some time prior to his death, I had always believed we would be together again and was finding it extremely difficult to accept the fact that he was gone. My aunt and uncle were extraordinarily helpful during this difficult time and nurtured me along without pushing too hard. I'm forever grateful for their incredible sacrifice. They were in their mid thirties, hadn't been married very long, had a new baby, a new house, relatively new careers, and they took on the challenge of raising a difficult kid. I learned somewhere along the way that my father always took care of Dick as a child and maybe Dick felt he had an obligation to do the same for me. However, I doubt it was done out of a sense of obligation, but, rather, simply because they were wonderful people who wanted to help. Whatever the reason, it made a tremendous difference in my life.

Following my dad's death, I gradually slid back into the routine of school life. I remember the first day I returned to school after the funeral. Kids seemed to steer clear of me. I doubt any of them had lost a parent, and they most likely didn't know what to say to me. Likewise, I didn't know what to say to them. However, over time everything got back to normal.

I made a lot of friends at Christ the King. My best guy buddies were Bill Flynn and Mike Downey. Being a thirteen year old, I also had friends who were girls—not necessarily "girlfriends" but girl friends. Linda Beauchamp was a lot of fun and hosted a few parties at her house. Meg Dunn was a tall girl with dark hair who I thought was quite pretty, and Cathy Link was an attractive shorter blond girl from Wisconsin whose father was a doctor.

Parties inevitably turned into "make out" parties—lights out and necking, but nothing too serious. Dating seemed like a big deal at the time, very adult and exciting. I convinced Uncle Dick and Aunt Jean to let me have a party at their house. Like other parents hosting parties, they went upstairs to their bedroom, and downstairs in the teenage party area, the lights went out. All was going swimmingly until the lights suddenly came on all around us, and there stood Uncle Dick at the base of the stairs. That was the end of the party and the last time I asked to have one there.

About this time I picked up the habit of smoking. Several of my friends at school were sneaking smokes, and—peer pressure being what it was—I started smoking as well. The popular brand was Parliament, which had a recessed filter that was very cool. I also tried Luckies (Dad's favorite brand). Cigarettes cost twenty-five cents a pack in those days, so they were easily affordable. I didn't smoke every day but I smoked enough.

Sneaking a beer now and then also seemed like a good idea. Uncle Dick had a beer refrigerator in the basement, and I'd have one every now and then. Apparently he was on to me and kept inventory, because we had a little chat about my newfound entertainment. Beer was no stranger to me since my grandmother would pour me a few ounces with lunch when my father and I would go there to visit. However, following the chat with my uncle, I made sure that was the last beer I took from the refrigerator.

I sometimes wondered if my aunt and uncle had second thoughts about having me live there. I was becoming a handful. However, we all made it through my various experiments, and I graduated from Christ the King in June 1961 at the age of thirteen.

Canisius High School

My uncle was very involved with the Canisius College Alumni Association and thought it would be a good idea for me to attend Canisius High School. Canisius was a Jesuit-taught boys' school on Delaware Avenue that had been in existence for some eighty years with an enrollment of approximately 600 students. The main building was built as a Masonic Consistory, which, in turn, incorporated the George Rand mansion prior to being purchased by the school. It was a most impressive stone structure with a large set of blue doors at the entrance. It contained a theater-style hall located in the main building, bowling alleys on the lower level, and an Olympic-sized indoor swimming pool adjacent to the bowling lanes. The classrooms were housed in a long two-story structure attached to the mansion, which had a much more modern and less attractive appearance.

I applied for admission and was accepted. The dress code called for blue blazers, gray wool pants, and a gold tie (school colors were blue and gold). My friend Bill Flynn also applied and was accepted. We lived about a half-hour drive from the school, and Uncle Dick or Mr. Flynn would take us there in the mornings. I'd ride two buses home and walk the mile to the house in the evening. While waiting for the bus at the corner of Ferry and Main, I'd hitchhike, and at times would get a ride part of the way home. It was much faster than the bus because of the many stops the bus made and the delays caused by transferring to the second bus at University and Main Street.

The Sturminator

Canisius was a rigid school with strict discipline. The Prefect of Discipline, Father John Sturm, was a Jesuit priest who was a Golden Gloves amateur boxer before becoming ordained. He was a rather short man with a generous gut, which hung over the cincture of his robe. He was a habitual cigar-chomping man who I came to believe had supernatural powers. He seemed to be everywhere at once with a nose for any trouble students dared even to think about. I got to know Father Sturm quite well and spent a considerable amount of time with him. After being caught, you had to see him face to face, at which time he would rant and rave, yell, and, if the spirit moved him, give you a good hard smack against the head or cheek. Sometimes he would ask you to sing what you did wrong, which wasn't any fun for me but most likely made for a good laugh at the rectory in the evening.

Punishment was doled out by sentencing the offender to varying numbers of days in "jug." Jug was held in the classroom next to Father Sturm's office and consisted of writing about a topic he dreamed up. He would write the topic of the day and the number of words required for completion on the blackboard. Topics varied, but generally they would be intellectually challenging assignments such as, "Why is an orange, orange?" or "Why is a doorknob round?" After spending an inordinate amount of time in jug, I started writing during class to speed up my exit time. He got wise to that, and had me read my work out loud, which of course had nothing to do with the topic. In those instances he increased the number of words to complete the assignment by a hundred or two. Another favorite trick he employed involved stylistic writing (of sorts). After he wrote the topic and number of words on the board, he added, "Write one line, skip two," or variations of that. In other words, as hard as I tried, I couldn't beat him. However, even when I was being punished, I couldn't help but admire and actually like him. He was above all, fair. I had to admit what I did, that I had gotten caught, and that I had to pay the price. But that didn't stop me from trying to get around him.

I think the person who best summed up Father Sturm was the late Tim Russert, the award-winning moderator of the television show *Meet the Press*. Tim was a 1968 graduate of Canisius, who, like me, got to know Father Sturm well. He told the story of getting into trouble and asking, "Father, don't you have any mercy?" Father responded, "Russert, mercy's for God. I deliver justice."

Hic, Haec, Hoc, and Summer School

My freshman Latin teacher was Father Pfeiffer, a balding, short, portly man. He was a nice guy—a good thing—since I had a terrible time with Latin. Father Mooney was the school spiritual director, and everyone loved him. He smoked like a chimney (cigarettes), and senior students were welcome to come to his office and fire up. You could smell the smoke from a long distance away. As a result of his smoking habit, Father Mooney died of lung cancer several years later.

During my first year of high school, I didn't have much of a social life. Between commute time, class time, jug time, and studies, there wasn't much time left. I did attend a few basketball games, among them a couple against St. Joe's High School from Kenmore, our rivals. My grades were average—not great but not awful—and I passed my freshman year. High school was quite an adjustment from elementary school, especially when thrown into a structured place like Canisius, but I managed to get through.

My sophomore year proved to be more of a challenge. The subjects were much more difficult, and as hard as I studied, I started, nevertheless, to fall behind with my grades. Geometry and Latin were especially difficult for me. In fact, we hired a tutor to help me with geometry. My geometry teacher was a lay teacher named Mr. Palisano, who I thought was a jerk. My distain for him only strengthened after one experience when he really went over the top with me. On that occasion he was distributing the grades from a test we took the prior week. I had received an F, and he called me to come to the front of the class. He instructed me to bend over, and then he kicked me in the ass.

All the boys laughed, but I was humiliated. It didn't bother me so much that the guys were laughing, as I probably would have done the same, but Mr. Palisano was laughing. I was right. He was a jerk. With the help of the tutor, I managed to get a passing grade but I recall it being something like 70 (65 was passing).

Latin was another story. I just couldn't get it and, ultimately, I failed with a 63, which was a real problem since it was an unbendable requisite that each student completed four years of Latin. In other words, if a student couldn't pass four years of Latin, he wouldn't graduate from Canisius High School.

I don't know why my second year was so much more difficult than my first. Admittedly, I was spending practically every day in jug, which distracted from my study time. Additionally, I had begun attending dances at Bishop Fallon and was thinking more about girls than books. I had to attend summer school to try to get a passing grade in Latin.

About this time I had begun returning to my old neighborhood and reacquainting myself with old friends and making new ones. I also began speaking with my brother and sister more often, and I broke the three-year silence with my mother. After much thought and discussion with Uncle Dick, Aunt Jean, and my mother, I decided to move back home to Evadene Street.

I still had the issue with having to pass second-year Latin, so I enrolled in a co-educational public high school. Bennett High School was located a couple of miles from my house. It had a large enrollment, was co-educational, and was multi-racial. By contrast, Canisius was small, had all male students, maybe one or two black students, and only white male teachers. The gender issue was a more significant change than I had imagined it would be.

A middle-aged woman who couldn't control the class of about forty students taught my summer school class. The type of Latin she taught was different from that I tried to learn at Canisius. The pronunciation was very different since the Canisius version had a much more religious tone and dialect. In addition to that, I was having a ball with my new environment, which consisted of very little discipline. More importantly, girls were on the scene. The end result was I received a grade of 36 in summer school at Bennett. A few weeks later I also received a letter from Canisius asking me not to return.

Bennett High School

Since Bennett was a public school, there weren't any grade requirements for admission. Going there seemed like a natural thing to do, and, frankly, it was the only alternative. I was persona non grata at Canisius, which meant I wouldn't be welcome at any of the other private or parochial schools in town.

I thought there were a lot of students at Bennett during summer school, but once the full school year kicked in, I was amazed at the numbers. As much of an adjustment Canisius was with its rigidity, Bennett was overwhelming in its laxity due to its sheer size. This was all new to me, and at the same time, very exciting.

Drinking, Dating, Driving, and Drive-Ins

One of the interesting things about living in New York State was the drinking age. It was eighteen. When I enrolled in Bennett, I was fifteen and soon to be sixteen. The standard procedure was to get phony proof so you could go to the bars and enjoy a few beers. Of course, this made sense to me. Phony proof of age wasn't a difficult or expensive thing to obtain. Smoking was also part of the drill, which was easy for me since I'd been doing it (moderately) since I was twelve or thirteen. Bennett really was a different world from Canisius and one I wholeheartedly welcomed. The natural thing to do after being thrown out of Canisius was to gravitate to my new surroundings, and the surroundings suited me just fine.

In addition to the Bennett High environment, the whole 1960s era was a thrilling ride. The 1950s were fun with Dick Clark's American Bandstand, dances like the Stroll, Twist (which I won a contest doing at a Bishop Fallon dance), and others; great music like "Great Balls of Fire" by Jerry Lee Lewis (still one of my favorites), Little Richard, Johnny Mathis, and other artists. But the 60s, led by the "British Invasion" of the Beetles, Dave Clark Five, Rolling Stones, and others, took things to a whole new level. It was an electric era fueled by Woodstock, hippies, drugs, coffee houses, a glacial movement toward open sex, and liberation from everything. The Vietnam War created a divisive galvanization of the youth and a different society from what America had seen before. John F. Kennedy brought enthusiasm to the White House when he was elected in 1960 and fueled the youth movement until his assassination in 1963.

I was easily distracted by this whole new world. I did attempt to do well in school and worked at it, but only in a somewhat reluctant way, doing the minimum amount of work just to get by.

I reacquainted with old neighborhood friends and made new ones. The usual meeting place was a restaurant named Colonial House on Main Street near Niagara Falls Boulevard about a fifteen-minute walk from my house. We met there after school on an almost daily basis. Pete Seereiter, Bill Walgate, Kathy Kelly, Ed Smolcrack, Terry Dwyer, Nancy Webdale, Carol DiJo, and others would show up most days, and if we didn't see each other after school, we'd surely get together at Colonial House on the weekends. We became acquainted with the wait staff there and one older woman in particular. We called her "Mom." She acquired this name because she regularly wrote letters of excuse for us when we played hooky.

Bill, Pete, and I became best of friends, and we ate, drank, dated, and played together all the time. Bill's father owned a Nash Rambler that was a great drive-in car since the back seat reclined, and four people could rest against the back seat and watch the movie, or… well… whatever.

Nancy Webdale lived a few blocks away on Larchmont, and Pete Seereiter lived across the street. Bill Walgate lived a few miles away in Eggertsville; Terry Dwyer and I lived around the corner from each other.

Sometimes Bill, Pete, and I would decide to go to a drive-in theater together to watch a movie and drink beer. Bill and Pete were a couple of years older than I, and they had driver's licenses. On more than one occasion Bill picked me up with a girl in the front seat and drove to Terry Dwyer's house to pick her up. Oftentimes, beer drinking with the guys was upset by other plans that Terry orchestrated. I realized I was being fixed up.

Terry was a beautiful girl with a great smile, long brunette hair, a structured face, and a willowy figure. She was smart, had a great sense of humor, and was always fun. I thought she was terrific, but I didn't like the idea of being set up. We went out several times following this arrangement until one night at the Mona Kai while having drinks with umbrellas in them, I told Terry I thought she was wonderful but that she should turn her attention to Bill who really loved her. It wasn't too many years later that I realized that was a big mistake—one that nearly cost me dearly.

In 1963, when I turned sixteen, I was eligible to obtain a learner's permit to drive. Jack Zack and my mother owned a used robin-egg-blue Nash Rambler. The law in New York allowed a person with a learner's permit to drive during daylight hours as long as a senior driver (someone over eighteen with a driver's license) was in the car. For the most part I adhered to this rule. However, on one occasion, I had other plans with Carol Johnston, who was a girl I had been dating. My plan was to drive her to the Lake Shore to my grandparents' cottage. So, on a rainy weekend day, off we went—just Carol and me in the Rambler. The problem was that Carol didn't have a driver's license. In fact, she didn't even have a learner's permit. Things were going along well, and we were more than half way there when a traffic signal began to turn red. It was slippery with the wet streets, and I was practically at the crossroad, so I ran it. A few minutes later

I heard this "beep, beep," which quickly annoyed me. Then I heard the siren from a motorcycle cop who was waving me to pull over.

The first thing he asked for was my driver's license, which I made a fumbling effort to "look for," and then proudly produced my learner's permit. The obvious question that followed was to ask Carol for her driver's license. Of course, there wasn't one. At that point, the cop gave me a ticket for running the red light, driving without a license, and driving without the registration, which couldn't be found anywhere in the car. As fate would have it, I was pulled over in front of a bar. So in we marched (Carol and I), where I produced a phony ID and ordered a beer to relax and determine my next steps. The cop was quite clear that I shouldn't even think about driving the car, advice that I respected. I called Bill and Pete, who showed up in about an hour (and three beers) later. Pete drove my mother and Jack's Rambler back to our house on Evadene, with Bill, Carol, and I following in Bill's father's Rambler. Later that day I told my mother what had happened. Of course, she went crazy, for which I didn't blame her. She promptly took my learner's permit away, and I promptly called Uncle Dick to see what I had to do from a legal point of view.

It turned out that driving without a license is a misdemeanor in New York. I had to appear in night court a couple of weeks later accompanied by Uncle Dick. The judge was a stern fellow. As I sat listening to cases preceding mine, I began to feel uncomfortable about the whole situation. When my turn came, he asked if I "did it." I said I had been driving without a license, and that the registration was missing from the car, but that the traffic light had just turned red when I was under it. He didn't seem to be interested. Next, he said I should reappear in a month, get a haircut, and take my driver's test. I didn't like the haircut part, but I did like the idea of taking my driver's test. His reasoning was that if I passed, I wasn't a menace on the road.

I reappeared in a month, freshly shorn with my driver's license in hand. I had to plead "youthful offender" to expunge the misdemeanor charge from my record. Uncle Dick and I had some discussion about this since you're only allowed to plead YO, or young offender, once, and I wasn't sure if we should waste it on such a trivial matter or save it in case I really needed it in the future. He convinced me I should use the "get out of jail free" card now, and I did. In the end, I wound up with a fresh haircut, a new driver's license, and a fine of around $75. I also lost driving privileges for a month or so, but time heals all wounds, and soon I was behind the wheel again.

A New Appreciation for Life

In March 1964, I experienced a life-changing event. I was a passenger in a Chevy Camaro being driven by Jimmy Starks, a friend of mine. It was a miserable night with heavy snow. I remember traveling on the New York State Thruway near South Buffalo, although I can't recall where we were going. Suddenly, a double-tandem tractor-trailer traveling in the opposite direction came over the median toward us. That was the last thing I remember.

Several days later, I woke up in Our Lady of Victory Hospital with facial lacerations, a few broken ribs, a broken knee, six teeth missing, and a lot of bumps and bruises. Apparently, there was some confusion identifying me since my drinking ID from St. Lawrence University had my picture but the name of Timothy Jay Espenlaub. I was told that I went through the windshield. I was also told that Jimmy died in the accident.

I spent a few weeks in the hospital in a three-man room, which was a good thing since I had company and didn't just lie in bed thinking about what had happened. I had a lot of visitors, which also helped. When I was released, I was a sight with scars, bruises, teeth missing, and I was walking with crutches. It wasn't possible to return to Bennett, so the City of Buffalo hired a tutor who came to the house daily. Daily attendance in a schooling environment was a novelty for me since I had adopted the habit of going only four days a week with a day off in addition to the weekends. I would typically go to Grammy and Poppy's house and do chores for them and enjoyed that a whole lot more than being locked up in school. I found school boring and felt claustrophobic while in attendance. The world was an exciting place. Being in school kept me from it. Nonetheless, in my new situation with a tutor I did reasonably well, and my grades for my junior year improved over the previous two.

By now I had healed and had a new partial plate that improved my appearance tremendously. The bruises were gone, but I still had (and have) a scar on my right cheek. I realized the doctors did quite an amazing job when I understood the extent of my injuries.

It wasn't easy to forget my brush with death and the death of Jimmy. As a result of the event, I found an entirely new appreciation for life. I was young, I was alive, and I was determined to take advantage of all life had to offer; that is, to fully appreciate friends and relatives and to move forward. That tragic event may account for my penchant for looking ahead and not looking back. I found a whole new zest for life. The following summer I spent a lot of time just trying to enjoy life. The beach was a popular spot—especially the beaches in Ontario, Canada. Our favorite spot was on Lake Erie called Sherkston, which had a beach and a deep, cold quarry. Needless to say, with my limited swimming prowess, I never entered the quarry. At Sherkston there was a gate with a toll charge based on the number of people in each car. Our regular drill was for two or three of us to climb into the trunk about a quarter mile before the gate. Once we were through the gate and out of sight of the gatekeeper, we'd escape. Fortunately, the trunks of the various cars we drove never malfunctioned, and we were always able to get out.

Another popular pastime was to sit on the sun porch on Evadene with Terry Dwyer's yearbook from Mount Saint Joseph's Academy, which was an all-girls school. I would select various girls and ask for a history on each, with the most important question being if they were dating someone regularly. Terry was a valuable source of information, and my mining for dates proved to be a good tactic since it provided several dates with several girls.

Gran Prix at the Glen

A favorite event in the fall was a road trip to Watkins Glen, also known as the Glen. Each year in September, the United States Formula One Gran Prix was held there, and we went two years in a row. Gran Prix racing at the Glen began in 1961, so it was a relatively new event.

The first year I went with my brother and a few of his friends. We rented and hauled a travel trailer. Once at the Glen, we set up at a trailer park adjacent to small lake. It was really quite a nice spot. Those were a wild couple of days. The racetrack was surrounded by storm fencing—no cement walls or barriers to protect spectators in the event one of the cars left the track. There were large crowds all over town and the locals were deputized for the event—a rag-tag bunch of wannabe cops. When you consider that the population would swell by multiples of thousands for the event, and everyone was there to have a good time, I admired the cops (long term and wannabes) for their restraint. It was party, party, party, all over town and especially inside the infield of the track. The first year we walked to the track and watched the race at turn Number 10, which was a hairpin turn—a great location since the drivers had to downshift to negotiate the curve, and then speed shift to regain speed. We watched these machines traveling at breakneck speeds and go around the track over and over again. The first day was for time trials, and the race was held the following day. Racing greats such as Graham Hill and Sterling Moss were crowd favorites. At night we changed venues from the track to local bars, but the activity stayed the same—drinking beer.

The following year in 1964, Pete Seereiter, Bill Walgate, and I rented a motel room. We pulled Pete's car onto the infield and watched the race while sitting on the hood leaning against the windshield at our favorite spot, turn Number 10. During the evenings we went to a particularly lively bar about a half-mile up a steep hill that I believe was called the Seneca Lodge. It was always packed to the gills, which presented a problem for people consuming large quantities of beer. The problem was the restaurant was so popular, the lines for the restrooms were endless. I had just as much fun that year as in the previous year. It's my understanding that the race is no longer held there, with the last year being 1980. It was fun while it lasted.

Back to School... Once in a While

That September I went back to Bennett High School for my senior year. Having successfully passed my junior year, I thought I'd breeze through to graduation. I also thought I could do it by attending classes three to four days a week. As usual, I'd typically spend time with other guys who had the same idea, or I'd visit with Grammy and Poppy on my "days off." Every two weeks or so I'd take the bus to their house and drive my grandmother in her car to Buffalo State Hospital, where her brother Hank had been admitted. It brought back memories of visiting my father there. The facility had not improved in the intervening years and was still an eerie place with many sad residents. After the visit, Grammy and I would stop at a local restaurant and have a sandwich and a beer.

I had a lively social life. One interesting fellow I met at Bennett was Bunny Jarrett. He was a light-skinned black fellow who was well connected and a lot of fun. Several times I went with him to the Bon Ton Jazz Bar on East Ferry Street, which was in an all-black neighborhood. The Bon Ton had excellent jazz with many different musicians, some of whom were quite famous. It was interesting to be a white (the only one) sixteen year old with illegal ID, drinking beer in an all-black bar, listening to jazz being played by all-black entertainers. Very interesting.

I joined a fraternity at Bennett that year, and we thought we were hot stuff. The fraternity wasn't nationally recognized, but that didn't matter to us.

Confessions of a Sixteen Year Old

About this time I convinced Terry to participate in a scheme to liven things up at Mount Saint Joseph's Academy where she was a senior. Each of us had a role: hers was simply to unlock the exterior door to the girl's locker room; mine was to open the door, run the length of the room, and exit the other side. The plan was executed with precision, neither of us was caught, and we provided a level of excitement rarely, if ever, seen at the school.

A favorite sport of mine was to sneak out of the house at night and head for Rossi's Tavern on Main at Minnesota. Rossi's was a nice bar with excellent food—most notably beef on kimmelweck. "Beef on weck" is worth a trip to Buffalo. A large round of beef is prepared and placed in a steamer. The chef thinly slices the beef and places it on a kimmelweck roll, which is a hard roll, similar to a Kaiser, baked with caraway and salt. To eat it, you dip the top of the roll into the juices, add some horseradish sauce, and dig it! Delicious! A local favorite.

But, to get back to my sneaking out at night, the fact that I regularly did it is not remarkable. What is remarkable is how often I did it and that I was never caught.

My brother's and my little bedroom on the second floor had three windows facing the street located just over the gable roof that covered the sun porch. On select nights I climbed out one of the windows, worked my way to the end where the gutters were, and pitched myself the three feet to reach the small roof over the front door. With one hand on the edge of the sun porch roof and the other on the roof over the entry, I lowered myself until my feet were resting on the wrought iron handrail; then gingerly I jumped down until I was standing on the landing. With that, I was off and running the mile or so to Rossi's. This feat was relatively simple in the summer but considerably more challenging in the winter with snow and ice on the roofs.

Once at Rossi's, I met others I knew. Most often it was Bill Walgate and Pete Seereiter. We would take our places at the piano bar, where Tommy Flynn played old-time favorites, such as "Toot Toot Tootsie," "Me and My Shadow," and "On the Street Where You Live." The more beer we drank, the more we thought we could sing. In hindsight, I feel sorry for the others in the bar. After those times I found the return climb up onto the roof and into our bedroom always exciting. I never did fall, since falling wasn't an option.

Sikora Says, "Sayonara"

Like most sixteen-year-old guys, I dated several different girls and had fun. All was going well until I went up against my nemesis, Mr. Leonard S. Sikora.

Mr. Sikora was the assistant principal at Bennett, and he was always on the lookout for truants. He was in his first year in this position, and it appeared he was trying to form a reputation as being a tough guy. This didn't deter me, because I thought as long as my grades held up, who cared if I skipped a few days here and there, even if it was every week? Early on, he called my mother and told her of my repeated truancy. She, in turn, had Jack follow the bus to see if I exited at school. He, in turn, dutifully reported back to my mother that I didn't. This drill of deception went on for the first few months of my senior year. In November, Mr. Sikora made an announcement over the public address system that anyone who skipped school the day after Thanksgiving would be suspended. For a guy like me, that threat amounted to a great challenge; so naturally, I took that day off. Shortly thereafter, my mother and I were in the assistant principal's office, where I expected to be suspended for a few days. I guess Mr. Sikora had had his fill with me, for he didn't merely suspend me. He expelled me. Expulsion meant, "Say goodbye to Bennett." It also labeled me as an unwelcome student at any of the city's public schools.

This turn of events I had not foreseen, so I had to figure out what to do. Not only had the public schools categorized me as unwelcome, but also I realized there really weren't any options available to me. I researched boarding schools, but even if I was accepted in one, we couldn't afford the tuition. At that point I knew I was limited to two choices: one was to find employment, and the other was to join the service.

Day after day I looked through the help wanted sections of both the *Courier Express* and the *Buffalo Evening News*. Either the positions offered weren't appealing to me or I wasn't qualified (typically the latter). It was then that I took it upon myself to go downtown and meet with the U. S. Army recruiter. I met with a sergeant who was quite likeable and who carefully explained various options. He also told me that since I had turned seventeen just a few weeks earlier, I needed parental consent to enlist. I assured him that I could obtain it.

The sergeant gave me tests to evaluate what type of work I might be qualified for, and we agreed that the Army Security Agency (ASA) would be a good fit. There was one difference between joining the ASA or a different area: I had to enlist for four years rather than the usual three. He explained that this was because the army was going to make a significant investment in training me, so I had to give them an extra year as repayment.

I took the paperwork home and told my mother about my plan. I thought since she had such a difficult experience trying to control me that it wouldn't be too difficult to convince her to sign. She was adamantly opposed to the whole concept. I explained that there really weren't any options for me. She conferred with Uncle Dick, who saw the merit in my joining the military, and ultimately, she signed. During this period I had a regular appointment with my doctor, who expressed doubts about my ability to pass the army physical due to the injuries I sustained in the car accident.

I carried the paperwork back to the recruiting sergeant who scheduled the physical. I took it and passed. The next thing I knew, I was scheduled to take a train to Ft. Dix, New Jersey, on January 11, 1965, for basic training.

Chapter 3

The United States Army Years

1965 to 1969

It's a story often told—maybe not told enough—how the military has the ability to take a kid without much going for him and turn him into a self-confident man with direction, determination, and drive. That's what the army did for me.

Ft. Dix, New Jersey
January 1965 to March 1965

I had about three weeks before I was leaving home for new horizons. It was an emotionally mixed time and my last Christmas in Buffalo as a kid. I was excited about the unknown adventures that lay in front of me but sad to be leaving a familiar environment. Regardless, I had enlisted and that was that.

On the morning of January 11, 1965, I boarded a train at the New York Central Terminal in Buffalo bound for New York City. Upon arrival there, I boarded a bus from Ft. Dix that was waiting with several other recruits to make the hour-and-a-half journey. Once we passed the gate and entered the base, all of us tried to take in everything we could as quickly as possible. We pulled up to a row of barracks and were greeted by a drill sergeant yelling for us to get into formation. It wasn't pretty, but at least we got into a line. We handed over our paperwork and began being processed in. This entailed getting a "haircut," which took about a minute, and lining up at the quartermaster's for our clothing, which included everything from boxer shorts to fatigues to boots. It was a very orderly and efficient process. Once we were finished with these tasks, we went to Easy Company for a day, where we were assigned to permanent barracks and to our company and had the pleasure of meeting our very own drill sergeant. Easy

Company was the calm before the storm. I clearly recall lying on a bunk bed with my fatigues and new, tight-fitting boots thinking maybe enlisting wasn't such a great idea—especially the four-year part. But it was what it was, and I was determined to be successful in everything ahead of me.

Our barracks were an old one-story building made of wood with large gaps in the walls. Since it was January in New Jersey, those gaps proved to be quite drafty. Cold in fact. We had a coal potbelly stove in the middle of the room, which was manned each night by rotating volunteers who kept the fire going, as it was the only source of heat. Every six feet or so there were support posts. A coffee can painted red was nailed to each post about four feet from the floor. These were called "butt cans," and that's where one would extinguish his cigarettes. Most mornings the butt cans had a fairly thick skim of ice on top.

The man who was to be our constant companion for the next eight weeks was Sgt. Green. I don't know if we even knew his first name. We didn't need to. He was absolutely and always Sgt. Green to us. That said, Sgt. Green slept in a small room at one end of the barracks. He was a black man, about six foot one, weighed about 175 pounds, and was as solid as a brick wall. His posture was so rigid that we wondered how someone could stand that erect for so many hours for so many days. This guy was a lean, mean, fighting machine. His vocabulary was slanted toward obscenities, his voice was thundering, and his demeanor was akin to that of a hungry lion. He was quite a bit different from Bunny, the only other black guy I had known from my high school days. This wasn't the Bon Ton.

There were about forty guys in my barracks who came from a variety of backgrounds. The draft was still in full force in 1965, so not all the guys were as "gung ho" as I was. After all, I had volunteered. Sgt. Green could care less whether you volunteered, were drafted, or were hiding from the law. From day one until graduation, we were his to shape and mold into soldiers. A few of the guys suddenly disappeared, presumably because they couldn't cut it, went nuts, or were in the brig for going AWOL. A few, but only a few. We'd notice when someone went missing, but never asked what happened to him or where he was.

Most of the guys got along well, and as time went on I think we all realized we actually needed each other. A big part of the training was to learn to trust and depend on fellow soldiers. One guy from New York City was difficult; he beat up some guys in our barracks. After witnessing several incidents, about six of us decided to take matters into our own hands. One night, while he was sleeping, we threw a blanket over him and dragged him into the latrine where we beat the crap out of him. He yelled and screamed, and we kept punching, kicking, and hitting him with a couple of "entrenching tools" (shovels) until he was bloody. I'm convinced Sgt. Green heard the racket, but there's a certain military justice that seems to work when allowed to work. As a result, the troublemaker from New York never bothered anyone again.

Sgt. Green's usual routine was to turn on the lights at some ungodly early morning hour and yell, "Mens, get your lazy asses out of those racks!" Not quite the same as having your mother announcing that breakfast was ready and asking how you slept. We had about fifteen minutes to make the beds, dress, and line up in (proper) formation in front of the barracks. Sgt. Green would conduct roll call and hold an inspection. If you missed buttoning a button, or your boots weren't really shiny, or he just felt in an ornery mood, he'd yell in your face, "Give me ten!" which meant ten pushups. Invariably, ten would turn into another ten, followed by yet another ten or so. Next, we lined up outside the mess hall. There were three rows of four-top tables, with each row having five tables. Each man would grab a mess tray and go through the mess line; then he would take a seat at the next table in a row. About five minutes after the last man was seated at the last table, the row would stand up and the process would repeat itself. The best seating placement was at the first table in a row, which allowed you a longer time to eat. After leaving the mess hall, there were garbage cans with heaters where we washed the trays with a brush and dipped them in clean water to rinse them off. Then we returned to the barracks for fifteen minutes only to line up in formation again. We went through this same process for breakfast, lunch, and dinner every day for eight weeks unless we were in the field.

The drills varied from day to day but most days included rigorous physical exercise. The sergeant who led this drill was not Sgt. Green, but rather a guy who made Sgt. Green look weak. He was a Hispanic man, short in stature but all muscle—truly a power machine. It's important to note that when I joined the army, I was six feet tall, weighed about 135 pounds, and I had a twenty-eight-inch waistline. I wasn't muscular, but I was nimble and had little difficulty with physical exercise. Others with weight problems quickly lost the weight and most got with the program fairly quickly. If they didn't, the exercise would be extremely challenging and the sergeant would be merciless. In addition to the regular drills with pushups, sit-ups, running in place, and crunches, every few days we would run a mile with a backpack filled to capacity. Guys would puke when we first began this drill, but later in the training, sickness would be a rare sight.

Constantly, we were marching to one place or another or riding in the back of a military truck that weighed about two and one-half tons (called a duce and a half) if the destination was especially far away. We endured memorable training sessions with equipment: gas masks, rifles, hand grenades, and bayonets.

For gas mask training, several of us were led into a cinder block building. A tear gas canister was tossed inside. Obviously, the thing to do was to put on the gas mask. I know it sounds easy, but in the heat of the moment, it can be tricky. In order to get out of the building, you had to do it successfully.

I especially enjoyed the rifle range. Prior to joining the army, the extent of my shooting experience was taking shots at jars and cans at the Lake Shore with my Daisy BB gun. Now I was handling a ten-pound M-14 with bullets about three inches long and a magazine holding twenty rounds. I did quite well with this weapon and was awarded an "Expert" medal for my abilities with the rifle.

The hand grenade range was an exciting place. Basically, we were given about fifteen minutes of instruction, and then handed a few grenades. We would pull the pin and throw the grenade while we took cover behind sand bags. Fifteen minutes may not seem like much training but it's really not difficult to grasp the concept of pulling a pin, throwing the thing as far as you can, and ducking.

Bayonet training was a lot more personal. The classes consisted of instructions on how to lunge at another man and plunge the bayonet into him. We had many practice drills. It was scary, but it got the adrenalin flowing.

My big day came in March 1965, when I graduated from Basic Training. I had never been in better physical health, and I was anxiously anticipating where I would be sent next. My orders came and showed I was going to be stationed at Ft. Devens, Massachusetts. There I was to attend school to become a Morse Code Interceptor.

Before going to Ft. Devens, I was given a fourteen-day leave, which I spent in Buffalo. Although I'd been gone for only two months, everything seemed quite different to me. I thought everyone had changed, but in fact, it was I who was now seeing the world in a different way. I felt I had purpose, and considering my life before joining the army, I certainly did.

Ft. Devens, Massachusetts
April 1965 to September 1965

I had an enjoyable time on leave, and after the fourteen days I boarded an airplane to Logan Airport in Boston. This was the first time I'd been on an airplane, and it was quite an experience. I took a late afternoon flight, and I remember it being a rocky ride. Landing over the water at Logan Airport was a nail biter.

Compared to Ft. Dix, Ft. Devens was an attractive place. There were large swatches of lawn, landscaping, and neat rows of two-story barracks, which were build more recently than those at Dix. I was on the first floor and assigned to an upper bunk. Life here was much more relaxed. We still had to keep everything neat, and we had regular inspections, but the emphasis was on education. We had classes five days a week for eight hours a day. I caught on quickly and excelled at my new profession. I led my class with speed and accuracy typing code on a "mill." A mill is a manual typewriter with only capital letters. We typed five rows of ten groups of five characters each, then double-spaced and continued in the same manner. Morse code is a language much different than any other, consisting of dots and dashes, with each character in the alphabet and numbers and symbols having their own sequence. The faster the code is sent, the more difficult it is to determine the characters, as the sounds blur together. My speed increased to sixty words per minute, and I found that when copying code being sent faster than sixty words per minute, I continued to type for several seconds after the sound of code stopped. It was all about memory retention.

We were free to come and go as we pleased over the weekends with the exception of the occasional parade, which I hated. We had a roster, which we checked daily to see if we had Kitchen Police (KP) duty. Once scheduled, it was best to volunteer for a job you knew rather than to wait to be assigned. I regularly volunteered for "pots and pans," which meant I was in charge of washing them. Other duties involved serving meals or preparing food. Peeling potatoes seemed like an endless task. The worse job was cleaning the grease pits where the sludge and grease collected. Cleaning it required getting into the job up to your elbows and pulling the mess out.

Side Trips

The closest town to Ft. Devens was Ayer, located just outside the base. We went there frequently to hang out at a diner. Unlike New York, the legal drinking age in Massachusetts was 21, and unlike Buffalo, the penalty for underage drinking was severe. We were allowed to drink 3.2 beer on base, which was a lot like drinking water.

I went to Boston a few times and found it to be a great city. My favorite place was the Commons, where people would stand on benches and wax poetically, holding court on subjects of all varieties. It was only an hour away, and sometimes I'd catch a ride from someone with a car or I'd take the bus. Once I rode on the back of a motorcycle, and I still remember how frigid the ride was back to the base. Another time I went to Concord to see Walden Pond. Concord was only about a half hour away and although it was interesting, the pond was rather small and the home where writer Henry David Thoreau had lived was nothing more than a few foundation stones.

I visited my cousins, the Lesniaks, in Syosset, Long Island, taking the train. I spent a Saturday night there and returned on Sunday.

Other Adventures

I attended just one United Service Organization (USO) dance on base. At those events, girls were bussed in. The scene was like a kid's first dance: the guys stood against one wall and the girls gathered against the other. I don't recall anyone memorable at that dance and consequently never attended another.

My pay ($68 per month) had not increased from when I had first entered the service, but I found a way to supplement my salary by giving haircuts. My barbershop was in the latrine in the barracks, and the barber chair was a trashcan. I purchased a set of clippers in town, and I was in business. It wasn't especially difficult to improve on the haircuts from the barbershop on base, and people seemed happy with my services.

While at Devens, I decided to take the General Educational Development (GED) test to obtain my High School Equivalency Diploma. It was a five-subject exam given on specific Saturdays without any study guide. I passed the test and added the diploma to my burgeoning education file.

I had been keeping in touch with Terry Dwyer while at Devens, and she asked if I would escort her to her senior prom from Mount St. Joseph's. Bill Walgate was in Korea, and I gladly accepted her invitation. I flew military standby from Logan Airport to Buffalo and dressed in a white dinner jacket my mother had rented for me. We double-dated and drove with a good friend of Terry's, Susie Matalone, and her date, Rob. That very night I realized maybe I shouldn't have told Terry to date Bill and to leave me alone. There was a certain chemistry between Terry and me—we just clicked. I was very happy being with her, and I felt great when I was near her.

On August 31, 1965, I graduated from the Army Security Agency School. I was officially awarded with my MOS of 05H20 (commonly referred to as 05B) Morse Code Interceptor, and I received my "Top Secret Crypto" security clearance. On the same day, orders were distributed. I found out my next assignment would be for three years in Bad Aibling, Germany. It was quite an exciting day for me.

Prior to going on leave, I was scheduled to attend a Tactical Training Course from September 4 to September 11, 1965. This training was required for all men going to Germany, Korea, or Vietnam. The Second World War in Europe ended in 1945, but the Cold War was in high gear, driven by the building of the Berlin Wall in 1961 and the Cuban Missile Crisis with the Soviet Union in 1962. There was a very unsteady peace between Russia and the United States. Korea, of course, had the demilitarized zone, the DMZ, at the 38th parallel separating South and North Korea, maintaining a tenuous peace arrangement. Vietnam was just beginning to heat up.

The Tactical Training Course was an infantry-based training program. That meant we fired more advanced weapons such as the rocket launcher; we had more gas mask training; and we participated in survival training. For the grand finale we were dropped off in a swamp at night and had to evade the enemy to reach our destination by morning. I was with a couple of guys, and we made it, although it took all night. Thank God for the other guys—my sense of direction was pitiful! (In fact, it still is.)

We did have a compass and the training on how to use it, so I might have made it alone, but that's questionable. Dodging the "enemy" was the easier part of the exercise. I found that my involvement in the course made me more self-assured and confident of my abilities.

Meanwhile, I had no idea where Bad Aibling was, but a couple of the instructors said they'd been there and it was a beautiful place. Prior to departing, I was given two weeks of military leave, and I flew to Buffalo via military standby from Boston. I spent almost all of my time during those fourteen days with Terry. We went out to dinner often, took drives, and did a lot of things together. Autumn is a particularly nice time in western New York. One day we drove to Letchworth State Park just to walk through the lanes and trails to admire the colorful fall foliage. Terry had begun college and had a much better regiment with regard to attending school than I did, so our time was limited but we made the most of the time we had. She was still dating Bill and I didn't discourage the relationship, but I didn't encourage it either. I knew my fondness for her had grown tremendously. I also knew I was soon going to Germany for three years.

While I was home, I did some research on Bad Aibling and found that it was located in the Bavarian Alps about an hour from Munich, Innsbruck, and Salzburg. In other words, Bad Aibling was located in one of the most beautiful parts of Europe, nestled in the middle of the Alps in sight of the Zugspitze, Germany's highest mountain. It sounded like an absolutely great place to be stationed.

Bad Aibling, Germany
October 1965 to January 1967

In early October, I traveled from Buffalo to Maguire Air Force Base in New Jersey, where I boarded a military transport plane to Frankfurt, Germany. It was a long flight, especially considering the farthest I had previously flown was from Boston to Buffalo. The plane landed in Frankfurt in the early morning, and a bus transported me to a base where I processed into the country. I stayed in Frankfurt for a couple of days, and then boarded a train to Munich, where I changed trains to Bad Aibling. While traveling, I couldn't help letting my mind wander, thinking about all the battles that occurred during World War II. I remember going through the Black Forest region and trying to imagine fighting in such dense terrain. When we were heading out of Munich, the Alps came into view, and with each mile I drew closer to their majesty. Again, I imagined how soldiers battled in such difficult conditions.

I arrived in Bad Aibling on a beautiful crisp autumn day. Everywhere I looked I saw the Alps. It was the beginning of a love affair that still exists. Men were dressed in lederhosen with Alpine hats holding long feathers, while women wore the traditional dirndls. Mercedes Benz cars were everywhere, along with Volkswagens, a few Opels, and the occasional Porsche. There were no American "yachts" with the big tail fins and sweeping hoods. I stood in awe on the platform at the train station for what seemed like an hour but I'm sure it was only a few minutes. This was an entirely different world from anything I had even seen or even heard of. It was wonderful.

I took a Mercedes taxi to the Bad Aibling Kaserne, where I was dropped off at the gate. This was a top-secret military base and outsiders were prohibited from entering without proper documentation. The Kaserne was a well-kept place with several two-story buildings that were our barracks. They were constructed of cement and stucco and painted a faint yellow color. They had been built during World War II for the German Luftwaffe, and an airstrip was also constructed there at the same time. Now the huge hangar and adjacent buildings were being used as our operations center.

Inside the barracks, I found hardwood floors and rows of two-man rooms measuring about fifteen by fifteen feet, with marble window casements and shutters on the windows. Rooms were on both sides with a wide hallway separating them.

Living here was more like staying in a hotel than in traditional army barracks. There wasn't any KP or motor pool duty. We were there to ply our trade; German civilians including putzfraus (cleaning ladies) fulfilled other duties. However, one notable exception was that I never saw a German in or near the operations center where classified activities occurred. Although I was an enlisted man, I was treated with respect like that afforded officers. The other soldiers were smart and had various skills, all of which related to intelligence work. Many had the same skill set I had, but there were also decryptors, linguists, and others with honed intelligence skills who worked with us.

In addition to the barracks and the operations center, there was an antenna field with a vast array of various long-range antennas, a post exchange, a movie theater, a laundromat, and a dining hall. To call the dining building a mess hall would be an insult to the cooks. Germans prepared our food and it was very good. We worked 24/7, 365 days a year, so the dining hall was always open.

The time of my arrival in Germany was perfect since it was right in the middle of the festival season. There's nothing like being in Bavaria in the fall. Every village, regardless of its size, had a brewery that had been in existence for centuries and held a festival resplendent with oomph pah bands, sweinwurst mit kraut (Bavarian sausage with sauerkraut), weisswurst (white sausage), brochen (hard rolls), and, of course, a lot of singing, dancing, and beer. I attended at least ten festivals the first month I was there.

I shared a room in the barracks with a good guy named Ed Hollo. He was a likable fellow, and we got along very well. Ed, Dan Alexander, and I became fast friends. I made many friends and really don't recall anyone I didn't like. It was an amiable group. Another friend was Ron Gilmore, who met a German girl and ultimately got married. Tom Howard and his wife were from Texas, lived off base, and drove a big Chevy, which stood out. Riley Self (I always loved the name) was a sergeant who was in charge of the evening shift. We had men from all over the United States with many different backgrounds but we all got along very well.

Work was great. It was intellectually stimulating, challenging, and rewarding. We worked rotations of six days from eight in the morning until four in the afternoon, six eves, and six mids. After the day and eve shifts, we had two days off, and after mid shift, we had three. This schedule provided time to see things and travel around the countryside.

My first long-distance trip was to Venice, Italy, via train with Ed and Dan. It took forever, and we changed trains several times. The trains stopped at each little town, where there would be a man with a white coat and a cart from whom you could purchase a sandwich or a beer by opening the window and waving to him. We did this at several stops. The last train we took was from Verona to Venice, and it was unlike anything I had ever experienced. Women were breastfeeding children in the aisles, others had live chickens with them, kids were running wild, and there was general pandemonium.

We finally arrived in Venice about six in the morning. As soon as the train door opened, we were greeted with an odor that would curl the hair in your nostrils. We quickly discovered the cause. During this time it was not at all unusual for people to open their windows and throw their garbage into the canals below. Additionally, the whole town was overrun with cats and their droppings. Venice was a garbage pit. But it was also a beautiful place. San Marco Square was magnificent and the uniqueness of the city surrounded by canals was beautiful. After a few glasses of wine, the smell seemed to dissipate and we adapted quite well. The ride back was a sleep-a-thon. We didn't patronize the men in the white coats as vigorously as we did on the way since we had to go back to work when we arrived in Bad Aibling.

About this time, I bought an Opel that was about fifteen years old. It had been sold from soldier to soldier and had likely called the Kaserne home for most of its life. I paid $200 for the car, which is also the amount I subsequently sold it for when I left Germany. This little dreamboat gave me freedom to explore the surrounding area. Its top speed was 160 km per hour (about 100 miles per hour), which was not especially fast on the autobahn. When reaching this speed, it would shake, rattle, and fortunately not roll. The floor behind the driver's seat had rusted out, and I put a piece of plywood over it to keep the snow out in the winter and keep people in while sitting there. It was a motley gray color. It was the first car I ever owned. I loved it.

The currency was Deutsche marks, and the conversion rate was four marks to the dollar. A half-liter of beer cost one mark, brochen (rolls) were five pfennig (just over a penny), a Wiener schnitzel dinner cost six marks. Germany was quite affordable even on the salary of an enlisted man. Of course we purchased more expensive items such as cigarettes, soap detergent, toiletries, and gasoline from the post exchange, or PX, which was considerably less expensive than buying these items off base.

A German-style inn or tavern with a bar, a restaurant, and rooms for rent is called a gasthaus, and the closest one to my base was affectionately referred to as "The Last Chance." It was a typical place with long wooden tables with benches on each side and a large ceramic stove in the middle to provide heat in the winter.

The floors were wood and the atmosphere was more like that of a being in someone's living room than being in a restaurant. Since it was so convenient and comfortable, many of us frequented The Last Chance on a regular basis. In the mornings after the mid shift, the chimney sweep would generally show up for a beer covered in soot. He, along with the farmers, added local color.

One night a few of us were engaged in a conversation with a couple of German men. They were conversant in English and brought up the topic of how poorly Americans treated blacks. This went on for some time until I had enough. I blurted out, "I don't understand why you are so upset about America's treatment of blacks. After all, you killed six million Jews!" Silence dominated the room that had been a din a few seconds before. Deafening silence. Looking back, I consider the remark a bit of a faux pas on my part.

The army ran a few hotels in Bavaria for the relaxation of its soldiers. One was the Lake Hotel on the shores of Chiemsee, Germany's largest inland lake, located about one-half hour from Bad Aibling. Chiemsee was an absolutely beautiful sixty-acre lake with an island where one of Mad Ludwig's castles was situated. Adolf Hitler built the Lake Hotel in 1936 as the first hotel along the autobahn, and he spared no expense. The U.S. military took over the property in 1945 at the end of World War II and commissioned it as a resort for servicemen and their families. The charge for enlisted men was $1 per night for a single room. I recall there being a total of about seventy-five rooms in the hotel.

I stayed at the Lake Hotel often. The rooms were modest but they contained double beds with wonderful down-filled duvets that were exceptionally comfortable, and they had private bathrooms. As nice as our living quarters were at the base, this was luxury. In addition to the rooms, there was a very nice dining room and a bar housed in a semi-circular room overlooking the lake. Outside was a large terrace facing the lake and the island castle. It was a wonderful place to unwind and enjoy the luxury of being able to sleep in a bedroom without roommates.

I telephoned my mother once and Terry Dwyer another time from the hotel. The process was to have the receptionist place the call and wait for an hour or two for the call to go through. In today's electronic environment when we can call all over the world on cell phones, it's difficult to imagine that forty-seven years ago it took an hour or longer to get a connection from Europe to the United States. The quality of the sound was not particularly good with high interference levels, and the calls lasted only a few minutes, but they provided happy memories that stay with me to this day.

In addition to the Lake Hotel, the United States took over a second hotel after the war called the Hotel General Walker in Obersalzberg. Originally one of the grandest hotels in Germany and the meeting place of the inner circle of the SS, it offered opulent accommodations and sweeping views of the Bavarian countryside and Alpine scenery. As beautiful as the Lake Hotel was, the Walker was stunning.

The hotel has a fascinating history. In the early 1920s, Hitler was a neighbor of the Platterhof Hotel (subsequently named the General Walker), and it's believed the first chapter of *Mein Kampf* was written in the Bavarian room of the original Steinhaus, which was the name of the original estate prior to the expansion of the property. The hotel has known three names: originally the Steinhaus Mansion, then the Platterhof Hotel, and finally, the General Walker. Once the Nazi Party took possession of the hotel in 1936, the entire property was renovated, and it became one of the most modern and luxurious multi-wing hotels in Europe. After sustaining heavy damage in a bombing raid in 1945, the hotel stood vacant and crumbling for several years. In 1952, the U.S. Army rebuilt the hotel and designated it an Armed Forces Recreation Center. I stayed at the General Walker several times, and while it was not as opulent as in its heyday, it was pretty damn nice.

We went to Munich, Salzburg, and Innsbruck regularly, as they were all in close proximity to Bad Aibling. Munich was the easiest to get to either by car or train, and we traveled there most often. A regular stop on our trips was the Hofbrauhaus, which was an enormous beer hall where everyone drank from liter mugs and enjoyed the brass bands. It was interesting to see the women (fraus) carrying four or five one-liter mugs of beer in each hand to serve the tables full of partygoers. I remember there was one table situated near the brass band that was rumored to be where former Nazi SS officers congregated. I don't know if that was true or not, but by the looks of the characters who occupied the space, it might well have been factual.

On one memorable trip we went to the Hofbrauhaus for a few hours, and then stopped next door at a small Hungarian gasthaus around the corner. A fight broke out that was very much like what I had seen in western movies—chairs flying, fists flying, bottles flying, and the large plate glass mirror behind the bar shattered into pieces after being struck by several chairs. It was one hundred percent pure chaos. After being thrown out the door, I had the presence of mind to stay outside. The other guys didn't have the same idea. Finally, when we heard the easily recognizable sounds of "dobie, dobie" (police sirens), we ran for it. The next morning we discovered that one of our guys had broken two fingers. We returned to Bad Aibling to have him medically treated.

We also frequented the neighboring villages. All these places were exceptionally scenic, and we enjoyed all our trips. I met several Germans and enjoyed their company despite the fact that most spoke very little English. This forced me to learn a bit of the German language, which I found challenging but rewarding. I never learned the proper tenses or how to be proficient, but I did learn enough to be somewhat conversant, get from place to place, and not starve.

The summer of 1966 my mother and sister visited me in Germany. They took a guided bus tour of several countries in Europe, and they arrived in Germany after a few days. This was their first time out of the United States, and it was very exciting for them. I took a train to meet them in Heidelberg. Upon arrival I found a gasthaus to spend the night and paid the matron fifty pfennig for use of the bathtub. Being "good as new," I went to the hotel where they were staying, saw them in the dining room, and said, "Guten Tag," which means "Good Day" or "Hello." It had been about eight months since I had seen anyone from my past, and it was wonderful to have family with me.

I negotiated with the tour company to accompany my mother and sister for about a week to various countries on the bus, but I had to arrange my own accommodations once we arrived in each town. We went to Geneva, Paris, and the Arlberg region of Austria, which left a lasting impression on me. We said goodbye when they were departing Paris, as I had to return to Bad Aibling.

The autumn of 1966 was a rerun of the previous festival season with visits to many surrounding villages. Interestingly, I never attend the Oktoberfest in Munich, preferring the smaller local venues.

Everything about my stay in Germany was beyond words. The scenery was spectacular, the work stimulating, the people friendly, and the food terrific. In spite of the lure of snowy peaks, crisp mountain air, the aroma of wood smoke in the winter, people in lederhosen and Alpine caps, my mind was drifting in a different direction. In the fall of 1966, the war in Vietnam was rapidly escalating. I'd read about it daily in the *Stars and Stripes* and became convinced that I should be there. I felt guilty about living in the lap of luxury while a war was taking place. I had joined the army to serve my country and it didn't seem right for me to stay in Germany while the United States was entangled in war.

With these thoughts in mind, I scheduled a meeting with the commanding officer and told him I'd like to be transferred to Vietnam. He advised me to think about it more. A couple of weeks later, I met with him again. I explained why I wanted to go and why I felt I had to go, and he submitted the paperwork requesting a transfer. A few weeks later he called me into his office and told me that my request had been denied. I made the request again, and the paperwork was submitted a second time.

This time it was approved, and the CO said something to the effect of, "If you're that crazy, then go ahead and go." I knew I'd miss Germany, but the fight in Vietnam was a time in history. I was in the time, and I needed to be in the place as well. I could always return to Germany at a later date. My orders provided for a two-week leave stateside and instructed me to then fly from Travis Air Force Base in California to Tan Son Nhut Air Base in Saigon, with my final destination as the 330th RRC unit in Pleiku, located in the Central Highlands.

Prior to leaving Germany I received a letter from Terry telling me Bill Walgate had proposed to her, and he wanted to get engaged. She asked what she should do. I wrote back telling her not to do anything, that I would be home soon, to keep it to herself, and that we would talk about it then. I also told her I loved her.

I packed my gear, said goodbye to my pals, stopped by the various gasthauses to bid adieu, sold my old gray Opel, and took a train to Frankfurt to board a military aircraft to McGuire Air Force Base in New Jersey.

I had decided not to tell my mother or other relatives that I was heading to Vietnam, but rather to say I was home on leave. I had devised a convoluted plan to have my mail sent to Germany, then forwarded, and reversing the order for my letters back home. I had decided to tell Terry the truth but only after she promised to keep it a secret.

Home on Leave

I arrived home for the leave and followed my plan. All was going well until some correspondence arrived at the house with Vietnam plastered all over it. The jig was up. My mother was beside herself, crying and repeatedly asking me how I could do this to her. It was not pleasant. I explained to her that I felt I had to go. It didn't lessen her burden, but at least I didn't have to repeatedly respond as to why I was doing this to her.

During my leave I spent every day with Terry. We went out to dinner most nights, and we had a wonderful time. We spent the last weekend together at Allegheny State Park, where we rented three cabins. Sounds romantic, and it was, but it would have been even more so if we didn't share the space and time with Terry's mother, Terry's friends Mary Balling and John Dobson, friends of Terry's mother Bill and Ethel Uhaus, and an exchange student named Jorge from Columbia, who was staying with the Uhauses.

Jorge was a teenager and John, Mary, Terry, and I introduced him to the sports of sledding and poggying. John drove as Terry and I were occupied in the back seat. When we returned to the cabins, Jorge couldn't wait to announce that Pat and Terry were "knocking" (necking) in the back seat. He also told everyone in great detail about his newly learned sport of poggying. Stern looks greeted these announcements. In spite of my missteps, however, we still had a good time.

The day came to say goodbye, and it was very difficult to do. I was grateful for the time we had together, but it didn't lessen the pain of leaving. Terry and I had conversations about the future. She agreed to tell Bill that she was too young and couldn't commit to him. She would also tell him about us.

We both realized we were truly in love and would one day get married. Lots of guys got married just before they shipped out, but Terry was still in college, and I was leaving for a year, so we had to wait.

Pleiku, Vietnam
February 1967 to March 1968

In February 1967, I packed my duffle bag and flew to San Francisco, where a military bus took other soldiers and me to Travis Air Force Base. This was the height of the Vietnam protests with hippies and anti-war dissidents everywhere. They were particularly noticeable in San Francisco. As we went by street corners in the military bus, all sorts of obscenities were flying—some directed *at* us, others directed *by* us.

A couple of days later, I boarded a military transport and took off for Tan Son Nhut Air Base. We landed in Alaska to refuel, and we disembarked from the plane. It was cold. I mean it was frigid. We were given army blankets to wrap around ourselves while we walked down the stairs from the plane to the mess hall during refueling. I recall it was thirty or forty degrees below zero, and the wind was howling. The mess hall was about fifty feet from the PX, but you had to walk to the end of a walkway, cross the fifty feet and walk back up an adjacent walkway to get there. Since I was low on smokes, I did it. In hindsight, I should have quit smoking. God it was cold.

I re-boarded the plane and took off for Saigon. All in all, the trip took about twenty-four hours. Nevertheless, my adrenalin was flowing, and the excitement of landing in Vietnam kept me awake and alert for most of the trip.

As clearly as I recall the cold in Alaska, I remember the heat in Vietnam. We landed, and as soon as the door opened, a burst of heat entered the aircraft. As I climbed down the stairs from the plane, the sun and breeze felt like the heat from a blast furnace hitting my face.

We lined up and boarded a bus to our barracks. I was housed in an eight-man tent very close to the end of a runway. F-14 jets took off and landed every few minutes twenty-four hours a day, every day. The roar of the engines with flames shooting out of the back and the rapid climb out of sight was absolutely awe inspiring. I had never seen anything so exciting and riveting in my life. I was mesmerized and thrilled by the power of our air force.

I spent a couple of days at the base, and then boarded a C-130 transport plane to Nha Trang, located on the coast of the South China Sea, where I spent four days. We sat with our backs against the sides of the plane harnessed in and facing each other. The interior was basic metal without any padding. Even more interesting to me was that the rear door remained open throughout the flight. We landed on a makeshift corrugated steel runway and boarded two- and one-half-ton trucks to the camp, which consisted of rows of tents that accommodated eight men each. The scenery was breathtaking with green hillsides and the sea. I remember remarking to others that one day after the war was over, Nha Trang would become a luxury resort. That, in fact, has happened with many top-notch hotels now dotting the seacoast. While there I waded into the South China Sea just to say I did it.

After my brief stint in Nha Trang, I boarded another C-130 transport and headed to my final destination of Pleiku, located a few hundred kilometers northwest. Again the rear door remained open, and the scenery changed from being verdant green spaces to thicker jungle terrain and higher hills and mountains. From time to time I'd see wide swatches of barren land in contrast to the greenery. These swatches were where napalm had been dropped, defoliating large areas of the hillsides. Once again we landed on a makeshift corrugated airstrip where there were two Quonset huts. That was about it—the airstrip and two huts.

Pleiku was famous for having seen the first open combat between American and North Vietnamese regulars after full American deployment in Danang. The American Seventh Cavalry, an air brigade, touched down south of Pleiku near Camp X-Ray in the La Drang Valley on November 14, 1965. The battle pitted 450 U.S. ground forces against 2,000 North Vietnamese regulars, resulting in a tentative U.S. victory. It wasn't a famous battle of scale but one of legend, because it was where both sides cut their teeth and sized each other up for what would be eight more years of war. The clash was also important because it made the war look "winnable" to Americans. It didn't actually prove to be a model for the war that materialized: combat in which the hit-and-run North

Vietnamese enemy was rarely in sight and engaged battles were only of their choosing.

Again we boarded convoy trucks for the half-hour ride to base. Along the way were acres and acres of rice fields with Vietnamese men, women, and children wearing the trademark conical Asian hats (more commonly referred to as coolie hats) while standing in water up to their knees.

We arrived at the base, which consisted of about thirty tents of the same type as I found in Nha Trang; that is, they slept eight men each. There were no buildings on base. Most of the tents housed the troops, but there also was a shower tent and a mess tent. Both officers and enlisted men lived in identical tents. Sandbags about three feet high with an opening in the front and the rear surrounded each tent. The tents were mounted on floorboards spaced about an inch apart. In the middle were support posts. Canvas folding cots with mosquito netting were arranged along the sides of the tents against the sandbags outside, which provided a degree of safety. I was fortunate to have a spot in one corner of the tent, which afforded me a little additional protection since I had sandbags along my right side and also next to my head. Each tent had electricity provided by gigantic generators. We had three or four light bulbs hanging from the tent cross supports. We also had a small under-the-counter-type refrigerator. I don't recall how we obtained it, but we had it, and it worked.

Along the perimeter of the base stood two towers about twenty-five feet high with 40-caliber machine guns. Between the towers were sandbag bunkers spaced about every one hundred feet with an interior that would hold two men and a position on top that would hold one person. Those were equipped with M-60 machine guns as well as each soldier's individual armament. Each evening at the start of guard duty, the men assigned to each bunker would string three claymore mines between the bunkers and the Concertina wire. A claymore mine is a directional fragmentation mine that contains seven hundred steel balls and has a range of fifty yards. It's activated by electric remote control and can be aimed in a specific direction. On the top of the mine is a socket that receives a wire with a plug on the end. On the other end of the wire is a trigger device that, when squeezed, detonates the mine. Arming the mines was particularly perilous during the rainy season as the detonators were sensitive to lightning and there was the danger they could detonate during the arming process.

We were assigned to guard duty every few weeks. When the moon was full, we had excellent night vision, but we also became easy targets standing watch atop the bunkers. On dark evenings both we and the enemy were much less visible. One night I spotted a blond medium-sized dog coming from outside our perimeter fences. I assumed he would step on one of the land mines planted there, but he somehow avoided them and was able to crawl under the wire with only superficial scratches. I called softly, and the dog came to our bunker. He became my pet. Dogs, like the people in Vietnam, were generally small. They were also a dietary Vietnamese mainstay. I named him "Big Dog."

Big Dog was an easy-going guy who loved almost everyone. He became the tent pet, and we all watched out for him. I thought about taking him home with me, but I realized he simply wasn't, and could never be, civilized enough to live in the United States. I discovered this because of an incident that occurred when General William Westmoreland came for a visit. On that day we soldiers were all lined up to listen to a talk the general was to give. Out of nowhere Big Dog appeared, chasing a small dog. Once he caught up with other pup, he cocked his leg and let loose. This happened in clear sight of everyone including the good general. At that moment Big Dog became destined to remain in Southeast Asia.

There weren't any latrines. Traditional toilets were replaced by fifty-gallon drums cut in half with a board placed across the top. Bomb casings situated into the ground served as vessels in which to urinate. Both contraptions were surrounded by boards on three sides built about three feet high to provide "privacy." As you can imagine, these were not places to read the Sunday paper, which was a good thing, since there weren't any Sunday papers. Actually, there weren't any regular papers other than occasional copies of *Stars and Stripes*. Toilet paper was at a premium and was often substituted by comic books, magazines sent from home, or, sad to say, copies of *Stars and Stripes*.

Following guard duty, each man was assigned a specific task. One task was filling lister bags, which are long canvas bags suspended on tripods containing drinking water. Another was going to the creek to fill a water tanker, which in turn filled the large cistern used for showers. A third (and clearly the most undesirable) task was commonly referred to as "shit burning" detail. There were also other duties, such as filling sandbags and picking up around the compound.

Shit burning was critical to keeping the cans emptied and for sanitation. This duty entailed pouring diesel fuel into the half fifty-gallon drums, lighting a piece of paper, and igniting the heap. The result was billowing black smoke and liquefied waste. Once the can cooled to the touch, it was loaded onto the back of a truck, taken to a deep trench, and dumped there. On one occasion one of my pals was behind the truck when the fellow getting ready to dump the can slipped, realigning his aim, resulting in dumping the contents into my buddy's face. From that day forward, he was referred to as "Old Shitface."

Another incident involving this detail happened when Bill Monk and I were assigned to do the burning. I suppose it's similar to witnessing a car accident where you really don't want to look, but you are compelled to do so. As we were pouring the diesel into a can, Bill looked in. He pointed out there was a half of a dinner roll there.

I said, "How in hell could someone eat while sitting here?" Bill, who had a slight stuttering problem, said, "Well, he wasn't all bad...he couldn't eat the whole thing."

Aside from these two guys, my other buddies were "Digger" Schmidt, who allegedly was an undertaker in his previous life (doubtful but it made for a good story), Jim Ward from Philadelphia, Fred Powers from Indianapolis, and his sidekick Harry Pierce, also from Indy. Fred and Harry had joined the army on the "buddy system," which meant they would be stationed together for the duration of their duty. Both had come from Korea before being assigned to Vietnam, and both lived in the tent with me. Harry could be a handful when he had one too many, and we all watched out for him when that happened, but he was really a nice guy.

Dining was a new experience. C-Rations came in small olive drab (what else?) boxes with the contents labeled on one side. The boxes contained one tin of meat with beans, meat with potato hash, or meat with vegetable stew accompanied by a tin of bread-and-desert, a four-pack of cigarettes, and a P-38. The P-38 was a small device that was used to open the cans. A civilian would refer to it as a small can opener, but the military had a different term for most items. The cigarettes were usually Lucky Strikes. Lucky Strikes changed their packaging somewhere in the 1950s using different colors on the boxes, but these small packs of four smokes still had the old wrapping, meaning they were at least ten years old. They were potent cigarettes and rough to smoke, but we managed to do so.

At each meal, large crates containing C-Ration boxes would be set out with the labels face down. I dreaded the thought of grabbing ham and lima beans, since that was absolutely the worst tasting variety. When that happened, I immediately searched out one of the few guys who actually liked it and tried to negotiate a trade. Fortunately, a few months after I arrived, we had a typical mess tent with typical army food, which, while not great, was a welcome improvement.

During the dry season, November through April, the climate was arid and the dust heavy, with temperatures typically in the nineties during the day and seventies at night. Due to the intensity of the heat during the day, the nights seemed much colder than they actually were.

Historically, Pleiku had the highest level of rainfall in the Central Highlands, and when the monsoons hit, a torrent of rain fell for months. I have a clear recollection of the first monsoon that hit us in May 1967. I looked outside the tent and saw a black wall coming toward the camp. The wall was dirt picked up by the wind and the swirling rain. It hit the camp with a vengeance and took down a few tents. Ours was on shaky ground but remained standing. The intensity was astonishing and the force, awesome.

Our operations area consisted of about twelve two- and one-half-ton trucks equipped with sophisticated equipment to detect and copy enemy signals, decrypt them, and communicate the information to affected units. Each truck was staffed twenty-four hours a day, 365 days a year by six soldiers each manning a station. Unlike Germany where the signals were sent at high speeds and with accuracy, this code was sloppy and difficult to copy. Also, the senders were usually in the jungle and had only weak antennae, which made hearing and copying a challenge. The key wasn't speed but the ability to mentally "tune in" to the type of code being sent.

One of the trucks was off limits to all but a handful of men. It was staffed by a civilian from the National Security Agency and six handpicked soldiers. I was selected to be one of the six a couple of months after I arrived. The equipment inside was exceptionally sophisticated. A small anteroom was erected prior to entering the truck. We had to remove our boots there to keep dust from entering. As an added benefit, the van was air-conditioned to further provide protection to the gear.

The area was known as Engineer's Hill. An artillery unit was located on a hill behind our base. It would fire artillery over our tents and operations center into the jungle beyond every night, all night long. In addition to posting our men along the perimeter nightly with machine guns, claymore mines, and other weapons, we were further protected by helicopter gunships and "Puff the Magic Dragon."

The gunships had various types of armaments, but generally they all had rocket launchers, M-75 grenade launchers that were belt fed and carried anywhere from 150 to 300 rounds, and four 7.62 machine guns (two on each side with swivel mounts).

Puff was another story of military might. The Douglas AC-47 Spooky had tremendous armament and firepower and was referred to by the North Vietnamese as "Dragon" or "Dragon Ship." The nickname caught on, and GIs referred to the plane as "Puff the Magic Dragon," named after a song made famous by the folk singing group Peter, Paul, and Mary in 1963.

In some situations in which ground forces called for close support, that is, more firepower than could be provided by light and medium ground-attack, aircraft was needed. The C-47 was a modified DC-3 with three 7.62 millimeter General Electric mini-guns to fire through two rear window openings and the side door—all of which were located on the left side of the plane. The guns were actuated by a control on the pilot's yoke, enabling him to control the guns individually or together. When we would call for help, Puff would show up, and when the plane tilted to the left all you could see were lines of red, which were tracer bullets from the machine guns. In researching for this book, I found that its coverage was over an elliptical area approximately fifty-two yards in diameter, placing a round every 2.4 yards during a three-second burst. The plane also carried flares, which it could drop to illuminate the area.

A third support included F-14 jets with napalm. You could hear the jets flying overhead and observe them off in the distance where they would drop napalm bombs. It was a terrifying sight, and the flames were never to be forgotten.

Life each day was similar to the day before. In the mornings, a duce-and-a-half would bring mama sons and baby sons (older and younger women), whose job it was to sweep the tent floors, wash our fatigues, and polish our boots. The women took the clothes to a nearby creek and beat them on the rocks. Nobody cared about shiny boots, but (especially during the monsoon season) keeping them clean held down the mold and mildew.

Our cots were the typical folding army type seen in movies with mosquito netting held in place by small wood frames. We slept on or under a sleeping bag, which never saw a cleaning for a year. Here mold and mildew became a problem during the rainy season.

We had rats the size of cats, and we would regularly shoot them with M-14 rifles inside the tents. Remarkably, nobody was ever injured by stray bullets. This practice was later disallowed, which was probably a good idea.

The best part of the day was mail call. We gathered at the same time every day. The orderly appeared with bags of mail and boxes, reading the labels and calling out the recipients' names. I was fortunate to receive mail more days than not and would covet the letter or package until I was back in my tent sitting on my cot. There I would carefully open the package or letter and savor every word. I had a tape recorder, and Terry and I would exchange tapes regularly. I'd turn the recorder on, close my eyes, and listen intently. Often she would record several of our favorite songs. On one occasion, she sent me a large tape packed in popcorn. I retrieved the tape and shared the popcorn with my tent mates, who all enjoyed it as much as I did. Much later I learned this delectable treat was shipping popcorn, but it sure tasted good to us.

On a typical night if we weren't working at the Ops (operation) center or on guard duty, we would be playing poker. Our tent was the designated place, and games went on late into the night. At the beginning of the month just after payday, the game was "pot limit," which meant you could bet as much as was in the kitty for the next card. As the month progressed the betting limit decreased until the end of the month when there was a twenty dollar limit. Since U.S. currency was used on the black market, we were paid in military script (commonly referred to as "funny money") to keep dollars out of Vietnamese hands. The maximum denomination was twenty dollars, so the sheer size of the pots was enormous, and often the amounts as well. I did very well playing poker, which I attribute to the lessons learned from Grammy Blewett, who was not only an excellent poker player but also an excellent instructor. I did so well that when I was discharged from the service, I was able to purchase a new car when I returned to the States with my poker winnings.

When I first arrived in Pleiku, we were allowed to go to town during daylight, which I did a few times. There was a market where people were speeding around on motor scooters, but overall most people just squatted and starred at us. Many of the inhabitants of this region were Montagnards or hill tribe people. They were ethnic minorities living in villages, housed in thatched single-family houses, and they didn't seem at all friendly. We had been in Pleiku for about a month, and during that time several GIs were injured or killed while in town. As a result the town was declared off-limits one hundred percent of the time for the remainder of my tour.

In order to periodically get off base, I often volunteered to either drive a jeep or ride shotgun to the Pleiku airport to pick up officers and, sometimes, civilians. They normally flew into Pleiku on military aircraft, but once in a while our guests would land in an Air America plane. If Air America was supposed to be a secret, it was the worst kept secret of the war. Air America was an American passenger and cargo airline that was covertly owned and operated by the Central Intelligence Agency's Special Activities Division. It supplied and supported U.S. covert operations before, during, and after the Vietnam War.

In our unit there were two grenadiers, a term that meant the men didn't carry the traditional M-14 rifles, but rather a much less heavy M-79 grenade launcher supplemented by a .45-caliber pistol. One of the guys was rotating home, and I maneuvered to get his grenade launcher. Although I was considered an expert marksman with the M-14 and had never fired the M-79 or a .45, I thought it would be lighter to carry and safer to have.

The M-79 was a single-shot, shoulder-fired, break-action grenade launcher that fired a grenade measuring about four inches long with a circumference of about three inches. It also fired a variety of 40-millimeter rounds including buckshot. It was a great weapon for riding shotgun on the airport runs. I never had any lessons with the .45, shot it a few times, and found it to be a good paperweight. My original thought that the grenade launcher would be lighter was correct. However, I failed to consider the weight of the bandoleers of ammunition. Overall, the M-14 would have been the lighter choice.

At the Pleiku airport we picked up the passengers who often arrived in starched fatigues, which we found hilarious. We would sit them and their gear in the back seat, and off we'd go. During the dry season we would run the jeep as fast as humanly possible, causing a mini dust storm until we arrived at the base, where we would slam on the brakes, which created a huge dust storm to back up into the vehicle. During the rainy season when the dirt became slick as ice, we would speed along, sliding sideways and enjoying the fright we caused our passengers. It was great fun.

After a few months we reached the conclusion that we should create a more civilized atmosphere, and to achieve it, we should build a proper shithouse. We obtained lumber and constructed an architecturally stunning eight-holer with four spots on each side facing each other. I don't recall exactly how we obtained the lumber but I do remember we swapped items we "acquired" with another unit for various items from time to time. It was a beauty and the pride of the unit. Constructed of two-by-four studs with a plywood façade, metal roof, and screening from the ground up to about three feet with hinges on the top, it was functional and a vast improvement from the half fifty-gallon drums with boards across them.

Now determining that we were accomplished designers and builders of impressive structures, we decided our next venture was to construct a club. We hand mixed cement and poured the floor. The structure was again framed with two-by-fours and had plywood siding and a metal roof. If people were excited about the new "men's room," they were delighted with the "club." It quickly became the place to see and to be seen. We frequently received shipments of greatly appreciated beer. Usually it was Crown, which was a beer from Korea. The beer was some of the worse tasting stuff any of us ever drank, but like the ten-year-old cigarettes we smoked, we drank it. The real value of Crown beer was the weight of the cans. If you had a good throwing arm and were accurate, it was possible to kill a giant rat with a direct hit even with an empty can.

A number of months into my yearlong tour, I decided it would be fun to see Bill Walgate, who had returned from Korea only to be shipped to Quy Nhon, which was about one hundred miles due east of Pleiku. There was a convoy that regularly traveled the route over the mountains through the An Khe Pass. I was able to convince a captain to let me borrow his jeep. His previous jeep had been blown up, and he told me if that happened to this one, I shouldn't come back. I laughed. He didn't.

My pal "Old Shitface" and I jumped in the jeep. We took off before the captain changed his mind and met up with the convoy not far from our base. We brought along our weapons, extra ammunition, a change of underwear, and several beers. The An Khe Pass was famous for ambushes; hence, we traveled in convoys and only during daylight. The trucks and jeeps totaled about fifty, and once we were lined up with jeeps in the front and rear with mounted M-60 machine guns, off we went. Initially my greatest concern was trying to avoid getting hit by the numerous flying beer cans, which we were successful in doing. Along the way we heard a lot of gunfire, and we picked up speed, stopped drinking and throwing cans, and concentrated on getting the hell out of there. Shortly afterwards, things calmed down and we were back to drinking beer and ducking cans.

We arrived in Quy Nhon safely although a bit inebriated. We headed to the CO's tent to inquire where we might find Bill. His aide pointed us in his direction and after we met, Bill asked to have the afternoon off and we went to town. Quy Nhon was on limits during daylight hours so we climbed back into the jeep and headed for a bar. Several beers later, I convinced Bill to demonstrate his prowess with karate by breaking the arms off chairs with his hands. The owner wasn't too pleased with this activity but backed off quickly when we all grabbed our weapons. Time flew by and before we knew it, nightfall was upon us, which meant we should have been back on base. We headed back in the direction we thought was correct but found ourselves in the middle of nowhere until we came to a bridge with a roadblock that was guarded by our South Korean allies. They didn't speak English, but Bill assured us he could speak Korean. I don't know what he said but it wasn't received well, and the guard pointed an AK-47 in our faces. Shortly after the Koreans had their fun, they pointed us in the right direction and we eventually found the base. Naturally, we didn't know the password, so we had another gun pointed at us, but eventually we were admitted and had a restful night's sleep. The next day we rejoined the convoy, which arrived back in Pleiku without incident.

A few months later, Bill came to visit me in Pleiku traveling by the same convoy. Although we had a great time in Quy Nhon, his mood was entirely different, and he was bitter about my stealing his girl. We had heated words, and it wasn't a pleasant experience. The relationship between Bill and me would never be the same, and I couldn't blame him for feeling the way he did. I didn't intentionally "steal his girl" but it happened, and I was not sorry that it did.

During their tour, soldiers were encouraged to take an R & R (rest and relaxation), leaving the country for seven days. Men had their choice of going to Hawaii; Sydney, Australia; Hong Kong; Kuala Lumpur, Malaysia; Bangkok, Thailand; Manila, Philippines; Singapore; Taipei, Taiwan; or Tokyo, Japan. Once you put in a request for R & R, you were assigned to the next available flight to your destination, issued orders, and flown to various airbases for the departure.

Terry and I planned a reunion in Hawaii. We were both nineteen, and her parents agreed but only with a chaperone, which turned out to be her sister-in-law Marilyn, her oldest brother's wife. For our reunion, I sent small amounts of money to Terry often since we were restricted in how much we could send out of the country at one time. Finally, she had enough money for Marilyn and her to take a tour to Honolulu, where we would once again see each other. My orders were cut, their tour was arranged, and we were set to go.

I flew to Cam Rahn Bay to depart for Hawaii. At Cam Rahn Bay, I was told the flight I was supposed to take was full, and I'd have to wait until the following day. The following day the same thing happened. I met with a chaplain who was going to board the flight and gave him a letter to give to Terry in Hawaii. I told her it didn't look like I'd be able to get there and that I loved her. After another day of the same, I flew back to Pleiku and skipped R & R. We survived the experience, but it was tough.

Meanwhile, Terry and Marilyn were traveling on a shoestring. I planned on replenishing money when I met them, but since that didn't happen, they were virtually broke. To add insult to injury, Marilyn came down with the flu and felt miserable. The only comedic part of the journey Terry shared with me later. It seems she and Marilyn went to a nightclub show where the comedian asked for volunteers from the audience. Somehow Terry wound up on stage, and she was asked a simple question, "Have you been leied in Hawaii?" She answered, "Oh yes, upon arrival." It was a crowd pleaser.

I was scheduled to return home in early February 1968. In the later part of 1967 and into the spring of 1968, our tents were being replaced with barracks. Superstitions abound when guys "got short," meaning they were winding down their tour. I didn't want to move into the barracks located about 500 yards from our tents, and we weren't scheduled to do so until after I was to leave. The last month I slept with my flak vest on, my bayonet with the scabbard tied to the frame above my head holding the mosquito netting, and my weapons, ammunition, and helmet in the cot with me.

On January 30, 1968, all hell broke loose all over the country with the onslaught of the Tet Offensive. The offensive was a military campaign launched by both the Viet Cong and the North Vietnamese. It was a campaign of surprise attacks launched against civilian and military command and control centers throughout South Vietnam during a period when no attacks were supposed to take place. The operations are referred to as the Tet Offensive because there was a prior agreement to "cease fire" during the Tet Lunar New Year celebrations. Both North and South Vietnam had announced on national broadcasts that there would be a two-day cease fire during the holiday. Nonetheless, the communists launched an attack that began during the early morning hours of January 30, the first day of Tet. The offensive turned out to be the largest military operation conducted by either side up to that point in the war. We were lucky to be reinforced by artillery, gunships, Puff the Magic Dragon, and F-14 jets throwing down napalm bombs in the distant hills.

Since the fighting continued and the Pleiku airstrip sustained considerable damage, my departure date was postponed. Eventually the fighting subsided, however, and I was scheduled to leave. I flew (once again) to Cam Rahn Bay, this time in a helicopter strapped next to the rear door gunner. My year was closer to thirteen months than twelve, and I was ready to leave. My orders were to report to Ft. Meade, Maryland, where

I was to work at the National Security Agency (NSA) after a thirty-day leave.

Once in Cam Rahn Bay, we boarded a chartered civilian plane bound for McChord Air Force Base in Washington State. There wasn't a sound in the aircraft until the pilot announced we were at 10,000 feet, at which time everyone cheered. We stopped in Japan to refuel and finally made it to McChord.

I recall boarding a bus and being taken to a barracks where we showered. There weren't any cots in the barracks but rather long rows of racks with dress green uniforms alongside tailors who measured us. We left there and went to "Murphy's Steak House," which was really a mess hall. We grabbed a tray and entered the chow line. Once we arrived to the front, the soldier behind the counter asked how we would like our steaks and how many we'd like. What a meal! After dinner, we returned to the barracks where the uniforms were on rows opposite where they originally were, and they had our names pinned to them. The level of efficiency was incredible—and greatly appreciated.

I left McChord via bus to SeaTac Airport and flew to Phoenix, where I changed planes to Chicago, where I changed planes to Buffalo. Once in Chicago, I called Terry and told her where I was and what time I expected to land in Buffalo. I asked her not to tell anyone and to meet me at the airport. Until that moment, she didn't know I was back in the States, safe and sound. We had a very emotional conversation and one filled with happiness.

Homecoming
March 1968

I arrived in Buffalo, climbed down the stairs from the plane, took a deep breath, and entered the airport expecting to see Terry. She was there, but so were my mother, my sister Patrice, Uncle Dick and Aunt Jean, and Terry's mother and brother Marty. She had rounded up everyone she could in an hour and a half! I had waited for this day for more than a year, but there's no way to prepare for the moment it actually happens. We all hugged, tears flowed, and then we all just looked at each other as if this moment wasn't really happening. Finally, I suggested we head for the airport bar and have a drink, which is exactly what we did. I was never overweight, but I had lost about fifteen or twenty pounds since we last saw each other, and everyone seemed to be looking me over.

I stayed in the apartment previously occupied by Mrs. Weeks across from the bedroom where my brother and I lived as kids. It was eerily quiet—without whirling helicopters, the omnipresent artillery shells flying overhead, or their explosions in the distance. Then too, it felt strange to be living in an apartment with walls and without roommates. My life for the previous year had been completely different in every way, and this dramatic change took some getting used to. Over time, I acclimated and spent much more time in the present and the future than in the past.

I was proud of the time I spent in Vietnam and felt I had made a contribution to the war effort. However, not everyone was pleased with our country's involvement in Southeast Asia. In fact, the majority of Americans were vehemently opposed to it. I found many people who were not only disinterested in my experiences, but who were actually repulsed. It was a common theme across America. The country was tired of the war, the economic drain, and, most of all, the death toll. They questioned why we were there and a majority of the American public lost its appetite to continue the effort.

The level of discontent was somewhat surprising to me. Of course, I realized there was a strong anti-war movement in our country prior to my departure, but I didn't realize how much strength the movement had gained while I was gone. The reality came into sharp focus a few weeks after my return. On March 31, 1968, President Lyndon Johnson addressed the nation, announcing steps to limit the war in Vietnam and also to report that he would not seek re-election to the presidency. The president of the United States—a man of exceptional will and strength, the former Master of the Senate—had been exhausted by the war and the discord it had created in the country. He was throwing in the towel.

During my leave, I focused my attention on Terry, and we spent every available minute together. She was a junior in college and an ardent student, intent on attending classes and doing well. She was also a young woman in love, so every now and then she would play hooky so we could spend even more time together. We often went out to dinner, walked, laughed, lived, and loved. It was a wonderful and magical time.

Engaged to be Married

While home on leave, the topic of marriage came up. Actually, Terry brought it up by asking if and when we should get married. I was game for sooner rather than later, but she felt it would be devastating to her parents if she didn't finish college, so we agreed to wait until after her graduation. I also needed to secure a job upon my discharge from the army before we could move forward. We agreed to become formally engaged and to set the wedding for August of the following year.

Terry explained that I needed to ask her father for her hand, which, frankly, scared me. Her father was a strong man in many ways. He had been brought up in an orphanage in South Buffalo named Father Baker's, which was a place known to me in a very different way. When my brother and I were kids and constantly fighting, there would come a time when our parents wanted to make a point. My father would tell us to get in the car, because he was taking us to Father Baker's. We would make what seemed to be a very long journey to the orphanage, where we would have a "Come to Jesus" discussion about our behavior, and we would swear we would never "do it" again. I recall two or three such trips.

Terry told her mother about our decision to become engaged, and she was supportive. The plan was set. Mr. Dwyer occupied his reclining easy chair, a Barcalounger, every night with his rosary in one hand and a quart of beer in the other. Sunday nights were very special since *Bonanza* came on the television, and it was one of Mr. Dwyer's favorite shows. We had dinner in the dining room, and Terry and her mother went into the kitchen to clean up. The first floor of the Dwyer house consisted of a front hallway and the living room, dining room, and kitchen, all of which were in very close proximity. The girls peered into the living room where I was situated on the sofa about three feet from Mr. Dwyer, who was glued to his show. Then the moment came. A commercial came on, and I spoke up (with the prodding of the girls about five feet away).

I said, "Mr. Dwyer, I have something I'd like to talk to you about. Terry and I would like to get married." At that very moment when I blurted out the last word, the commercial ended and the show came back on.

Mr. Dwyer replied, "That's fine with me," and became again fixated on the adventures of Ben Cartwright and his sons Adam, Little Joe, and Hoss. The permission was granted!

Not long after that, Terry and I decided to go to Gamlers (commonly referred to as "Gamblers") Jewelry Store downtown on Main Street to select an engagement ring. Terry was very fond of diamonds with a marquis cut, and we narrowed it down two different rings, one with a diamond about half the size of the other. I wanted the larger one, but Terry insisted that it would look too large on her hand, so we bought the smaller version. Many years later Terry admitted she really liked the larger ring, but she didn't want me to spend the money. We were officially engaged on Washington's birthday in February 1968, and we set a wedding date for eighteen months later in August 1969, allowing time for Terry's graduation and time for me to secure a job.

While on leave I bought a new car—a Mercury Cougar XR-7 with an eight-cylinder 302 cubic-inch engine and a three-speed shift on the floor. It was British racing green, had tan leather interior, and was a very flashy car. Many people loved the Ford Mustang, but I thought the Cougar was really something. I used my poker winnings from Vietnam to make the purchase.

The weeks flew by, and suddenly it was time for me to pack my duffle bag and report to Ft. Meade. Leaving Terry was never easy, but it wasn't nearly as difficult as when I was going overseas. This time I wasn't halfway around the world. We would be only 400 miles apart, and I could easily fly or drive to be with her.

Ft. Meade, Maryland
March 1968 to December 1968

When the day arrived, I drove my Cougar to my new assignment in Laurel, Maryland. The drive took me through the southern tier of New York, through eastern Pennsylvania, and into Maryland. The trip began with a short stint on the New York Thruway to Batavia then onto Route 63, passing Letchworth State Park, which held many pleasant memories, and through Mt. Morris, where my father had spent so long recuperating from tuberculosis. The rest of the journey through New York and most of Pennsylvania was Route 15, which was primarily a two-lane road with an occasional "suicide lane" through the mountains, concluding with the last one hundred miles on Route 83 into Maryland. The trip took about eight hours and was a scenic, memorable, pleasant ride—one that I would become very familiar with over the next eighteen months.

Ft. Meade was approximately the same size as Ft. Devens, and substantially smaller than Ft. Dix. It consisted of various units, but the Army Security Agency had a large presence there since the

National Security Agency (NSA) was located at the edge of the base, as well as at an annex near Friendship Airport (now named Thurgood Marshall Baltimore-Washington Airport).

The NSA complex was enormous, with a high fence around the perimeter and armed guards at every entry point. Inside were cavernous hallways with large swinging doors spaced about every couple hundred feet, and closed doors all along the way. Although the building was enormous, the work inside was carried out in a portioned manner with entry only into the area a person was assigned to. I had no idea what was going on in the offices adjacent to my area, and nobody ever discussed what their job entailed or what type of work they were doing. Even when with people in my unit, the only time anything regarding our work was discussed was while we were in our own area. I suppose the best way to keep a secret is not to tell anyone, and that was the motto we all lived by.

I worked alongside other military personnel as well as civilians, but our work group was primarily civilians. Jim Ward, my pal from Vietnam, was assigned to the same unit, and we had great fun pulling practical jokes. One of Jim's favorite things to do while walking in the hallways was to follow closely behind older women, who invariably didn't hold the door for the person behind. Jim would set his foot about two inches in front of his face and act as though the door had hit him in the nose. He'd fall to the floor holding his nose, and everyone would flock to his rescue. Jim became quite proficient at this stunt.

Another one of Jim's favorite pranks was to put green tape across his front teeth. When a co-worker named Mike (who actually had green teeth as well as other significant hygiene issues) faced me with his back to Jim, Jim would flash a huge green grin.

As an aside, Mike was an interesting fellow. Once a cockroach crawled out of his boot only to meet with a deadly stomp. Mike allowed as how those critters were rampant in his house, and how he and his lovely wife occasionally had to hose down the furniture.

Meanwhile, a few months after we arrived at NSA, Jim met a girl who was a former nun. They fell in love, she became pregnant, and she and Jim decided to get married. The legal age for marriage in Maryland was twenty-one, and Jim and I were twenty. I went with him to the county offices in Annapolis and dutifully signed an affidavit stating that I was twenty-one, that I knew Jim, and that I knew him to be twenty-two years old. Jim walked out with a marriage license. Just so you know, they were married, had a child, and lived happily ever after.

During this time I befriended several likeable guys, including Mike McClellan, Lenny ("Crazy Lenny") Kreman, John Maher, and others. The only person I knew when I arrived at Ft. Meade was Jim Ward, but my circle of friends grew rapidly between the guys in our barracks and those at work.

Ft. Meade was located just outside the town of Laurel, which was (and still is) famous for the Laurel Race Track. I went to the track a couple of times but didn't have a lot of spare time. Other than the racetrack, the town was rather nondescript and not particularly enticing.

Weekends in Buffalo with Terry

I was initially assigned to the day shift at NSA but later requested, and was granted, the eve shift with hours from four in the afternoon until eleven thirty in the evening. This schedule change enabled me to travel to Buffalo on the weekends and have more time to spend with Terry. The first year I was in Maryland, I drove the 400 miles each way every weekend except two. As a result, I logged 52,000 miles on my new Cougar.

On those weekends I'd leave Meade after work at eleven thirty at night and arrive in Buffalo at about seven the following morning (my best time was six hours and fifteen minutes). The roads along Route 15 during the winter could be tricky, but I had studded snow tires to cope with snow and they worked quite well. I ran off the road only once and had to be towed out of the snow, whereupon I continued on my journey to Buffalo.

On one of my trips, I arrived in Buffalo, opened the front door of the house on Evadene, and there, sitting on the living room floor with a case of beer between them, were my good friends Harry Pierce and Fred Powers. I had not kept in touch since Vietnam, and I was surprised and happy to see them. Apparently, the night before they were in their hometown of Indianapolis having a few beers when they decided it would be fun to see their old pal, Pat. I joined them in the impromptu celebration, and Terry and I spent that day and the evening with them. The next morning they drove back.

On my trips to Buffalo, typically Terry would meet me in the morning and we'd go places, see people, and just hang around together. Saturday nights usually meant a trip to Santora's

Restaurant on Main Street for pizza. We often went to a restaurant named John's Flaming Hearth in Niagara Falls, an elegant spot with a piano player and excellent food served by tuxedoed waiters. Our favorite place was the Old Orchard Inn in East Aurora, where the owners, Chuck and Joyce Roof, befriended us.

On Monday mornings I'd leave Buffalo about seven and arrive at Meade around three in the afternoon, leaving me time to shower, dress, and report to work by four. The next week I'd do it all over again. In hindsight, I suppose it was a bit much to make that trip every weekend through all kinds of weather, but I was in love and it all made sense to me. I did this for eighteen months, and if I could to do again, I would.

Civilian Life Just Around the Corner

I had applied for full-time civilian employment at NSA and was told I would be hired as a GS-7 upon my discharge from the army. This was a big deal and it fulfilled what I needed to do to move forward with our wedding plans. The salary was $6,742 annually, which seemed like a million dollars compared to my military wage. The same amount would equate to $43,428 in 2013 dollars adjusted for inflation.

My four-year tour of duty was up on January 11, 1969, but Uncle Sam must have had the Christmas spirit as I was discharged on December 20, 1968, allowing me to spend Christmas with my family. What a terrific surprise! And a great Christmas present—a twenty-two day early release! Before leaving Maryland to go home for a few weeks, I signed a month-to-month lease on a very small one-bedroom apartment in Laurel.

My army adventure came to an end. I entered the military as an E-1 private and left as an E-5 specialist fifth class. While in the army, I was awarded the Expert Rifle Marksmanship Badge, the Good Conduct Metal, The Meritorious Unit Commendation, the National Defense Service Metal, and the Vietnam Service Metal with two Bronze Service Stars.

When I entered two months after turning seventeen, I didn't have any direction or idea of what I'd do or how I'd do it. The U.S. Army taught me discipline, self-assuredness, self-confidence, independence, and the value of teamwork and reliance on others. I stood tall and ready to find success in whatever I did. Now, one month after turning twenty-one, my life had purpose. I had a good job with NSA. I was engaged to be married within eight months, and I was about to spend my first Christmas at home since 1964. Life was good. Very good, indeed.

Chapter 4

A New and Exciting Time
1969 to 1974

Although I had secured a position with NSA, Terry wanted to stay in Buffalo if possible after we were married. I spent time job searching for local employment while home but found it very difficult since I couldn't discuss what I did while in the service, and, even if I could, my experience didn't have any direct application to the civilian world. At one point, we explored buying twenty acres near Colden in the ski area outside Buffalo, but fortunately, we walked away from the deal when we discovered it involved building an access road to county specifications. Finally, we accepted the fact that I would be working in Maryland and that Terry would join me there after we were married.

In mid January I returned to Maryland and reported for work. I was assigned to the same unit I had worked for while in the military: same place, same people, same work, different clothes, and vastly different compensation.

I went about setting up my apartment that was in the middle of a cluster of antiquated two-story, red brick buildings in Laurel. The apartment consisted of a living area, galley kitchen, bathroom, and a small bedroom. I furnished the living area with two folding TV tables, two folding lawn chairs with multi-colored vinyl webbing, and a television set with rabbit ears and aluminum foil to improve reception. The bedroom housed a folding cot. I equipped the kitchen with a frying pan, two sauce pans, a few sets of silverware, four dinner plates, glassware, and assorted utensils. The bathroom had two bath towels and two hand towels. The place was hardly ready for a spread in *Better Homes and Gardens,* but it was adequate, convenient, and inexpensive. Besides, I spent most of my time at work, on the road, or in Buffalo.

Spring arrived and the weather was beautiful. The Mercury Cougar had served me well, but with its high mileage, I knew it was time to say goodbye. The replacement decision was easy. I bought a new 1969 Chevy Corvette with a 350 cubic-inch engine. It was silver with a gray interior, a four-speed manual transmission on the floor, and a T-top to enjoy the sun. It looked like it was speeding while parked at the curb. Beautiful!

Recognizing that Laurel wasn't the place Terry and I wanted to live, I explored the area to find a more suitable place to set up house. I looked at every town within a reasonable driving radius and kept coming back to Annapolis, a beautiful historic town located on the Chesapeake Bay and home to the U.S. Naval Academy. I discovered a relatively new garden apartment complex named Spa Cove and learned that a second floor two-bedroom apartment was going to be available in a month. Although I didn't need the place until August, I decided to rent it then and there since we didn't know whether another apartment would be available later. As an added benefit, we could furnish it before we moved in, so it would be ready when we arrived.

Terry had majored in elementary education. She sent her resume to Anne Arundel County, which in turn contacted her for an interview. She and a girlfriend flew to Baltimore where we met. She had a successful interview and was subsequently offered a job as a first-grade teacher in Parole Elementary School. Parole was a section of Annapolis and was aptly named. Recently integrated, the school was slowly converting from an all-black institution to one with whites. Unbeknownst to us, the principal, Mr. Walter Mills, a black man, was renowned as a tough disciplinarian, who thought it a grand idea to leave the public address system turned on while disciplining children.

Terry had concerns about Parole Elementary, but she also wanted to get started on her new career and our new life together. When she heard about Mr. Mills's methods, she said to me quietly, "We'll see how it goes. I suppose I can always quit."

With that caveat in mind, we agreed we now had all the pieces in place. I had a job with a good salary, Terry had a job with an even better salary, and we had signed a lease for our first apartment. The only thing left was the wedding itself.

Wedding Plans

I found it fortunate that Terry and her mother were immersed in planning the wedding without consulting me. We did discuss and agree to have the wedding at St. Joseph's Church where we had both attended elementary school, and we also agreed to have the reception at our friend's restaurant and our favorite spot, the Old Orchard Inn. The last major detail was where to go on our honeymoon, and we decided that Bermuda would be the perfect place. Terry and her mother made the decisions regarding colors of dresses for the bridesmaids, flowers, transportation, the brunch menu, the reception menu, the music, and all the other details. I simply asked them to tell me where to be and what time to be there.

I asked our old friend Bill Walgate to be my best man. He agreed, which pleased me since I hoped that time had healed all wounds. However, shortly before the wedding, he telephoned and told me he simply couldn't do it. I scrambled and asked Tom O'Connor, a bartender friend of mine from Santora's, if he would be willing to step in. He agreed. The groomsmen were my brother, Jim Ward, and Phil Seereiter. Terry's maid of honor was her longtime childhood friend Mary Balling, and her bridesmaids were her two sisters-in-law, Marylyn Dywer and Karen Dwyer, and my sister Patrice.

Wedding Bells

August 2 was a particularly hot day for Buffalo and especially hot in a morning suit with tails. Our friend Father Bob Beiter presided at the marriage ceremony. Terry arranged the music, and it was very special.

Terry had spent six years taking voice lessons. The nun who taught Terry in high school also directed the nuns' choir at Mount St. Joseph's. When Terry asked Sister Gertrude Mary and her choir members to sing at our wedding, she and the other nuns enthusiastically agreed. Our wedding music was not typical church hymns, but rather a selection of songs that had very special meaning to us. The processional song was "A Time for Us" from *Romeo and Juliet*. The offertory song was "One Hand, One Heart" from *West Side Story*; the communion song was "Lara's Theme: Somewhere My Love" from *Doctor Zhivago*; the meditation hymn was "Ave Maria" and the recessional song—the grand finale—was the theme from

A Man and A Woman (one of our favorite movies and soundtracks).

Due to the heat (and maybe the excitement of it all), my hands had become swollen. Terry found it difficult to put my wedding ring on, but ultimately she was able to push it over my knuckle. The crowd seemed amused.

We practically skipped out of the church to the theme of *A Man and a Woman*, stood in the greeting line, poised for pictures, and left for a brunch gathering at the Continental Inn on Sheridan Drive. From there we drove to the Old Orchard Inn for the reception. Everything about the party was terrific, and several of the guests did their part in holding up the bar. Finally the moment arrived for us to leave. We changed out of the wedding attire and made the grand entrance down the stairs from the owner's residence for our departure. The night before I had hid the Corvette in the barn to avoid soaped windows, tin cans, and other foolishness. We walked briskly down the stone path from the restaurant to the barn, jumped in the car, and left with a flourish as we sped in the direction of the Little White House restaurant in Williamsburg. Following a light dinner we departed for a hotel near the airport where I carried Terry over the threshold. Terry spent about an hour soaking in the tub with all the bubble bath and oils she had brought with her, while I watched a pre-season football game. Once she finished the bath ritual, we sipped Lancers Rose. Suffice it to say, we had a wonderful night.

Honeymoon

The next day we arrived at the Castle Harbour Hotel in Bermuda and were greeted by the doorman. "Big Daddy," as he was called, was all decked out in a white shirt, white Bermuda shorts, white shoes, and brilliant white teeth, which stood out dramatically against his dark black skin. Big Daddy was a jovial and courteous man, custom-made for his job and delightful in every way.

After sorting out why our "ocean view" room actually had a view of a vine-covered wall and moving to the correct room (after a bit of a ruckus at the front desk), we adjourned to the lounge where Terry ordered a drink with an umbrella in it. The only other time I recalled her drinking a cocktail with an umbrella was at the Mona Kai years earlier when I told her to date Bill and leave me alone. Times had changed.

We spent a memory-filled week on the island enjoying the beach, the swimming pool, the drinks, the food, the motor scooters, and, of course, each other. On our first excursion riding scooters, I had difficulty driving on the left side of the road, so Terry took the lead. That first day I fell off my scooter, and she kept on going thinking I was right behind her. Once she arrived back at the hotel, she realized I wasn't there, and thoughts of becoming an early widow crept into her mind. She put Big Daddy on the case, and as they were about to send out a search party, I showed up.

We enjoyed many fine meals and various types of entertainment, but the most interesting evening was spent at a nightclub with a voodoo act. A native with a crazed look took the stage and started writhing and crying out to the loud beat of a drum. He then spread a mat on the floor, grabbed several beer bottles, broke them into small pieces on the mat, poured a flammable liquid on top, and lit it. At that point his mind seemed to be in another place as he slowly walked across the glass and flames. The crowd was full of oohs and aahs, but the coup de grace occurred when he picked up the flaming broken glass and rubbed it into his face. That's when the crowd went wild.

Settling in Annapolis
August 1969

The week flew by and it was time to return to Buffalo for a couple of days before heading to our new home in Annapolis. The Corvette didn't have the space to carry wedding gifts, clothes, and everything else we had accumulated, so Terry drove the car and I drove a rented U-Haul truck. We were about fifty miles into the 400-mile trip cruising along on the New York Thruway when two of the four folding tables that were wedding gifts flew off the car luggage rack and were obliterated when they crashed onto the pavement. Fortunately, nobody was hit by the flying debris. The rest of the trip was uneventful, and we arrived at our little apartment in Spa Cove safe and sound.

We had furnished the apartment a couple of months earlier, although I had never stayed there. Everything was new and fresh—not just the apartment and the furnishings, but also we as a couple. There is something very exciting about starting a whole new life, and we both found it exhilarating. Terry did miss

Buffalo terribly, but we were thrilled to be starting our lives together.

I started my job at NSA in mid August. We only had one car, but I found a used Rambler that was pretty beat up but ran well, and it was cheap. The parking lot at NSA was not the place to park a Corvette, so I drove the Rambler, and Terry had the Corvette. In hindsight, it's interesting how many times Ramblers were a part of our lives. First it was Bill Walgate's father's Rambler we used for drive-ins, then it was my mother and Jack's Rambler I was driving when awarded a fistful of traffic tickets, and now as newlyweds, another Rambler. This one was not the pick of the litter.

A couple of weeks later Terry started her job as first-grade teacher at Parole Elementary about a mile from our apartment. She was quite a hit driving the "silver bullet." I was always amazed at how many cars were in the school parking lot considering it was an elementary school. I've heard of being held back, but…nah, it couldn't be.

Moving On

All was going along swimmingly until around October when I announced that I thought we should look for a house. I had more flexibility with my work schedule so I took on the task of searching for the perfect place. I found a reputable realtor who was most accommodating, and we looked at a lot of properties. Then one day he called and said that he had found a house that would be perfect for us. I met him at his office to take a look. The house was located in an area named Arnold, about ten minutes from downtown Annapolis in a small community with three different styles of houses. The house was about eighteen months old, and it was about to be foreclosed on. I had the opportunity to assume the owner's mortgage with very little out-of-pocket expense, but I had to move quickly. So I bought the house on the spot, signing the contract, and anxiously awaited Terry's arrival from work to break the good news. When she arrived home, I asked her to sit down as I had some wonderful news. I was having a difficult time containing myself and blurted out that we were now the owners of a house. At first she thought I was kidding, but I assured her I wasn't. She was astounded. Absolutely astounded. She couldn't believe that I would buy a house without her seeing it or even calling her to discuss the purchase! I decided we'd drive past the house and thought that would soothe her astonishment. We couldn't go inside since the owners were still living there with their herd of children. A month later, on December 19, 1969, we moved into our new home that I had bought for $31,300.

In my exuberance over having the opportunity to buy the house, I overlooked a few things…like the lack of air conditioning, the fact that the owners took the refrigerator and the washer and dryer, that the kids had left thousands of fingerprints (and other non-descript items) on the bedroom walls, the lack of curtains, the existence of a leak in the front foyer ceiling, and other things. Given the above, it was decision time, so I decided to sell the Corvette to fund several items we needed. This was a difficult decision, but I was trying to gain favor over my impetuous purchase, and it seemed a small price to pay. Not only did I part with my beloved sports car, but also I traded it in for a brand new red Fiat station wagon. What a culture shock!

About the same time we moved into our new house, we experienced three significant events.

First, I decided that, although I loved the nature of the work at NSA, I didn't see it as a career. Government work was very different from the private sector. The most important differences were the lack of ability to progress in terms of challenge and salary. I knew that if I stayed at NSA much longer, I would get sucked into the pay scale and the security of a government job.

Second, I met a fellow who lived at Spa Cove apartments and was a manager at the local Metropolitan Life Insurance Company. He convinced me that I was a natural insurance salesman. I resigned from NSA and embarked on what turned out to be a not-so-successful career in insurance sales that lasted only five or six months.

Third, and the really BIG news around that time was that Terry became pregnant. She met me at the Metropolitan Life Insurance office and gave me the good news on New Year's Eve. I drove home, and I was so stunned that I missed our turn and almost arrived at the Bay Bridge before I realized it. Terry and I were filled with joy. Here we were with a mortgage payment, a shaky insurance job, and a baby on the way. Most people might have been concerned about all that, but we were happy and overlooked the scary confluence of events.

In April I admitted defeat as an insurance salesman and started looking for other employment. I knew I could return to

NSA but still felt I could be more successful with other opportunities outside of government work. The problem was I wasn't quite sure what these opportunities might be. Fortunately, Terry continued to work until the end of the school year.

Major Finance

I went to an employment agency, and they had a position as a collector with a finance company headquartered in Silver Spring, Maryland. I didn't know anything about finance, banking, or, most of all, collecting debts. I interviewed for the position with Major Finance and was hired at a salary of $7,200 per year, which was just about what I had earned at NSA. Terry stayed home while I commuted over an hour each way, leaving home about seven in the morning and returning around seven or eight in the evening. To break up the loneliness, Terry occasionally drove me to work and picked me up so she would have use of the car. The problem was, I was never sure when my day would end.

My starting role at Major Finance was to collect delinquent accounts. I learned that most competitors had inside collectors but they also hired an "outside man" to knock on doors. Major didn't believe in this approach. Their method was for the collectors to try to collect the money by phone, but if that wasn't possible, then the collectors had to make the field calls themselves. This approach did make me a much better telephone collector, but at times when calls weren't effective, I'd find myself in Washington, D.C., or Prince Georges County, knocking on doors. Generally, I'd make those "field calls" on late

Friday afternoons since most of our customers were paid on Fridays. These trips were always exciting, sometimes scary, and generally successful.

Typically, loans were secured by "household goods," a term that was purposely non-descript. One of our favorite tricks with especially difficult customers was to make a field call with a "stick list." I'd knock (or more likely bang) on the door, and when our customer answered, I'd identify myself and announce I was there to make a list of our collateral. I'd walk through the premise listing every single item including silverware and dishes. Whatever the customer owed was what my total would be. Normally at that point there would be an offer to make a payment or two, to which I replied that I wasn't permitted to accept payments, and the customer would have to come to the office to stop the "action." Once in the office, I'd call Mr. Roper (also known as El Roper), who was a counterpart in another office. I would ask him to try to stop the writ of mandamus.

A writ of mandamus has absolutely nothing to do with collections or debts, but it did have a nice ring to it, and it scared the hell out of people. We generally put the customer on the phone with Mr. Roper, and the customer would beg for forgiveness and promise never to miss a payment again. Customers would do anything to avoid the writ of mandamus.

Another vengeful activity was the "army game." I have no idea how this name became attached to the activity, but it stuck. Major Finance (and every other finance company) belonged to a "lenders exchange." When we took a loan application, the first thing we did was to call the lenders exchange and provide the name and address and other information of our applicant. The exchange, in turn, provided information such as where the applicant had open loans or where he had applied for a loan.

Sometimes we discovered the customer had an old loan with us, which had been charged off as a bad debt. More often we received the call for a reference from another company from which he was applying for credit. Naturally, when they learned of our charge off, the company where he had applied would decline the application.

We would then follow up and call our customer, remind him of the old loan that we never fully collected, and tell him if he paid off the old loan we were "ninety-nine percent sure" we could provide a new loan. It was remarkable how many people bought into that concept. At that point, we would accept payment (cash only) of the charged off balance and tell him we were submitting his new application to the "loan committee." Then we'd sit the applicant in a closing booth and let him sit… and sit… and sit… for hours. Every once in a while a head would pop up from the booth, and we'd reassure the customer that we were waiting for an answer and apologize, explaining that the committee was meeting for an unusually long time.

Ultimately (usually at closing time), we would walk into the booth and tell our waiting customer that the loan committee declined his request, at which time he would ask for his money back. This request was met with the same answer every time: We deposited the money earlier; we didn't have any cash in the office; and we couldn't get the money back from the bank. Ruthless—absolutely. Effective—always.

At Major Finance I met several fascinating people. Mort Stuart and Al Abramson started the company many years earlier, and they were the honchos. Mr. Abramson was the more likeable of the two, but Mr. Stuart was more involved in the day-to-day operations. Bob Railey, Dick Greene, and Bill Shanahan were office managers. Joe Stemmy, Len Kidwell, Ned Hensley, and Jerry Dunne were collectors, and various others had been there for years. I still keep in touch with Jerry, since he married my wife's sister, and Laurie Hawald (previously Sullivan) and I still exchange Christmas cards. By and large, they were tough businessmen and -women, but you had to be tough in this business to succeed. It was rough and tumble.

Baby Due Soon

Meanwhile, our baby was expected to arrive in mid August. The temperature was hot as hell, and we still didn't have air conditioning. We had limited health insurance covering the birth of the baby, but it was *very limited*.

August arrived but the baby didn't. Terry's mother and father drove to Maryland to help in anticipation of the birth. Tensions ran high, the temperature was even higher, and one night when Terry went to bed early, her mother and I engaged in an unpleasant discussion. She made a comment regarding the competency of our doctor; I made a comment that I wasn't aware that she was a doctor. It went south from there.

The next morning I rose early as usual and left for work. About nine o'clock I received a call from Terry seeking clarity on driving directions to Buffalo. Her parents had also risen early and packed the car before Terry got out of bed. Needless to say, I received a chilly welcome when I arrived home that evening and the chill remained in the air for several days. Finally on September 13, Terry was ready to go to the hospital. After being there for several hours, the decision was made to induce labor but that didn't yield results right away. The doctor told Terry that if she didn't give birth by the next morning that she would be discharged. I stayed with her until the evening and went home only to be awakened in the middle of the night by a call from her saying she was in labor and about to give birth. I sped to the hospital and sat and paced in the waiting room while smoking cigarettes. Michelle Lara was born September 14, 1970.

Terry stayed in the hospital until September 16, when she and Michelle were discharged. I met them at the front door of the hospital and took them home. A whole new world began for us. I didn't know anything about babies, including how to hold them, feed them, and, most of all, change diapers for them. I was a fairly quick learner with the exception of the changing part, which usually resulted in the diaper being around the baby's ankles fifteen minutes after I changed it. I never learned how to change a "Number 2" diaper, and when Terry wasn't available, I imposed on our neighbor Bette MacWilliams to step in and get the job done. Thank God for Bette.

Family Life

Adding to the challenges of having a new home, a new job, and a new baby, we decided to purchase two German shepherds. The male was Ingo and the female was Fusty (quickly renamed

Sark). I built two runs in the backyard where the dogs spent much of their time. Ingo was beautiful, resembling the television shepherd, Rin Tin Tin, but he had one major flaw—he was nuts, which I assume was caused from too much inbreeding. Sark was a smaller dog but attractive and very intelligent in addition to being paranoid. Basically, one dog was an idiot and the other needed a psychiatrist. I began to wonder which camp I fit into.

We quickly realized we needed more money than I was earning. There were many times when we had eggs but no butter. Spam, Chef Boyardee Pizza Mix, and Shake 'n Bake chicken were becoming staples at our house. However, I had a BankAmerica credit card (now VISA) that had a $500 credit limit. About once a week we'd hire a sitter for an hour or two and go to the Oxbow restaurant about a half-mile from the house and share dinner on the card. This worked well until we hit the $500 limit. We didn't have any debt other than the one credit card and a mortgage, but the mortgage payment was more than my take-home pay every two weeks. I thought about getting a second job but Major Finance was taking more and more of my time.

The only solution was for Terry to return to work, but if she went back into teaching, it would mean a full-time babysitter, which would offset most of the additional income. In addition, she had such a terrible experience in her first year with Mr. Mills and with the educational structure in Anne Arundel County that she lost her desire to teach. New York State was only a few hundred miles away but the two educational systems were worlds apart. Adding to the significant differences in teachers' qualifications, Mr. Mills had his way of doing things, and he wasn't going to change. He was an old-style disciplinarian whose methods Terry could no longer tolerate.

Meanwhile, the local newspaper, the *Evening Capital* (widely referred to as the *Evening Crap Wrapper*) was looking for a proofreader, and Terry applied. If ever there was a newspaper that needed a proofreader that was it. The paper was regularly riddled with typos, poor sentence structure, stories ending in the middle, and other maladies. She met with the editor, who asked for her qualifications. She provided her college GPA and her work background, and also discussed her academic awards, not the least of which was being named to "Outstanding Young Women in America" and "Who's Who in American Colleges and Universities." The editor had not heard of these awards and asked why she would even mention them. At that point Terry told him she was no longer interested in the job. We needed the money but not that badly.

We concluded that if she could find a night job, I could be home either before she left or shortly thereafter, which would reduce the monies paid for sitting. We thought about it and decided that a job as a waitress would fit our schedule and needs. The one problem was we had only one car. Terry spoke with her mother, who said she was getting ready to trade in her Chevy Malibu convertible, and we agreed that we would buy the car from her for the trade-in value. She was kind enough to accept a very liberal payment schedule, and we ultimately paid it off.

Terry worked nights at a family-oriented restaurant near the Chesapeake Bay Bridge in which she wore a Dolly Madison-type outfit. Typically, I would arrive home as soon as I could, relieve the sitter, and stay with Michelle, feeding her, changing her, calling Bette when needed, and putting her to bed.

While the waitress job helped tremendously, it was a night job, and the next day Terry had her day job of raising Michelle. We decided she should look for a regular job, and she applied for and was hired as a teller at Farmers National Bank in February 1971. The extra income paid for a babysitter, and the remaining monies were greater than her waitressing income. My hours were long, and I wasn't getting home as early as I previously had, so this was the answer. We seemed to be on even keel financially but we had a limited social life. We both belonged to card clubs in the neighborhood—Terry to a pinochle club and I to a poker club. Our outside activity primarily consisted on going to town to hear Dick Gessner.

Dick was an extremely talented guy who played the piano and sang classic Cole Porter, Rogers and Hammerstein hits, and Broadway tunes. He rarely played from music sheets and had a repertoire of several hundred songs. In addition to his talent, the local thespians would join him; in fact, anyone with a voice was welcome to stand by the piano and join in with Dick and the audience. We had many, many wonderful and fun-filled evenings with Dick. The night after Michelle was born, I went to the restaurant where Dick was playing. As soon as he saw me, he knew our first baby had been born. He stopped what he was playing and started playing "Michelle," which was a Beatles hit, and then he followed with the theme from a favorite movie of ours, *Doctor Zhivago*, titled "Lara's Theme." We became great friends and still stay in touch.

In the fall of 1972, we discovered that Terry was pregnant again, and the baby was due in June. We were delighted. Terry came from a family of five children, and I was one of three. Before we were married we thought having four or five kids would be great. Now the reality of supporting a large family was sinking in.

We decided that maybe the best course was to sell our house and look for a smaller place. We didn't really need four bedrooms. We could have our bedroom, the kids could share a second, and we could have a third for guests. We listed the house and the realtor's sign was prominently posted on the front lawn until one night when I came home from work after having a few beers and defiantly yanked it from the lawn. *So there—take that!* I said to myself. It felt great. We decided to tough it out and stay in the house.

I decided to take a second job to help with expenses for our new baby. I applied for and was hired at Archie's Beef and Beer on West Street in Annapolis. The owner was a likeable woman named Ella Hart, who was trying to make a go of it running a bar and restaurant that served soups, submarine sandwiches, pizza, and beer. My work schedule became intense: I'd work about fifty hours a week at Major Finance, commute sixty minutes to Annapolis, and work three nights a week until eleven or twelve. I also worked every Saturday and some Sundays when Terry and Michelle would visit and enjoy one of my "world famous" pizzas. I used to pound the dough and then throw it in the air several times to form the crust. Michelle was a little girl and enjoyed watching her father tossing the dough. Once I tossed it too high and it stuck to the ceiling for a few seconds until it fell. Her expression was priceless as she said, "Oh! Oh!"

Ella and I hit it off well, and before long, I was making the nightly deposit at the bank. I did everything from making pizza and sandwiches to pouring draught beer to mopping the floor at closing time. Our arrangement was I'd work until I had enough money to pay for the baby's delivery and hospital bill. That took about four months, and I resigned.

Terry continued with her teller job until close to the due date, and we were making ends meet. Joanna Christie was born on June 23, a healthy and beautiful baby. Terry spent the minimum amount of time her doctor allowed in the hospital, and I anxiously arrived at the appointed time to bring them home. Now we had two babies and two nutty dogs, which created a bit of a circus on a regular basis. But we were happy, and our new addition was wonderful.

As time went on, my job at Major Finance became more and more demanding. Since I began working there, I had been assigned to each of their four offices—Silver Spring and Mount Rainer in Maryland and Alexandria and Arlington in Virginia. After a couple of years, I was promoted to manager of the Arlington office, which meant more challenges, more salary, more hours, and the longest commute among the offices. I'd leave for work early, arrive home late, and frequently didn't see the kids during the week other than to peek into their cribs and catch a glance. The strain was more difficult for Terry, who had to manage the household, bring up the kids, and cope with my schedule. It was a challenging time for both of us. I deeply regret all the time I missed during the kids' childhoods and am tremendously grateful that my wife did such a wonderful job raising them. The time I missed with them is something I can never recover. I wish I could.

Once Joanna was born, Terry resigned her position at the bank. Now Terry was spending virtually all her time with our children, and, to supplement our income, was babysitting for neighborhood children as well. That occupied her every waking moment with very little adult interaction. She attended a regularly scheduled appointment with her doctor and broke down in tears. Dr. Monias told her she had to do something just for herself—not for the kids or for me. She mentioned our lack of money; nevertheless, he demanded that she listen to him and do what he said. She desperately needed an outlet.

As a child Terry and her best friend Mary Balling saved their money, and when they had saved enough, Mr. Balling drove them into the country to a stable where they would ride horses western style. She always loved horses so, following Dr. Monias's advice, she decided she would take lessons to learn how to ride dressage. She found a stable in Davidsonville named Idlewilde Farm with an up-and-coming rider named Linda Zang. Terry signed on for a one-hour lesson once a week, initially joining a class with four children. She quickly progressed, and we leased a horse, which we named Dante (we lived on Via Dante Street). We couldn't afford to own a horse, but wanted continuity with the same horse for lessons, so I devised and sold the idea of a lease. It worked well for both parties.

The red Fiat station wagon was beginning to give us serious problems. More and more often it would require repairs, which in turn required money to pay for the repairs. Shortly after we were married and moved to Maryland, my stepfather, who was working for Lane Bryant, was transferred to Washington, D.C. Fortunately, he introduced me to a man who was the branch manager at Riggs National Bank's main office. When household emergencies arose, I went to see him and he would provide a ninety-day loan. These loans were usually for a few hundred dollars, but they got us over the hump, and I always repaid promptly. They were lifesavers.

The Fiat was on its last breath when we took it to Rogers Chevrolet to discuss a trade-in for a new car. I propped the carburetor open with a ballpoint pen that kept it running for their inspection, and we drove off in a new Chevy Vega, a compact car with a stick shift and no frills. Now we drove a car that ran, but we also had a car payment.

Major Finance was a well-run company, but it had only four loan offices and one sales finance office. I was a manager of one of the offices and the men over me were young and deeply entrenched. This meant they weren't going anywhere, and I had progressed as far as I could for the foreseeable future. Further growth in terms of my position or salary I predicted would be very slow. I decided it was time for a change.

Major Finance provided me with valuable experiences and lessons I couldn't buy or learn in school. I developed further respect for the value of a work ethic; that is, obtaining results, perseverance, and determination. Finance companies were the basic training for banking, and Major Finance was an extremely well-run company that taught me well.

Chapter 5

Out of Small Loans, Into Banking

1974 to 1978

There was an ad in the paper for a position at Maryland National Bank in Baltimore. Maryland National was a large regional bank, the largest in the state. I applied for the job and was called for an interview. I met Ted Kozak from the personnel department and was routed around the building for additional interviews with Charlie Cawley, Ray Nichols, and Tom Mulford. Cawley was in charge of what was then called Master Charge. Nichols ran the special lending area, which entailed loans for equipment; auto leasing; overseeing the regional lending offices; accounts receivable factoring; inventory financing for cars, boats, and recreational vehicles; and other specialized lending activities. Mulford ran consumer lending.

Charlie Cawley looked like an Irishman from Boston, which was exactly what he was. He was about six feet tall with a waistline of about forty-four inches. His complexion was ruddy, and his hair wavy and reddish. He had a deep voice, he was articulate, and he could easily flash a big smile, but he had an aura that said he was in charge. He was a cigar-chomping guy whose intensity was readily apparent.

Ray Nichols was an entrepreneur. He was about five foot eight, practically bald, impeccably dressed and manicured, spoke fast, and gave the distinct impression of a guy who knew how put a deal together.

Tom Mulford was the oldest of the trio and was a quiet, gentlemanly fellow. It was obvious that Charlie and Ray were the shakers in the group. They were very focused and had aggressive personalities, while Tom was demure and more the stereotypical banker.

I thought all the interviews went well, and a few days later, I was asked to come back and meet with Charlie and Bill Melville, who was Charlie's boss. Charlie had previously worked at a bank in Boston, preceded by a stint at Beneficial Finance, and we told war stories about our finance company days, something guys with that experience typically do. Mr. Melville was a refined gentleman with a warm personality and was instantly likeable. At the end of the interview, Charlie offered me a position in charge of credit and collections for the credit card department. He also offered me a salary that was $5,000 higher than I was earning at Major, as well as a company car. I accepted on the spot.

I couldn't wait to get home to tell Terry the good news. Not only did I have an increase in salary, but also the commute was about half that of the trip to Arlington. The car was a big plus. We were delighted and happy to be moving on. I had spent my time learning the business from the ground up, and now I could utilize my skills at a much higher level. The education from my experience in the small loan company could never be taught in any other environment. I learned how to lend, and, of equal importance, I learned how to convince people to do something they didn't always want to do—pay. I knew I would miss Major and the people who had afforded me the opportunity to learn the business, but it was time to move on. I gave them two weeks' notice and immediately thereafter began working at Maryland National. It was April 1974.

Working with Charlie

I reported to work earlier than normal, expecting to be the first one there, but Charlie was at his desk behind a full glass wall facing the elevator. He was very intense, writing something and pressing down hard on his pencil. The look on his face showed a high level of concentration. He caught sight of me and was welcoming, showing me the various departments that occupied part of the sixth floor in a building located at 225 North Calvert Street. I estimated there were about 150 people in the entire credit card department.

Maryland National was the only Master Charge issuer in the state. Credit cards were relatively new financial products in 1974, and they were introduced before the age of widespread use of computers (well before personal computers). Copies of all charges were kept in huge drums, stored alphabetically, and manually sorted each month to send copies of the charges with the bills to customers. This practice was referred to as "country club billing." We had a customer service department but no automated messages. Customer service representatives handled each call. Collectors called every past due customer, and each credit card application was reviewed by credit analysts without tools such as credit scoring, which was developed later. The credit card business was a manual operation requiring sufficient manpower to cope with the massive flows of paper.

I was situated in a cubicle located just outside Charlie's office. I jumped in with both feet, and we were humming along at high speed. Credit and collections were the heartbeat of a credit card operation. Of course, operations, systems, and marketing were critically important, but credit and collections were the guts. We hired outside telemarketing firms and sent massive amounts of direct mail soliciting new cardholders. Typically we were flooded with responses. We had a policy of making credit decisions within three days, which created a big challenge when both the direct mail and telemarketing campaigns were in full swing, which was most of the time.

I soon learned that Charlie was a workaholic with a quick temper and a short fuse. He didn't have any tolerance for errors and was as demanding of himself as he was of all those around him. I often tried to arrive before him or work later that he did. It was impossible. On one occasion we were absolutely swamped with applications, and Charlie suggested the two of us use his office the next day to plow through them. I thought it would take days to accomplish the task, but I went along. He asked what time I'd like to start. Since I really didn't know what time he arrived at the office, I thought I should make it earlier than my usual 7:30 a.m. and suggested 6:30 a.m. We agreed.

I can count on one hand (with fingers left over) the number of times in my life I have overslept. The next morning the phone rang about 6:35 a.m. Terry answered and the only thing she heard was Charlie's bellow asking, "Where is he?" I jumped into my suit and raced to Baltimore. When the elevator door opened, there was Charlie writing something with a pencil and bearing down so hard that I don't know how the lead didn't break. He was gritting his teeth and was much redder than his trademark scarlet color. I spurted out, "I'm sorry," to which he responded, "Well so am I, because now you're going to do them all yourself and not leave until they're done!" I was relieved he didn't hurl something at me, which he was known to do, along with ripping telephones from the wall, or his rarely used, but most demonstrative anger-releasing maneuver of tipping over the bookcases in his office.

I raced through several hundred applications and finished about nine o'clock that night. As I walked toward the elevator, the roar came from Charlie's office, "Where are you going?" I responded that I had finished and I left. I always took pride in my skill in making credit decisions, but I am certain the level of delinquency from the batch of applications I approved that day was extraordinarily high.

One day a collector called Charlie's mother, whose account was past due by about a week. Charlie found out about it and went berserk. The collector, the collection manager, and I were in Charlie's office in no time. He slammed the door and yelled, ranting and raving at the top of his lungs. I never understood why he closed the door since he could be heard across the floor, and the full glass wall made the tirade visible to all. After you underwent Charlie's wrath, people came in and asked if you were all right. It was a real bruising to have him about two inches from your face, beat red, and bearing down hard.

I soon met Tom Groft, who had previously been with Eutaw Savings Bank, subsequently acquired by Maryland National. Tom had a terrific personality and a sense of humor that I found refreshing. We became, and still are, best friends. Perhaps the reason we're still close friends is due to the beatings we sustained together. Charlie would call us both into his office on a regular basis and work himself into frenzy over one thing or another. If he called us in and asked a question to which we gave different answers, he would tell us to get out, get our story straight, and come back in. If we again had differing stories, he would remove his eyeglasses, lower his head into his hands, say, "Mother of God!" and conclude with his usual, "I ought to fire you!" That comment was better than his other favorite, "You're fired!"

As intimidating as Charlie's intensity was, it was infectious. I never had a high level of patience, but I found I was getting worse, becoming more demanding of others and myself. Major Finance had an exacting atmosphere, but Charlie took it to new heights.

About this time, both of our girls were enrolled in school, and Terry looked for a regular job. The money she earned babysitting helped tremendously, but I'm sure it wasn't easy for her to spend days and most evenings with our kids as well as the neighbors' kids. As I mentioned earlier—for her, adult conversation came at a premium. So when she heard about an opening at a local saddlery store, she applied for the job and was hired. There she enjoyed the interaction with adults and with those who shared her affinity for horses. The downside was she was like a child in a candy store. Terry would receive her weekly pay envelope, and it wasn't unusual for there to be an amount owing, since she spent more than she earned. It didn't matter to me. What did matter was she had an outlet, and she was happy.

At Maryland National, Bill Melville decided after a few years to bring in another person from California, to run the card business. He transferred Charlie to operations, while Ray stayed in special lending. The first inkling we had that Bob was different was when he had the desk removed from his new office and replaced it with a high table where he would stand all day. Next he propped up "Thank you for not smoking" signs all over the office. He arrived at work around 8:30 a.m., and he left around 5 p.m. You would think this pattern would be a welcome relief for us after Charlie's antics, but, believe it or not, we missed Charlie.

Charlie talked to me about transferring to operations with him, but I hated operations, finding the work too tedious and with not enough interaction with people. I spoke with Ray, and he asked me to work in his department, which I did. Initially, I took over the credit area for indirect (dealer) car lending, and it was there that I met Harry Schmidt, who would later become known as the "Car Czar." Harry was a genuine character who was the hands down best dealer automobile credit man who ever existed. Dealers either loved him or hated him; there was no in between.

My Friend Tom Hudson

About this time, a sweeping federal law was enacted called Regulation Z, Truth in Lending, which affected virtually all forms of consumer lending. Especially onerous to me was a provision known as the "Holder in Due Course," which gave headaches to all of us who were engaged in indirect (third-party) lending.

The bank's primary outside law firm was Semmes, Bowen, and Semmes. Our lead attorney was Geoff Mitchell. I met Geoff and a young associate named Tom Hudson to figure out how we were going to deal with this issue. Geoff was a very good lawyer, but it was Tom who impressed me the most. For years, whenever I told an attorney I wanted to do something and asked for a way to do it, he always began with, "The prudent thing to do is…" My reaction? Hell, I knew what the "prudent thing to do" was, and it meant, "Don't do it!" Tom was refreshing in that he had a way of triangulating issues and coming up with creative approaches while providing the upside gains and downside risks. He'd leave me with a path forward and enough information to make the right decision. I liked Tom's legal savvy, and his personality was magnetic. We became, and still are, best friends.

Tom and I met regularly at the Playboy Club on Light Street on Fridays for its roast beef buffet luncheon. We loved the roast beef. We also attended Orioles games often, enjoying the game while passing along jokes. We both enjoyed practical jokes. Once I addressed an envelope to his office that had the words "Confidential—VD Test Results Enclosed" in bright red capital letters on the front. By the time the mail person got to Tom's office, there was a parade of lawyers following.

Tom had a great sense of humor and was no stranger to wreaking havoc upon others. He could take it, but he could also dish it out. One barely noticeable peculiarity about Tom is that he is missing his right thumb, the result of a childhood accident. It was great fun when I'd introduce him to someone and watch as they shook hands. The expression was always the same when they realized the "stopper" wasn't there. It was particularly entertaining when the shaker was the type to give the really strong shake and would wind up about ten inches inside Tom's coat sleeve. Tom took it all in stride; he even named his sailboat "Thumbthing."

Charlie Again

It was 1977 and Bill Melville decided it was time for yet another reorganization at Maryland National. The nut from California stayed with the card business, and the state was divided between Charlie and Ray, each taking over several regional offices. I was transferred to the Annapolis office in charge of Anne Arundel and Prince George's counties. The move suited me fine—the office was about fifteen minutes from home. Once again, I reported to Charlie.

The regional offices operated somewhat independently from headquarters and were responsible for business development, credit, and collections. Annapolis is a Mecca for sailboats in the country, and numerous boat dealers occupied the city. I spent many hours cultivating relationships with those dealers and manufacturers and met with a high degree of success. We had the "floor plan" (inventory financing) lines of credit for most dealers around town. Along with that came the first crack at all applications for potential purchase. At least, that was how it was supposed to happen. I visited the offices on a regular basis, and if I found out any retail business was going somewhere else, we'd have a intense meeting in which I'd explain the unwritten "rule" that the bank that provided the financing for the inventory had first shot at retail applications. The profit margin on the inventory lines of credit was slim; therefore, we needed the loan business from consumers to augment the income from the relationship. At those meetings, either we ended with a clear understanding as to how the game was to be played—our way— or I suggested that they find a new home for the inventory line of credit. In addition to the boat business, we also had a strong presence with automobile dealers in both counties.

The Boat Dealer Crowd

I made many friends doing business in Annapolis. One of the most colorful was a fellow named Harry Barrett, who together with George Patton (no, not *the* George Patton) owned a company named The Yacht Yard. They sold Endeavours, Irwins, and a couple of lesser-known sailboats. Both Harry and George were graduates of the Naval Academy and were fighter jet pilots while in the Navy. Harry was a wild man in every way, but he had a cherubic face that enabled him to get away with more than most men could. One of his favorite things to do was to sit just inside the door of a popular bar in downtown Annapolis named McGarvey's Tavern. Harry took it upon himself to grade each lady as she entered the bar. His grading system was simple. He would either let out a loud "Mooooo" or conversely make the announcement, "Nice tits." Back then, all the girls smiled. Today, he'd be in trouble. I'm sure if I tried something like that, I'd come home with a couple of shiners.

Harry's taste in booze was also simple. It was always silver bullets, which translates as "straight gin on the rocks and hold the fruit." Harry had a wooden leg, and I never met anyone who could come close to his outstanding capacity. However, everyone has his limit, and when Harry would finally reach his, he'd suddenly just fall asleep. One minute you'd be talking to him and the next he'd be snoozing. He always made great transitions.

In addition to The Yacht Yard, Harry owned a couple of bars, which came in handy. When it came to working a deal, he was at the top of his game. I'm sure his extraordinary drinking capacity netted a few sales along the way.

Others I befriended were Al Jacuwicz, who, together with his brother-in-law, owned Atlantic Sailing Yachts. Al was also a fun guy but more serious about the business than Harry. His brother-in-law Frank Pennington lived in Point Pleasant, New Jersey, and had a branch of the business there along with another on Narragansett Bay in Rhode Island. We had the floor plan, there again, the inventory financing lines of credit, at all three locations.

Curly Burgreen (bald of course) owned Annapolis Yachts Sales and Service, and Art Burr and his wife Maryann ran Burr Yacht Sales, selling Bertram Yachts exclusively. Tom Trainer owned McDaniel Yacht Basin and was a good friend, as was Tom Frank of Shady Oak Marine Sales. We had a lock on about eighty percent of the market with the inventory financing and the retail loans. I worked hard developing these relationships, but also I enjoyed knowing and working with these characters.

The most grueling time of the year was the fall when the boat shows would be held in Annapolis. The first show would be for powerboats for four or five days, followed a couple of days later by the sailboat show lasting the same number of days. These were the largest in-the-water shows in the United States, and every inch of water in the harbor was filled with boats—hundreds of them ranging from fifteen feet to one hundred feet. Dealers from all over the United States would be there, as well as manufacturers and vendors from around the world. We'd set up a booth selling our "boat show special" rates and always generated a lot of business over those two weeks. I'd work the manufacturers and dealers to deepen relationships and develop new ones. Parties were a big part of the show, and there were several every night. All in all, the boat shows provided a strenuous liver workout.

I often had business meetings with the dealers at The Library, a favorite place for lunch and dinner, located about one hundred yards from my office. Tom Groft, in College Park, called regularly only to be told that Mr. Blewett was at the library. When he finally caught up with me, he said I must be the smartest guy in the world after spending so much time in the library. I told him I spent as much time as possible there and found it enriching. Only later when he came for a visit did he understand.

The Eastern Shore of Maryland

During these years, life seemed to calm down. I'd been promoted several times and my income was steadily increasing. The crazy commutes were behind Terry and me, and we could afford to go out for dinner every once in a while. We had made friends and had a little time just for us.

Then things changed. I was asked to take over as the regional manager of the Eastern Shore with offices in Salisbury, Maryland, reporting to Ray Nichols. I always believed that when "asked" it really meant "you're going," and to refuse meant your career would take a hit. Salisbury is located about ninety miles from Annapolis on the opposite side of the Chesapeake Bay. This translated as a two-hour commute each way and necessitated crossing the Bay Bridge. I should note that I'm not comfortable with heights, especially crossing bridges, and most especially, the scariest of them all—the Chesapeake Bay Bridge. The alternative, however, was relocation.

Salisbury's claim to fame is that it is the home of Frank Purdue, famous for raising chickens. Tractor-trailer trucks plied the highways filled with chickens with feathers flying out the sides and an unmistakable odor trailing behind. It took about three minutes to realize that relocation was clearly not an option; instead, I negotiated with the bank to rent an apartment for me where I stayed during the week. Monday mornings I'd leave the house at six and return home that evening at eight. Ray Nichols held regularly scheduled Tuesday morning meetings in Baltimore that I was expected to attend, so Tuesday mornings I'd drive the forty-five minutes to Baltimore, attend Ray's meeting, and then drive to Salisbury, where I'd stay until Friday evening when I'd drive home for the weekend. This routine went on for about six months.

I met several interesting characters while on the shore. Maryland National had a large presence with automobile, boat, and mobile home dealers in the area. Of all the various dealers I'd met over the years, mobile home dealers were a breed apart. One notable owner was a fellow named Herb Gregory, who controlled a large dealership named Blue Hen Mobile Homes.

Maryland National had the floor plan at Blue Hen, and, as a result, the bank had a large mobile home portfolio. Herb was a wheeler-dealer and fun to be around but also a guy to be closely watched. It wouldn't be beyond him to stick it to you.

Once when I was on a dealer call, Herb mentioned he had won a trip to Curacao in the Netherlands Antilles. He went on to say that he and his wife had won so many trips that he wouldn't be able to leave the dealership again, but he wanted to know if my wife and I wanted to go on the trip. I immediately thought it would be a conflict and didn't want to be beholding to Herb. However, we'd been married for nine years and, other than our honeymoon, hadn't taken any trips other than camping in a state park or trips home to Buffalo. Beyond that, we normally didn't take vacations since I could collect vacation pay at the end of the year if I didn't use the days. But, thinking it over, it was winter, it was cold, and Terry and I had been apart for most of the previous six months. The temptation was great, and I decided to ask Ray what he thought of the idea.

Curacao Bound

Although Ray was a banker, he was also an entrepreneur who ran an auction company, among other endeavors. He drove a high-end Ford car to work, which was on perpetual loan to him from Ford Auto Leasing Company, while others drove mundane vehicles more akin to the banker image. Apparently, Bill Melville didn't take exception to Ray's making a living in addition to his bank job. Ray said he thought it would be all right to go on the trip, but he suggested I keep it quiet. I'd cleared it with my boss, fulfilling my obligation to keep everything above board, so Terry and I decided to take the trip. We arranged for Terry's mother to come to Maryland to watch the kids and made the necessary arrangements to leave. At the last minute Herb said it was too late to change the tickets to our names, so we had to go as Herb and Carol Gregory. Curacao immigration didn't require passports for entry, and the only identification we needed to enter the country was a Voter ID, which Herb supplied for both Terry and me.

Terry's mother arrived in town just as it was beginning to snow quite heavily. We had a flight the next day aboard KLM out of JFK airport, and we had intended to drive there. However, the snow was creating havoc on the highways, so we decided to take Amtrak from Baltimore to New York. It turned out that our train was the last to leave Baltimore because of the storm. We arrived at Penn Station only to find New York paralyzed. I finally found a cab driver willing to drive us to our hotel near the airport, but he charged us twice the normal fare, which I readily agreed to. I was determined not to miss the flight and would have paid triple had the cabbie asked.

We finally made it to the hotel, but it was one hell of a ride. The taxi couldn't make it up the driveway to the hotel door so we got out and lugged our suitcases up the hill to our destination. The entire trip reminded me of living in Buffalo. The snow kept falling and the airport was closed and remained closed for three days. We were stuck in the hotel and met several of our fellow travelers, introducing ourselves as Herb and Carol Gregory until one evening when someone challenged our identities. He was a friend of Herb's and knew we weren't the Gregorys. The jig was up before we even landed on the island. I confessed to him who we were and the circumstances that necessitated our changing our names. He thought it was good humor. We grew increasingly concerned about being arrested in Curacao, but we were determined to go.

Finally the snow stopped, the airports reopened, and we boarded our flight. It was nerve wracking as we waited our turn to go through customs, but we sailed through without a hitch. Once in the country we relaxed and enjoyed our abbreviated vacation.

Chapter 6

The Entrepreneur—
Part One
1978 to 1980

During the previous several months I had been working on a plan to start a small loan company. I developed spreadsheets to determine cash flows, formed a business plan, and felt the time was right to leave the banking cocoon and go off on my own. Between living in Salisbury more than half the time and my restlessness to move forward more quickly than was possible at Maryland National, I felt that starting my own business was the right course to take.

An accomplice, John Eckenrode, who also worked for the bank, was going to be my partner. Although John had never worked in a small loan company, he was a smart, energetic guy with drive and a lot of good ideas. The day finally came when I felt I had done all the work necessary to pull the trigger. I scheduled a time to meet with Ray to resign. At the eleventh hour, John backed out. I decided to proceed on my own. Ray took it well, but he tried to talk me into staying. His motivation surprised me. He told me that he was also close to resigning to start his own auction, leasing, and insurance company. He wanted me to partner with him. This was a twist I hadn't expected, and I gave the idea some thought. Ray was a very sharp guy with great business sense, and I was honored that he asked me to join him. On the other hand, I worried I might have another Eckenrode experience, where, at the last minute, I would be standing alone. Ray made compelling arguments that his lines of business weren't capital intensive or sensitive to interest rate fluctuations and therefore much less risky. After giving it much thought, I decided to go it alone and resigned to start The Money Tree Finance Company. His comments regarding capital intensity and interest rate volatility always stuck with me, however, and his words proved to be prescient. As an aside, Ray subsequently chose John Eckenrode as his partner. They resigned, started all the companies we had discussed, and were wildly successful.

Both Terry and I were excited about our new venture, but first there were some issues with our daughter Michelle that needed to be resolved. She had started school in kindergarten at Belleview Elementary and had just completed second grade. She was struggling with class work, and we met with her teacher to discuss the possibility of holding her back a grade. The school refused. Terry met with our pediatrician, Dr. Srsic, who recommended that Michelle take a battery of tests with a local company named Up Start. Following the tests, they recommended Michelle attend their classes over the summer. We saw improvement, but we felt she needed more individualized attention. We applied for her to attend St. Mary's Elementary School in Annapolis, and after consultations with the principal and a review of her tests, she was admitted. Our other daughter Joanna was ready to begin first grade, and she was also admitted. We felt fortunate to have the kids in Catholic school although it meant tuition payments that we didn't have before.

I left Maryland National in April 1978 with some money in the bank, but not much. I had to move fast to get the new company up and running. The first person I spoke with was Jay Schwartz, who was an attorney with Semmes, Bowen, and Semmes. Jay's primary concentration was lobbying during the

Maryland General Assembly session, but he had a corporate law background and agreed to help me incorporate the business. That was the easy part. Next I had to determine how much money I needed to raise and how to raise it. Again, Jay's advice proved valuable. We discussed a recent Securities and Exchange ruling that permitted me to put forth a stock offering to a maximum of thirty-five potential investors without registering the securities. After many discussions, we decided this would be the most expeditious and efficient way to raise capital. I spent several weeks putting together a stock prospectus in which I described the business plan in excruciating detail, complete with five-year projections and five years of pro forma financial statements. I then developed a target list of people who I thought might be willing to take a flyer. I decided I needed to raise at least $100,000, and if I was unable to raise that amount, I wouldn't pursue the venture. It would have been safer to raise the money while still employed, but there was an ethics issue as well as the fact that it simply wasn't practical to be out raising money when I was still employed.

I made several calls and appointments to discuss my proposal. I structured the deal in such a way so that we had two classes of stock with one subordinate to the other. I owned the common stock and sold preferred shares, thereby retaining ownership. My sales calls proved successful, and in a month I had stock subscriptions for $120,000. All the investors who subscribed put up twenty-five percent of their committed amount with a promise to fulfill the obligation when the monies were called. Every one of them came through.

I next met with various lenders to secure a line of credit, ultimately striking a deal with Commercial Credit Business Loans out of Wilmington, Delaware, for a $500,000 line secured by the receivables and carrying an interest rate of prime rate plus five percent.

With the finances taken care of, I rented office space on West Street in Annapolis, purchased office furniture, opened checking accounts, had the lawyers draft contracts, had them printed, developed all the forms, and set up everything we needed to do business. I hired two employees, Ruth Trovato, whom I had known from Maryland National, and my wife. We opened The Money Tree in June 1978, two months after I left Maryland National.

The primary source for loans was automobile dealers, and I knew them all since I had done business with them while at the bank. My niche was used car financing. We held title as collateral, and we also provided unsecured down payment loans to people who were seeking traditional bank financing but didn't have the cash necessary for the down payment. Our average loan was around $1,000. Business boomed. Not only was business very good but the quality of the portfolio was as well.

We worked hard with the office open Monday through Friday and two late nights as well as Saturday mornings. Ruth took care of all the bookkeeping duties. Terry worked part-time while the children were in school and became a proficient collector. I managed the overall business from making credit decisions to dealing with our investors and financial sources. The end game was to build a quality portfolio of loans, open another two or three offices, and sell the business to a larger competitor for a profit in about five years.

Our tenth wedding anniversary was coming up in August 1979, and I planned a surprise for Terry. I had sent away for several brochures from various hotels in the Pocono Mountains, a famous destination for honeymooners. I decided to reserve the "Adam and Eve" suite for a weekend. Terry's sister agreed to watch the children, and we made the drive to Pennsylvania. When we opened the door to our suite, there was a small sitting room and down a few steps was the largest heart-shaped bed I'd ever seen. As a matter of fact, I'd never seen a heart-shaped bed of any size, but this one was enormous. The bathroom had a heart-shaped Jacuzzi tub and was decorated with mirrors—mirrors on the wall, on the ceiling, and on the floor. This was an entirely new designer collection to me.

We had dinner in the dining hall and met several people who were mostly newlyweds from New Jersey. All in all, it was a novel experience. We had fun but decided we'd never return. I was glad we had the chance to get away from the strains of the business and have some time alone, but the hotel reminded me of the hotel in the movie *Dirty Dancing* with a younger crowd.

Finance company guys always like to tell collection stories. My favorite story from The Money Tree was about a customer named Robert. Robert had borrowed money from us for a used car and he was in default. I'd spoken to him often when he'd repeatedly made a "promise to pay," and then he would repeatedly break that promise. The only remedy was to repossess his car.

There were plenty of repossession firms, and I knew several from my Maryland National days. One particularly colorful repo man was Walt Gonturek, who was creative, inventive, and generally successful. Walt did whatever it took to bring in the bounty, usually staying inside the law, but nevertheless doing what he had to do to get the job done. But people like Walt cost money, and I was determined not to spend money on jobs I could do myself.

I hired a teenager from our neighborhood, and we drove to southern Maryland to collect the past due payments or repossess Robert's car. If I had to repo the car, then the kid would drive my car back and I'd drive the repo. Robert lived in a hovel in the country on an isolated dirt road, and when we pulled up there were several guys hunched over in a circle about one hundred yards away. I told the kid that if anything happened to get the hell out of there and go the sheriff's office located a few miles away. I called out saying I was looking for Robert. A guy stood up with a long knife with blood dripping off it. It turned out the guys were slaughtering a pig, but the bloody knife did cause us an anxious moment. Fortunately, the kid didn't flee. Robert and I had the usual discussion in which I offered two options—the money or the keys. He called a few people on the phone looking for money, but in the end, the car had to go. I asked for the keys, which he provided, and I climbed into the banger. About half the stick shift had been sawed off, and I couldn't figure out how to drive the damned thing. I told Robert to drive the car to the sheriff's office and we'd follow him. I also told him not to try to outrun us. We all arrived at the sheriff's, where Robert parked the car and we drove him home in the backseat of my car as promised. Upon returning to the sheriff's to report the repo, the sheriff told us Robert was out on bail for shooting at an old woman and killing her dog. That was the last time the neighborhood kid helped me with repos.

At the time I wrote the stock prospectus, the prime rate was 8.75 percent and the interest rates we were allowed to charge under Maryland law were in the neighborhood of twenty-eight percent. Even with Commercial Credit's line of credit at five points over prime (13.75 percent), the interest rate margin was a healthy 14.25. I recall pointing out in the stock offering documents that, in the unlikely event of prime going up five percentage points, our margins would still be 9.25, affording a very comfortable cushion. The prime rate in the United States ranged between 2 and 7.50 percent from the late 1940s until the late 1960s. From the late 1960s until mid 1970s, rates bounced around from a low of 4 percent to as high as 11.75 in 1974, which was an all-time high until 1979. Recall that the prime rate was 8.75 percent when we opened The Money Tree and the all-time high was 11.75, which occurred four years earlier. From June 1978 until April 1980, the prime rate in the United States steadily climbed month after month, and several times within a month, until it hit an incredible new high of 20 percent.

While this escalation occurred, I continued to think it was an anomaly and that rates couldn't just keep increasing, assuring myself they'd settle into a much lower range. But they kept climbing! We reached the point where if we made a loan we lost money, and if we didn't keep lending, we would seriously hurt our cash flow. Since we couldn't control the prime rate, the only course we had was more funding at lower rates than prime plus five.

I went to our investors and others offering subordinated debentures at rates of prime or prime plus one and issued bonds totaling $75,000, which provided relief. But the relief was temporary, as rates remained stubbornly high. Commercial Credit was getting nervous since the division that dealt with finance companies and accounts receivable factoring was experiencing an increasingly high number of defaults across the country. We kept our interest payments current, but that didn't allay their fears. I drove to Wilmington for a meeting, and while they agreed we weren't in default, they froze our line of credit. This action translated as a death knell for our company.

I went to the General Assembly in Maryland and testified before committees seeking regulatory relief in the form of interest rate increases, but I didn't find any sympathy. The only remaining alternative was to sell the company.

I put the word out that we were for sale and became reacquainted with a gentleman I had met while at Major Finance. He was the president of another long-standing finance company in Maryland, and he was interested in purchasing our book of receivables. I would have approached Major, but they had previously sold when the market was in good shape and acquiring finance companies at high premiums was in vogue. We had about 600 loans with assets in the range of $600,000 with low delinquency and loss rates, but ours was a "fire sale," and purchasers knew we didn't have bargaining power. I sold the receivables at a small premium, sold the office equipment, and terminated the lease. I was on the hook for monies I borrowed for the company from Annapolis Bank and Trust, and, under the terms of the sale, I was also on the hook for losses sustained for the trailing six months after the sale and for any loans with documentation deficiencies. The purchaser was quite intense in reviewing loan files and quite liberal in charging back loans to me for minute documentation flaws. I don't know if they had the same intensity in collecting the loans, but, in any event, I didn't have the money to pay for the loans the company tried to charge back to us. We were broke.

Having been in the banking business, I had great disdain for people who filed for bankruptcy. However, as the liability from the company kept mounting and my ability to meet the obligations kept declining, I met with an attorney who was a friend of Harry Barrett. I absolutely wanted to keep the house, partly because of my ego, but mostly because we had two small children who were comfortable in their little neighborhood. After several meetings with the attorney and having no alternatives, I filed for bankruptcy. It was devastating. It was even more devastating than losing The Money Tree. This was the lowest point of my life.

In June 1980, Terry and I looked around and considered our horrible situation. We were unemployed, broke, and, even worse, bankrupt. I wasn't quite sure where to go from there. We needed jobs, and we needed the salaries jobs could provide, but the economy was in rotten shape, and jobs weren't that easy to come by. I asked myself, *Maybe go back to Maryland National or even*

NSA? No. I decided I wasn't going back. I had to find a way forward. Maryland National was one of the creditors I discharged in bankruptcy, and I couldn't face them even if there might be a job available. Also, you'll remember, I had already determined that government work wouldn't get me to where I wanted to go.

Chapter 7

The Entrepreneur— Part Two

June to November 1980

Two of my investors, Harry Barrett and Ed Dyas, had formed a partnership in the United States Virgin Islands (USVI) on St. Thomas, where they set up a charter boat business complemented by various water sports, rental cars, and condo rentals. Ed (more commonly referred to as "Frog") built large residential homes. He was also involved in commercial development and enjoyed toys like his beloved Porsche and his Bertram fishing boat, "The Hooker." He was the primary investor in these businesses, while Harry took charge of the sales and marketing aspects. They hired a manager and his wife who were supposed to run the businesses and watch over Frog's investments. Instead, they fleeced him and absconded with a bundle.

I was out of work and broke, and Frog needed someone he trusted to figure out a way to salvage his investments. I agreed to go to St. Thomas on a six-month management consultant contract to sort out the finances. The agreement also provided housing in one of Frog's condos, the use of a car, and airfare for Terry and the kids.

The following week I flew from Baltimore with Harry and Frog to St. Thomas via Puerto Rico, with the understanding that Terry and the girls would come in a week or so. The flight from Baltimore was the usual. The flight from Puerto Rico was aboard a World War II vintage de Havilland twin-engine prop plane operated by Print Air. Prior to boarding in San Juan, everyone was asked his or her weight. I thought the rather heavy stewardess was kidding, so I told her I'd tell her mine if she'd tell me hers. She didn't appreciate the humor and was insistent about my weight. I finally realized that since the aircraft was so small, they had to distribute weight evenly to get the plane off the ground. The plane sat about a dozen people and shook and rattled the whole way to St. Thomas. There were two single rows of seats each with a vent that opened and closed manually to permit air to enter from outside. I found this a rather interesting way to provide ventilation. Two characters handcuffed to each other boarded the flight. It was readily apparent which man was the law and which man was the criminal.

We landed in St. Thomas safely, although I had doubts along the way. The St. Thomas airport consisted of a large Quonset hut that served as the terminal. Inside was a ticket counter for Print Air and Virgin Air, a roped off area for arriving baggage, a few benches, a lot of people just hanging around, and a bar named Sparky's. It was July, and it was hot as hell. Frog suggested we head to Sparky's for a drink since it would take at least a half an hour for the bags to get unloaded and carried the one hundred feet to the roped area. That assumed the bags arrived with us. Often there was too much weight on the plane, so the bags would show up on a later flight. Sparky's smelled like it had recently been sprayed with a couple of cans of Raid, but it was an oasis in the desert. After about forty-five minutes, we moseyed over to the baggage area and, incredibly, our bags were sitting there. We were off to a good start.

We took a taxi to the Frenchman's Reef, where the water sports operation was located. There was a counter in the lobby staffed by two people per shift with placards advertising half-day sails, full-day sails, half- and full-day fishing trips, rum cruises, scuba diving, and charter boats for minimum one-week trips. The Reef was perched high on a hill overlooking the Caribbean, and it was a classy hotel. A short walk down the hill past the swimming pool brought us to the end of a cement pier with a small two-story wooden building at the end. The ground floor was a storage area. There were circular steel stairs to access the second floor, which had two desks, a shortwave radio, and a small table. This was to be my office.

Harry and Frog decided we should go into Charlotte Amalie to meet with the banks where they had checking accounts and complete the documents to add me as a signatory. Although the town was only a couple of miles away, it could take half an hour to drive there, and parking was always a challenge. We decided to go via a small powerboat. There was a floating dock adjacent to the cement pier that we gingerly walked on for about twenty feet to board the boat for the five-minute ride to the harbor.

The first bank we visited was Bank of America. They were happy to see us, not because we were premium customers, but because my predecessor had written hundreds of bad checks. We had a similar experience with our second bank, Chase Manhattan. We had long discussions with both banks and explained my role was to sort out the mess and get things back on an even keel. The fact that I had a banking background seemed to help. Surprisingly, the banks allowed us to open new checking accounts with the understanding that I would meet with them every other week to apprise them of our situation. While the meetings were long and sometimes a bit tense, I felt we had accomplished what we had set out to do:

We re-established a level of trust, and we kept checking accounts in St. Thomas.

Later that day we jumped on the launch for the quick trip back to the Reef. I stood on the bow and jumped onto the floating dock when, suddenly, upon landing, my left leg collapsed beneath me. A wave had heaved the dock at the same time I landed, creating an unsteady landing surface. I was in serious pain and thought I had broken bones. I crawled off the floating dock into the backseat of a jeep for the trip to the hospital.

The hospital consisted of two very small one-story buildings surrounded by benches. I took my place at the end of the furthest bench, scooting and inching my way along to the front of the line for a couple of hours. Finally I was seated in a wheelchair and taken into the first building, where the nurse took an X-ray. I remember the machine was an ancient Picker model. My Uncle Jim from Rochester had worked for Picker for several years and the name brought back fond memories of visits there. I was wheeled back outside, where I sat for another hour or so. I had asked for something for the pain and was given two aspirin. Finally I was wheeled into a small office to meet with the doctor, who told me I had broken my ankle and that he would be putting my leg in a cast up to my knee. About this time a native strolled in, sold the doc a few lottery tickets, shot the breeze for fifteen minutes, and strolled out. While he was there chatting, I observed king-sized cockroaches climbing up and down the walls. Everything (except the cockroaches) moved at a much slower pace on the islands. The doctor went about putting on the cast, provided me with a crutch, and after about four hours, I left the hospital. It was hard not to think about my earlier comment about being off to a good start.

Frog drove me to one of his condos where my family would be staying. It was at the east end of the island in an area referred to as Red Hook, in a complex called the Anchorage. Each condo building was two stories with one unit on the ground floor and the other above. Ours was on the second floor in a building named "Ranger." After managing to climb the stairs, we entered a very nicely furnished apartment consisting of a small kitchen, combination living and dining area, two bedrooms and baths, and a balcony with views of the beach. Farther across the sea were fabulous views of St. John's. To the left was a very pretty swimming pool and just beyond that was the St. Thomas Yacht Club.

I settled in, but despite the beautiful views, I was depressed. We had sunk so much time, energy, and money into The Money Tree only to see it evaporate. Not only was the venture unsuccessful, but also now we didn't have a clear path forward. I enjoyed taking calculated risks, and I had thought I covered all contingencies, but the historic and rapid rise in interest rates blindsided me. Interestingly, shortly after the unprecedented rise that topped out at twenty percent, rates started to decline. It didn't matter. The several months of increases had taken their toll. My thoughts reeled: *Perhaps if we had been in business a couple of years longer we could have weathered the storm. Maybe I should have sold more bonds.* Now I had a broken ankle to add to my worries. I called Terry from a pay phone between the condo and the pool and tried to sound upbeat, but it wasn't easy.

After a night of self-pity, I decided to thrust myself into my new project. I arrived at the office at 8 a.m. after an interesting ride from the condo. People in St. Thomas drive on the left side of the road, but since the roads are loaded with potholes, the natives could care less about which side of the road they're on. They swerve left and right constantly to avoid the craters in the roadway. About an hour after I arrived, so did about fifty people who were holding bounced checks in their hands. Apparently there was no discrimination regarding the recipients of the non-sufficient funds. I met captains of our charter boats, captains of tour boats, the scuba diving team, the garbage collectors, the guys who ran the rental car business, and, last but not least, the finance manager of the Frenchman's Reef, who informed me we were six months in arrears in our rent. Frog and Harry were nowhere to be found. I later discovered they were out most of the night partying; consequently, I didn't see them until later that afternoon.

I told everyone the same thing. We would work things out, but I needed some time to assess the extent of the damage. Some seemed sympathetic while others were belligerent. It was a challenging day.

The next day Harry and Frog were heading back to Maryland, and I drove them to the airport. On my return through Charlotte Amalie, people who had bad checks chased my car down the street, as word had rapidly spread that there was a new guy in town. Over the next several days, I discovered that virtually every sub-contractor had been cheated. That was bad enough, but then I found out the IRS and local taxing authority were also due monies. Although Frog had deposited $10,000 in both bank accounts, I needed to be judicious in doling it out, since it was clear that the funds needed far surpassed the amounts currently in the accounts.

Life on "The Rock"

After about a week, Terry and the kids arrived from Baltimore via San Juan. Despite all the negative events, I was elated with the prospect of being with them again. I picked them up at the airport (the bags arrived with them, thank God), and we were off to the condo. The kids were ten and eight—very excited about living on an island with the beaches and swimming pool. That made our situation much more bearable. I dropped Terry and the kids off at the condo and returned to work.

We had a few employees who were a curious bunch. The lead guy was John Green. He was an illegal immigrant from the U.K., and Green was a pseudonym. John's talent lay in understanding mechanical issues and keeping the equipment in fairly good repair. His weak side was management of people. Under him was another fellow from the U.K. named Dick, who was a handsome guy. When casual, he constantly wore a very small bathing suit typically referred to as a "banana hammock." The visiting ladies loved the guy. Both these men worked on boat engines and repaired whatever needed to be repaired to keep us operating. That was challenging due to the constant deterioration caused by the salt water. We also had two cleaning ladies, Annie and Mary, who scrubbed the charter boats upon their return to prepare them for their next charter. They worked at a steady but slow pace, which drove me crazy, but they always got the job done. Aside from the operating group, we had six sales people who staffed the counter in the lobby of the hotel and several sub-contractors who operated the tours and trips.

Cash flow is critical in any business, but this operation took cash flow to a higher level of urgency. When we would book an activity, the guests would pay us in cash, credit card, or travelers checks. All these items were immediately negotiable. We would take a cut of the total price and pay the captains or vendors the remainder for their fee. Prior to my arrival, the subs typically would wait for a week or two for their money. However, having experienced the flood of bad paper, their new rule was cash up front. This practice necessitated my making several daily trips from the dock to the lobby sales center, as there weren't any cash reserves. When cash was short, I often had to wait for my salary, but ultimately I always received it.

There were no refunds for seasickness. That was our policy. However, if our equipment failed, we would give full refunds. One day a couple booked a full-day fishing trip aboard our twenty-eight-foot Bertram named *Chicky*. The boat had a shortwave radio, and the base station was in my office. The couple left early in the morning and went around a bend out of sight for their fishing trip. A couple of hours later the captain radioed saying they were coming in. I immediately called the sales desk in the lobby to see how much money they had in reserve, only to discover we didn't have enough for a refund. I pulled the binoculars up to my eyes, watching the bend until

Chicky came into view and saw both the husband and wife leaning over the side, barfing. I remarked out loud and joyfully, "Thank God, they're sick!" This was a typical day spent operating a company where pennies and dollars were in short supply.

Meanwhile, Terry and the kids settled in. On their first full day, Terry went to the pool with the kids where an American lady, reclining on a chaise, struck up a conversation. Her unsolicited advice was, "If you have a headache, take an aspirin, but if you have anything else, take Pan Am." These words of wisdom didn't help with the transition.

Terry and the girls spent time at the pool, on our beach, or in Megans Bay, a picturesque cove on the island. I spent virtually every day at work. There's only so much to do with two children and no husband around, so Terry and I decided to ask her mother to come to St. Thomas for a few weeks. About a week later, she showed up for what turned out to be a month's stay. We tolerated each other, and I was happy she was there.

One day I arranged a sailing trip to Buck Island with Terry, her mother, and the kids. The captain was a fellow named Dick Gizetti, who, with his wife, had retired at an early age. They had decided to live on his sailboat and use it as a source of income, providing half- and full-day sailing trips. There were also a couple of gentlemen on the trip. They were gone for several hours and returned in a jovial mood. The rum swizzles helped with the joviality, but the best part was Terry kept trying to fix up her mother with the two guys. It turned out they were priests. I had to laugh.

One larger-than-life guy on the island was Leroy—about six feet, five inches tall and solid as a rock. Leroy ran the ferry between St. Thomas and St. John's along with other business pursuits with his brother. He was the stereotypical island man, difficult to figure out and very intimidating. Terry saw his soft side and we eventually got along well.

There was a boat captain, John Brower (The Crazy Frenchman), who, along with his wife Chippette, lived in a nice home in the hills. They were an interesting couple, welcoming to us, and they had us to their home for dinner.

Cruise ships arrived every week to drop off thousands of passengers at the harbor. Two ships, the *Queen Elizabeth II* and the *Norway*, were so large they had to anchor at sea and transport their passengers to shore by jitneys. It was exciting to see these majestic looking ships silently cruise into sight. However, we generally tried to avoid Charlotte Amalie while they were anchored or docked. The town was always crowded, but when these enormous ships were in, it was jam-packed.

I was still lugging the cast on my left leg when Hurricane Allen hit the Caribbean. It was an extremely intense storm, ultimately classified as a Category 5. We had several days' warning and moved our boats to an area called Hurricane Alley, which was a small bay protected on three sides by land. The boats were anchored offshore and survived without significant damage.

Meanwhile, back on land, we were trying to move parts and tools from the ground floor and documents from the second floor of our little building at the end of the dock. I wrapped a heavy plastic bag around my leg, and John, Dick, and I timed the waves. They worked on pulling outboard motors and tools from the ground floor, and I hobbled down the hill to the building and up the spiral steps to retrieve papers. Once the waves became too frequent, we headed uphill, abandoning whatever we weren't able to carry. We left all the doors and windows opened, hoping the waves would wash through the building rather than wash the building away.

The following couple of days were turbulent. When the weather calmed down, Terry, the kids, and I drove to the Frenchman's Reef. Our building was still standing, but it had sustained some damage, and a large section of the cement pier was missing. We began the process of fixing what we could fix, and we moved back in.

A short time after the hurricane, I met another fellow named Gordon Brown, who owned an insurance agency. One night we were at a party at his house, and he asked how much longer I had to have the cast on my leg. I told him I thought it would be another three to four weeks, and he suggested I make an appointment with an American orthopedic doctor who had recently arrived on the island. I followed his advice and met with the doctor later that week. He sent for my X-rays from the hospital prior to my arrival, and he took new X-rays while I was there. Then he said cautiously, "I don't know how to tell you this…" Immediately I thought bad news was coming. He finished his sentence by saying that my ankle had never been broken; the technicians had misread the X-rays at the hospital. He removed the cast. What a godsend! I had spent several weeks trying to scratch my leg with a coat hanger. Trapped sand had irritated the sole of my foot, and I couldn't get to it. When the doctor removed the cast, I had foot blisters the size of silver dollars. Soon they healed, however, and I was up and running again.

Let's Make a Deal

By now I had been in St. Thomas more than a month and finally had my arms around the extent of the financial problems. I estimated the company owed several hundred thousand dollars in past due debts, but I thought I could work out settlements for about half that amount. I called Frog and broke the news to him. We went over the list in detail and he agreed to wire the money necessary for the settlements.

I spent the next several weeks meeting with what seemed like everyone on the island as I negotiated one deal after another. My usual offer was forty to fifty cents on the dollar. If pressed for more, I'd tell them they were driving us into bankruptcy. Or I would say if they didn't play ball, we would simply shut the doors and leave. As much as many people disliked us because of their negative financial experiences, still, they needed us. We had the best and most complete water sports packages for tourists, and without us, their source of marketing would dry up. Even the Frenchman's Reef waived four months of back rent. The IRS waived penalties and Island Revenue agreed to a two-thirds settlement without penalties. I used every cent of the money Frog sent, but the company survived, and we regained some degree of stature on the island.

The summer was coming to an end. Terry, her mother, and the kids had to leave to get the children back in school. It had been a unique summer. We had many good experiences, and I was thankful for the time we had together. Nevertheless, once again, like so many times in the past, we were saying goodbye. I had committed to staying until December and didn't have another job to return to, so I was stuck on the island for another few months.

Frog discussed the idea of my staying longer. I appreciated his providing a job, but also I realized that at the end of my commitment, I had to return to civilization and get settled. I'd seen too many people on St. Thomas whose stop on the island was the end of a rough road. Many alcoholics and drug users called the island home, and it was dangerous to stay there for too long.

Frog set out to find a replacement and received an application from the comptroller of Rock Resorts on St. John's. He arrived on the ferry, and we scheduled an interview on the beach at Cowpet Bay, the location of another of Frog's condos. When in the United States, Frog was pretty much all business. He enjoyed a good time but didn't drink very much and kept his mind occupied with his various ventures. However, when he came to the islands, he was a wild man. The night before he had a party at his condo, and when a neighbor banged on the door complaining about the noise level, Frog punched him in the nose.

The next morning at eleven o'clock, we met the job applicant from Rock Resorts. He looked every bit the part of a CPA—neatly dressed, well groomed, and well spoken. Frog asked if anyone wanted something to drink and proceeded to order three Elephant beers for himself. I had had Elephant beer once. It is brewed in Denmark and is a very strong lager, too strong for my taste. When the waiter appeared with the three bottles, Frog took off his left shoe and poured in one bottle, then followed the same ritual with his right shoe and finally drank the third and last bottle. This happened several times, and each time I found it hilarious. The guy from Rock Resort seemed curious about the ritual. I thought for sure he was going to walk, but soon he started drinking Elephant beer along with Frog (without the shoe trick). They hit it off. Frog made the offer, and he accepted. Frog was happy, the new guy was happy, and I was happy. We had my replacement.

Chapter 8

Looking for Work
November to December 1980

Terry didn't waste any time looking for a job upon her return. In October 1980, she started as an account assistant in the accounting office of Sam Davis, who handled bill paying and tax matters for various clients. The office was located in Severna Park, not far from our house.

My time on the rock was ending. I was looking forward to returning to the States, although I was somewhat concerned about work and money. I arrived back home in November 1980 and starting networking. One of my first interviews was with a company located in Sparks, Maryland, named PHH, which was involved in providing financial and management services for commercial vehicle fleets. I interviewed with six or seven people for most of a day and ended with the CEO. We were having a relaxed chat when he casually asked where I received my MBA. I responded I didn't have an MBA, and that brought the conversation to a screeching halt. He explained that the department they were thinking about for me to run was full of MBAs and that it simply wouldn't work having me oversee them without having an MBA myself. We shook hands and that was that.

One of the investors in The Money Tree was Frank Wells, a man I had met while at Maryland National. Frank was a good friend of Joe Mosmiller, chairman of Loyola Federal Savings and Loan, the largest such organization in the state with about $1.2 billion in assets.

Rules for savings and loan institutions had recently changed. Historically, they were restricted to mortgage lending, but the changes permitted them to engage in consumer lending as well.

Frank spoke with Joe and convinced him he should meet with me. I went to Loyola's headquarters on Charles Street in Baltimore and met first with Tom Marvel, the senior vice president in charge of mortgage lending, and next with Jim Johnson, the president, and finally with Joe. We had long and interesting conversations regarding how I might go about forming a consumer lending operation at Loyola and how it could make money for the organization.

Joe Mosmiller was a square-shouldered man with silver hair, tailored suits, and an intense personality. Jim had more of a slight build, was balding, and down to earth. Tom exuded warmth and a genuine smile that was disarming. They were a diverse trio, but I was quickly convinced that they knew their business inside out and they worked well together. Every detail was at their fingertips. They were quick to probe when I brought up a topic they didn't have familiarity with and quick to grasp and understand the cause and effect of various topics we discussed. I was impressed with them and thought they had the same feeling about me.

We had meetings on three occasions over a two-week period, and each time I felt comfortable with the organization and with the players. Apparently they felt the same since they offered me the job. We agreed on the salary and the title (vice president), but when I asked for a company car, they balked, saying everyone wanted a company car. I had become accustomed to the perk since I was afforded a car while at Maryland National and The Money Tree and even while in St. Thomas. They said they'd think about it. I wasn't in a strong negotiating position so I accepted their offer, and we agreed on a start date the following week. I felt renewed and anxious to embark on my new adventure.

At the same time, Terry had heard of a position as the high school secretary at St. Mary's where the children attended the elementary school. She applied, interviewed, and was hired. This was the perfect job for the perfect time. The salary wasn't terrific, but part of her compensation was half tuition for the children, which more than made up for any shortfall in salary. Also, she would have summers off, which helped tremendously with the kids.

I called Jim Goosen, a friend of mine in southern Maryland who wholesaled cars for a living. I explained I needed a car that would run and cost less than $1,000. He assured me he could meet my needs and called me the next day saying he had a green Mercury Cougar with high miles, but it ran well. I went to see it. What a sight! The car wasn't just green, it was *lime green*. Jim had failed to mention it had a half landau white top and that it was missing an antenna but the coat hanger worked just fine for reception. I bought it.

The following week I pulled into the parking lot behind the headquarters on Charles Street in my new old car. It wasn't hard to spot, and if you looked down from the executive offices on the fifth floor, it *definitely* was not hard to spot. I drove that car for a few months before Jim Johnson called me and told me to go to the Buick dealer and select a Le Sabre as my company car.

My first office was in a conference room across from Tom Marvel's office, and I quickly learned that Loyola wasn't just a mutual savings and loan, but rather, very much a family affair. Most employees had been there for several years, and there was a high level of familiarity. I found everyone to be welcoming and inquisitive about what I intended to do. The Major Domo was a lady named Helen Hansard who ruled the roost. Helen was about five feet tall and a bit portly, but she was not someone to mess with. It was apparent that everyone, including Jim and Joe, not only respected her but also were a bit afraid of her. She had absolute control of the entire mortgage operation—a force to be reckoned with. But, to tell the truth, it didn't take long to realize that she also had a heart of gold, and everyone loved her, including me.

I went about putting my business plan together, detailing the types of loans I thought we should originate, the yields and interest rate spreads available in the marketplace, the competition, and pro forma financial statements for three years. Once complete, I met with Jim McElvency, who was the chief financial officer (CFO), and incorporated my numbers into the company's overall plan to determine how much of a funding commitment I'd need. The yields on consumer loans were considerably higher than residential mortgages, and the gap between funding and loan maturities were much better, but, of course, the default rate was higher.

I met with Tom, Jim, and Joe for a couple of hours, detailing my business plan and what it could mean to the association. They gave me a green light on virtually everything we discussed. We planned to start with indirect (dealer) automobile loans and second mortgages, followed by boat loans and unsecured lines of credit.

The first person I contacted to join the team was Harry "Car Czar" Schmidt from Maryland National Bank. He was comfortable there, but we knew each other well, he trusted my judgment and commitment, and he made the decision to come on board. Next I needed an experienced consumer finance person to handle all direct lending. I called Ted Kozak, who used to be in charge of executive hiring at Maryland National but had since left and started his own executive recruitment firm. He came up with three or four candidates, and I decided to hire Doug Perkins, who had about fifteen years' experience in consumer finance. After interviewing him, I determined he was an excellent credit guy who would approve the right applicants and not get us into delinquency and loss problems. We needed a person to run operations, and I selected Roxanne Whitney, who was working in the mortgage department at Loyola. These were the initial key players, and we hired clerical staff both from within and outside the association to start the department with twenty people. I moved to a different floor and occupied about a quarter of it.

Chapter 9

Growing the Business at Loyola Federal
1980 to 1986

Harry and his network of car dealers got out of the gate in a hurry. His contacts and experience guaranteed rapid growth. Right from the beginning, we received more than one hundred credit applications daily from a multitude of dealers. I had relationships with many dealers from Anne Arundel and Prince George's counties and brought them into the fold along with Harry's Baltimore base. With that we quickly built a network of more than a hundred dealerships. The number of daily applications soon doubled.

On the boat side of the business, Doug didn't have prior experience or contacts, but I did. We started doing business with all my old dealer friends from Annapolis and the Eastern Shore. Second mortgages were sourced from our large residential mortgage portfolio, and, to a much lesser extent, the branches. Branch originations were always a disappointment to me both at Maryland National and Loyola. When we would look at the number of customers each branch had and assumed even a one percent penetration rate, the opportunities were overwhelming. The math problem worked but, in reality, originations from bank branches rarely did.

The FBI Knocks
March 1981

It was about this time that I received telephone call from a friend of mine telling me that the FBI was looking for me. I thought it was a practical joke, but he assured me it wasn't. I don't know why I was difficult to find since I was listed in the phone book, but I guess they didn't think of looking there. I called the regional office in Annapolis and said I heard they were looking for me, still thinking it was a joke but not completely sure. The agent said they would like to talk to me regarding Herb Gregory. I thought, *Oh shit! The Curacao trip!* I made an appointment and went to the FBI office. The agent said Herb was under investigation for bribing a state senator in Delaware and that I was not a target. He went on to say that Herb told them that Maryland National Bank provided the money to bribe the senator to encourage him to support raising interest rates in the state, and that Ray Nichols and I were aware of it. I assured the agent that I knew nothing about the matter and most seriously doubted that Ray did either. He said he would keep me advised of the proceedings.

At home, I called Tom Hudson, the attorney whom I had consulted in the past. He suggested that I call him from a pay phone and hung up. I went to the 7-Eleven near our house and called again, asking him why the hell was I calling from a pay phone. He said he was concerned that my home phone might be tapped. I thought that was nuts, but who knows? He advised me not to talk to anyone about the meeting and especially not to talk to Ray or anyone from Maryland National.

A few months went by with no word from the FBI, and I thought the matter had died. Then the doorbell rang at our house, and I was served a subpoena to appear before the grand jury in Wilmington, Delaware. I immediately drove to the 7-Eleven and called Tom.

Subsequently, I told Joe and Jim what was going on. The day before I had to appear before the grand jury, I recall them saying, "Don't let them keep you," which I appreciated.

Maryland National agreed to pay my legal fees, and Tom and I drove to Wilmington. Tom advised me that I had to appear without counsel, but if someone asked a question that I was uncomfortable with that I could leave the room, consult with him, and return with my answer. My reaction was that move wouldn't look good to the jurors, but I kept it in mind. I went into the room and sat in the middle of it in a straight-backed chair with several people around me in a half circle. The questions started flying. I knew I wasn't involved with anything related to bribery but I was afraid the Curacao trip would come up, and that wouldn't be a good thing. The hearing took about an hour. I answered all their questions without leaving the room, and Curacao never came up. With that behind me (what a relief!), I could go back to building a new business.

Home Equity Lines of Credit in Maryland

There had been some interesting developments on the West Coast. A new product was being offered in a very limited way. It was a second mortgage, not a traditional closed-end loan, but a revolving line of credit secured by a recorded second mortgage against a residence. I had read about it in a trade publication and quickly became intrigued by the concept. I spoke with Tom Hudson, and he told me it was against Maryland law to offer such a product. A couple of days later we spoke about it again. I could see the popularity that a product like this would have and wanted to find a way to offer it. He agreed and said maybe we could obtain a federal pre-emption from the Federal Home Loan Bank (FHLB) in Atlanta that would supersede Maryland law and allow us to move forward with the product.

Tom contacted the FHLB, writing them to describe what we wanted to do and conceptually how we would do it. After almost a month of back and forth, they granted their consent. About the same time, a bill had been introduced in the Maryland General Assembly, which would eliminate the prohibition from offering the product. Even if the bill passed, it would be some time before it would be enacted, which gave me about six months to make hay. We had to move fast before competition entered the arena.

Jim and Joe bought into the idea, and I met with Chuck Schmidt, who was in charge of systems. Most systems people are cautious and averse to thinking "outside the box." I suppose it goes with the mindset and generally is the right approach. In this case, we didn't have the time or luxury of dotting all the *is* or cross all the *t*s. I thought the reward far surpassed the risk, and with prodding from me (and Joe), he got with the program. It was necessary to piece together various systems to develop a program that could track multiple loan advances against a line of credit. We recognized it wasn't a long-range solution, but we needed to move fast. Despite the initial blowback, our systems people made it happen in about thirty days. At the same time Marshall Moore, who was in charge of marketing for the association, had worked with an outside ad agency and me to develop the marketing plan. Marshall was a middle-aged fellow who had been with Loyola for years, but he moved with the vim and vigor of a man thirty years younger, and he had an intensity level that matched mine. He produced an excellent and effective direct mail, radio, and print campaign.

There are difficulties associated with rolling out new products. Before you can sell them to potential customers, you have to explain how they work and what the benefits are, and often the explanation gets in the way of the sale. Marshall found the right balance, and we named it "Home Made Money." The logo was a large jar full of "funny" money. Although I never counted on branches for loan generation, when customers spotted that large jar on the counter, it piqued their interest. The newspapers ran stories, and television stations interviewed me and aired the story on their news shows. We hit a home run. Knowing all good things come to an end and that the clock was ticking, we did everything we could to originate as many loans as was humanly possible. I would arrive at the office at 7 a.m., and Doug and I would make credit decisions all day long and into the evening. Applications were flooding in. What a fun time we had!

Now the association had multiple vibrant credit businesses: automobile, boat, second mortgage, and home equity lines of credit. We started giving thought about where to go next. My original plan called for unsecured lines of credit. All our loans thus far were secured, and our delinquency and losses were well in control, so it was time to take a little more risk and gain the financial reward from doing it well.

Before we moved forward, I hired a collection manager named Bill Rickenbach, an old-time Baltimorean with a depth of collection experience. He had a heavy Baltimore accent, was large in stature, gruff and rough, and he could drink anyone I knew (but probably not Harry Barrett) under the table. He was a champion dart thrower and at one time was the Baltimore City champion. Rumor had it, the more he drank, the better he threw. In short, he was a wild man but, in spite of his foibles, he was an excellent collection manager and a perfect fit to our group. Marshall had a fellow working with him in marketing named Bill Van Blarcom, who had produced much of the work on Home Made Money. I thought it would be appropriate to have a marketing person on my staff that could interface with Marshall and the marketing department on all our products. I wanted the continuity of having the same person working on all our campaigns, and Marshall agreed to have Bill report to me with a dotted line to him.

Bill was a very intelligent guy who could think out of the box and who had a high degree of creativity. We started designing the new unsecured product and structuring a marketing program. We named it Dollar Sign and began offering lines of credit up to $20,000. It took off and soon we had a fifth product in our lineup that was contributing profits to the organization.

The group now totaled about sixty people. I thought we needed more management depth. I went back to the well at Maryland National one more time and convinced Tom Groft to join us as the number two guy. Tom was a well-rounded banker who understood all aspects of consumer lending. The one question he asked before deciding whether or not to come onboard was if I planned to stay at Loyola for a long time. My response was, "Loyola is my life." He accepted the position and made a wonderful addition.

About this time the glue and paper clips holding the computer systems together were starting to unravel. The software we were using wasn't designed to do what we were using it for, and the stress was showing. From the beginning I had sub-contracted with a company named Southwestern States Bankcard Association (SSBA) in Dallas to perform our data processing for the automobile business, since that business needed very specific capabilities that Loyola couldn't produce. We now had to discuss and make the decision whether to give all our business to SSBA or make the investment in software and personnel to perform the function in-house. Naturally, Chuck Schmidt wanted it in-house. I wanted to move it all to SSBA. A battle ensued, and I won. It's easier to win when you're on top, and I had the ear of the president and chairman.

Shortly thereafter, I was promoted to senior vice president, which really meant something at Loyola. The hierarchy consisted of the chairman, the president, and eight senior vice presidents. The eight SVPs were Bob Schultz, who handled mortgage operations; Jim McElveney, the CFO; Tom Marvel, in charge of mortgage originations and secondary markets; Marshall Moore, in charge of marketing and advertising; Mr. Pierce, a retired executive who had the honorary title; Bill Wycoff from personnel; Chuck Schmidt from systems; and me.

One of the perks associated with the title was daily lunch in the executive dining room. This was a nicely furnished room on the top floor where we were expected to meet daily and enjoy food prepared by Donald the chef. Donald was a large black man who had a devilish smile and an experienced skill in the kitchen. The camaraderie and food were excellent, but I found that the daily exercise was a bit much. Typically I attended three to four days each week. The topics generally evolved into the latest round of golf or fishing escapades. Frankly, I was too busy to take an hour a day to hear fish stories or tales of the fifty-foot putt.

As another very nice perk, we went with our spouses to the Greenbrier Resort in West Virginia for a few days each year for an executive physical. Typically, three or four couples went at the same time and spent a few days with one-half of a day dedicated to an extremely thorough physical. The rest of the time we played golf, ate, drank, and were merry.

The night before the physicals, the diet was restricted to liquids (which included alcohol) for those going through a colonoscopy. Jim McElveney was along with us one year, and he and I were scheduled for the dreaded test the next morning. We took the pill at exactly the same time and wagers were placed as to who would break for the men's room first. We surveyed the location and sat relatively close so when the medicine kicked in we'd have a fighting chance of making it. I won but only by a few minutes.

Back in Baltimore, we soon outgrew our square footage and there wasn't enough contiguous space in the building to house the division. Across the street there were three dilapidated row houses in desperate need of repair. Loyola bought the buildings and renovated them, which was good for Loyola, good for the city, and good for me.

Once the construction was near completion, we made the move across the street. The space was chopped up with walls separating the three buildings allowing access through two portals. There were two floors, which made for good exercise since the elevator was the hydraulic type that took forever to get from one floor to the other. Some windows were drafty since the building had historic significance and the Historical Society dictated they had to remain original. Despite these minor inconveniences, everyone enjoyed the increased space, and I enjoyed the privacy from the rest of the organization. Mayor William Donald Shaffer dedicated the building at a reception held for the executives, our entire department, and other city dignitaries.

Next door was a deli and a bar named Jay's. Every once in a while I'd ask my secretary to go there to pick up a six pack of Budweiser bombshells (16-ounce cans) for marketing meetings that took place in my office after hours. Bill, Tom, and I would brainstorm over a couple of beers. The creativity for Dollar Sign came out of one of those meetings. Business was going well, Terry and I had good incomes, and it was time to celebrate.

Fifteenth Anniversary in Europe
Summer 1984

It was 1984 and our fifteenth anniversary was coming up that August. I bought several Michelin roadmaps and various tour books and spent months planning a three-week trip to Germany, Austria, and Switzerland. I started saving the year before, and by the time August arrived we had sufficient funds for the trip. The kids stayed with Terry's mother and we flew out of Baltimore to Frankfurt, Germany.

We landed early in the morning, and the first people we saw after exiting the baggage area were German policemen with dogs and machine guns. Not particularly welcoming and most likely not sanctioned by the Chamber of Commerce. We went to the Kemwel rental car booth where I had reserved a car. We were given an Opel, which brought back memories of my car in Bad Aibling. Fortunately this one was brand new, clean as a whistle, and it didn't have a hole in the floor behind the driver's seat.

Our trip took us down the Romantic Road with Heidelberg as our first stop. We then continued southward along the Romantic Road to Munich and on to Bad Aibling, where I was stationed in the army. After that, we moved on to Austria before heading to Switzerland.

We ordinarily stayed only one night in each town. One of our favorites was Rothenburg on the Tauber River in Germany. There we stayed at a very nice little inn named the Hotel Burg. Another stop was just outside Munich in the town of Berg on the Starnenberger Sea. Our lodging looked more like a two-story American motel than a German hotel, but the views were great since it was located on the shoreline. Terry and I had lunch consisting of some nondescript meat, which later had an adverse effect on her. This was on a Saturday and the following morning she was nauseous. I found a little chapel in the village and attended Mass, but Terry couldn't make it. Our plans called for us to move on to Bad Aibling, and Terry said she thought she could make the trip. It turned out to be a mistake for us to travel, as Terry was really sick.

We finally made it to Bad Aibling and booked a room at the Hotel Lindner. I explained as best I could to the desk clerk, "Mein frau ist krank." She suggested we go to the krankenhaus (hospital). We entered the building, and I repeated what I had said in the hotel to a small nun dressed in white and tried to explain it was stomach pains caused from eisen (food). She immediately grasped Terry's arm and whisked her down a long hallway with me trailing behind at a fast gait. A few minutes later a doctor appeared, and I tried to explain the problem to him in my broken German. I kept saying eisen until finally, in perfect English, he said, "Eisen is steel. I believe you mean essen." It would have been nice if he had spoken up before I struggled with German, but I guess he needed some entertainment that day. He provided us with some tablets and told Terry how often to take them. There wasn't any charge and we returned to the hotel.

I stayed with Terry for a couple of hours and she urged me to see the town since I had spent more than a year there in 1965 and 1966. I took her up on her suggestion and visited several spots. It had been almost twenty years since I was there and the visit brought back many pleasant memories.

I returned to the hotel and Terry seemed to feel a little better. The clerk asked how she was and suggested I bring her a bowl of oxtail soup. I brought it to our room explaining it was broth. One spoonful and she was off to the races. She has never eaten oxtail soup again. That evening there was a zither concert scheduled in the hotel, and again Terry urged me to go downstairs and attend. I missed not having her join me but I enjoyed the concert. While downstairs, the clerk asked how Terry was feeling. I bent the truth and told her Terry loved the soup and was on the mend.

The next morning Terry felt much better. We speculated that maybe it wasn't the food but just her nerves since we had never left the kids that long and she missed them dearly. In any event, we were off once again on our way to a small village named Bayrischzell, about an hour from Bad Aibling.

That night we were sitting in a gasthaus enjoying dinner when we heard the dreaded question, "Is that American I hear?" The people in the next booth were from Massachusetts and decided to join us. They were interesting, but we would have preferred to be alone. We parted company the next day and made our way to Innsbruck and then on to Salzburg, where we stayed in a small inn.

That afternoon after returning from sightseeing there was a knock on the door. It was our new pals from Massachusetts. To this day we have no idea how they found us. They asked where we were going next, and we told them we would be heading north to Berchtesgaden. We awoke the next morning and headed south.

We kept traveling, enjoying the lakes area outside Salzburg, and then we headed toward Switzerland. We climbed up a steep alpine road outside Interlaken when the car began making strange noises and overheating. We pulled into the parking lot of a small inn and had lunch. The views of the Jungfrau, the highest peak in Switzerland, were spectacular and the food was equally impressive. The car had cooled down and we drove down the mountain to town where I purchased a gas can and filled it with water to be used if the car overheated again.

Over the course of a few weeks we made a big loop and spent the last night in Heidelberg as we had the first. We stayed in the Zum Ritter Hotel where we stayed a few weeks earlier. On our first night we ate dinner at the hotel and Terry insisted I leave a big tip. I tried to explain that waiters in Europe were compensated differently than in the United States, and if one left any amount, it would only be pocket change. She didn't buy it. I gave up and finally left a tip that would be customary in the United States. When we returned for our final night, the waiters were climbing over each other trying to get to us.

We drove to the Frankfurt airport the next morning and returned the rental car. They asked if everything had been all right with the car. I told them about the overheating issue and offered to donate my water can, whereupon they told me the car was air cooled without a radiator. I'm sure they had a good laugh after we left the counter.

Our return flight was uneventful, and we landed safely in Baltimore. It was a wonderful anniversary trip and certainly more enjoyable then our tenth in the Poconos.

Back at work, everything was humming along. I was happy to have Tom Groft onboard, as I would never have been able to leave without him. We kept making loans and eventually in 1985 we had $250 million in consumer loans on the books, which represented about twenty percent of the assets of Loyola. More importantly, our earnings represented about a third of the overall earnings of the association. Life was good.

I bought a new Mercedes Benz 300 turbo diesel, which was like owning a land yacht. It was huge and rode like a dream. I still had my company Buick, and Terry usually drove the Mercedes.

Jim and Joe began having conversations about converting Loyola from a mutual savings and loan to a stock corporation. The senior team discussed various structures, and we hired financial advisors. The personal benefit of converting to stock was the probability of being granted stock options or grants, which could be lucrative. I thought Jim and Joe would probably want to sell Loyola and collect a windfall, which would allow them to dedicate even more time to golfing and fishing. It all sounded like a good idea to me.

Time for a New House

Terry and I had been looking to move out of our original house that I bought in 1969, and we found a building lot in Annapolis on a peninsula between Church and Crab Creek, just off the South River. There were a total of ten acres that two admirals had purchased years before with the idea of building their houses there when they retired. Their plans had changed, and they subdivided it into nine lots each consisting of approximately an acre. Three of the lots were directly on the water, but two were sold, and the third wasn't on the market. We bought a lot about one hundred yards from the water and the community dock. Frog was still building houses, but his were of a much larger variety. He recommended we meet with another builder named Russell Daywalt. I fancied myself an amateur architect and drew a sketch of the house on large pieces of graph paper. I also had diagrams of room locations and sizes. Russell provided these drawings to a draftsman who developed the elevations and structural drawings, and soon we were clearing trees from the building site and beginning construction.

We had never built a house before, but we enjoyed the process. We visited the site most days, since it was only about ten miles from our house. It was also important to be on site regularly, since we didn't have architectural drawings and several decisions had to be made on the fly. The project took about six months from start to finish. The outside was light tan vinyl siding with a brick foundation, and we had a two-car garage, which we never had before. The ground floor had a spare bedroom and a full bath, a family room with a stacked stone fireplace and cathedral ceiling, a screened porch off the family room, a large eat-in kitchen, a living room, a dining room, and a master bedroom suite with a sitting room and a deck. The girls' bedrooms were upstairs, separated by a bathroom. We bought several new pieces of furniture and new drapes, and the home was complete. We loved our new home, and we loved living in a very small development near the water.

My Baptism. Poppy, my father, and me at the occasion of my baptism in 1948 on the front porch of my paternal grandparent's home at 907 Prospect Avenue on the west side of Buffalo.

NFL Bound. Me at age 2. Even though it appears that I'm destined for a lucrative career in the NFL, I never pursued the sport.

What a Handful! Me at age 7 trying to corral my sister Patrice at age 2.

Home Sweet Home. The house I grew up in at 26 Evadene in Buffalo. Notice the three windows over the roof. That was the "escape hatch" that I regularly climbed out of for nighttime activities.

Joie De Vie. Uncle Dick and Aunt Jean enjoying an evening cruise on the Seine in 1972.

Wedded Bliss. My Grammy and Poppy on their
sixtieth wedding anniversary.

South China Sea. Me on a terrace in Nha Trang
shortly after arriving in Vietnam in 1967.

My Canine Friend. "Big Dog" and me in front of our tent, the "Pleiku Hilton." A loving pet that was meant to stay in Southeast Asia.

A Little Worse for Wear. Picture of me in front of our tent with the perimeter of the base in the background.

THANKSGIVING DAY DINNER

Shrimp Cocktail

Crackers

Roast Turkey

Turkey Gravy   Cornbread Dressing   Cranberry Sauce

Mashed Potatoes   Glazed Sweet Potatoes

Buttered Mixed Vegetable

Assorted Crisp Relishes

Hot Rolls   Butter   Fruit Cake   Mincemeat Pie

Pumpkin Pie w/Whipped Topping

Assorted Nuts   Assorted Candy   Assorted Fresh Fruits

Tea w/Lemon   Milk

PRAYER

Father of mercies and giver of all good, by whose power we were created, by whose bounty we are sustained, and by whose spirit we are transformed, accept, we beseech Thee, our prayer of thanks.

For those who love us and of whose love we would be more worthy, for those who believe in us and whose hopes we cannot disappoint; for every good gift of healing and happiness and renewal, we bless Thy name, we thank Thee for our homeland, for all that is just and true, noble and right, wise and courageous in our history. We praise Thee for our place in the community of nations and we invoke Thy blessings on men of good will wherever they may be and who labor for a world of justice, freedom and fraternity.

Most of all, Eternal Father, we thank Thee for Thyself, the nearness of Thy presence and the warmth of Thy love, whereby our minds and hearts find joy and peace. Freely we have received, O God, freely let us give ourselves to Thy gracious purposes. For Thy love's sake. Amen.

COMMANDER'S MESSAGE

On this traditional Thanksgiving Day, as we find ourselves half way around the world from home, we should pause for a few moments to count our many blessings as Americans. We should never forget that in Vietnam, our actions are defending free men everywhere. We pray that peace will come to all the world and that all of us can return to our loved ones in the not too distant future.

W. C. WESTMORELAND
General, United States Army
Commanding

A Great Spread. The army knew how important Thanksgiving was to the GIs in Vietnam and spared no expense in preparing an excellent holiday meal. I thought General Westmoreland's message was heartfelt and sincere.

Our Wedding Party. From left to right: me, Terry, Terry's maid of honor Mary Balling, my best man (and great bartender) Tom O'Connor, Terry's sister-in-law Karen Dwyer, my pal from Vietnam Jim Ward, my sister Patrice, my neighborhood friend Phil Seereiter, Terry's sister-in-law Marilyn Dwyer, and my brother Tim.

Courier EXPRESS
AUG 3 1969

Mrs. Blewett
. . . Miss Dwyer

Miss Theresa M. Dwyer and Patrick M. Blewett exchanged wedding vows at 10 Saturday morning at St. Joseph's Church in Main St. The bride is the daughter of Mr. and Mrs. Michael A. Dwyer of Englewood Ave. The bridegroom is the son of Mrs. Jack Zack of Eva-dene Pl. and the late Timothy Blewett. After a honeymoon in Bermuda the couple will make their home in Annapolis, Md.

Wedding Announcement. This notice appeared in both the *Courier Express* and the *Buffalo Evening News* the day after our wedding while we were in Bermuda on our honeymoon.

Lucky. One look at this picture and you'll understand why I consider myself lucky.

Teenage Buddies. Bill Walgate on the left, Pete Seereiter in the middle, and me on the right at a reunion at the Stuffed Mushroom on Main Street in Buffalo in 1990. Obviously, Budweiser was the drink du jour but it looks like Bill had something with a swizzle as well.

Silver Anniversary. Father Bob (later referred to as Roberto on our vacation to Italy and Hans while traveling in Germany and Austria) visited us in our home in Chadds Ford, Pennsylvania, in 1984 when we reaffirmed our wedding vows after twenty-five years of marriage.

The Big Apple. Our friends convinced Terry to take a Christmas train trip from Chadds Ford to New York while I was in the U.K. I flew in from London to surprise her and met them at the top of the stairs at Penn Station. From left to right: me, Nancy Lee Groft, Terry, Tom Groft, Julie Van Blarcom, and Bill Van Blarcom at Rockefeller Center.

Dinner in Bermuda. Terry and I flew from the U.K., while Michelle and Joanna flew from the United States, to spend a few fun-filled days together in Bermuda in 1997.

Show Time. Wendel and Terry in England with her trainer getting some last minute tips before a dressage competition.

Eliten. More commonly referred to as Wendel, or as he came to be known, Wonderful Wendel. He was a true competitor, never disappointing in the show ring, and a great friend.

Putting on the Strut. I never gave thought to spending time with the Queen of England while growing up in Buffalo but it happened in 1997 when Terry and I were invited to a Garden Party with Queen Elizabeth at Buckingham Palace. It was a wonderful experience.

Riding in Style. Terry in front of one of the Bentleys at Buckingham Palace. It was often difficult to choose between one of the two blue Bentleys or the green Rolls Royce. Decisions, decisions! While our chauffer left something (actually, many things) to be desired, it was a hoot.

Presidential Times. President George H.W. Bush with Terry and me at the Samoset Resort in Camden, Maine. He and Barbara were frequent guests at the annual MBNA Management Conferences and a joy to spend time with. Both Terry and I have deep admiration for both of them, for their integrity and for their service to our country.

Mr. Bush. President Bush and me in Maine at another MBNA conference. A true gentleman.

Stiff Upper Lip. Leaving MBNA International was difficult but, I felt, necessary. I'm thankful to the senior management, their talents, and the dedication they displayed. They were a great team.

New Challenges. This small group headed up a big undertaking in establishing Bank One International in 1998. From left to right: Jeff Courtney, Bill Van Blarcom, me, Helen Williams, and Sue Wildman. Another great team.

Oudie the Wonder Dog. Every night Oudie would sit on a small desk at the kitchen window of the Tower House waiting for me to arrive home from work and display her joy upon my arrival. A little dog who displayed bravery in the face of ghosts and bats.

A Godsend. Terry, Oudie, and Bette MacWilliams on a visit to see us in the U.K. Roger was the best neighbor in the world—he knew how to fix everything! As for Bette, they say "Face your fears." I was able to do that in Vietnam and later with heart problems, but thank God for Bette when it came to help with changing diapers.

Kids and Kids. Michelle, our oldest daughter, and her two children Tyler and Joelle, along with her best friend Rob, who is a surveyor, a farmer, a chef, and an all-around good guy. What a blessing to have children and even more so to have grandchildren.

Gone Fishing. Tyler is not only a "jock," a walking sports encyclopedia, and a really nice young man. He's a fisherman! Here he is with his catch of a Spanish mackerel on a family vacation to Panama City, Florida, in 2013.

Free Spirit. Joelle is an adventurer, an animal lover, and a girl anxious to explore all life has to offer. And…she's a delight. One look and you sense the energy!

Our Little Girl. Joanna's a gal who's figured out how to juggle many things and stay happy while doing so. Michael is an adventurer—experienced wake boarder, airplane pilot, and medevac helicopter pilot. Together they enjoy life to the fullest.

Talk About an Adventurer! Bridget follows in her parents' footsteps. She loves taking chances, having fun, and all things exciting.

My Brother. Tim and his wife Florence travel to London frequently to visit their daughter who lives and works there. Tim and I are different in almost every way. We have differing views on politics, books, movies, and, well…just about everything. But he's my brother and I'd do anything to help him in any way. The best part is I know he would do the same for me.

Mom! They're Doing it Again. My sister Patrice and her husband John on a convention trip to California. She was a little girl when I left home to move in with my uncle and aunt, and I left for the army at age seventeen just a couple of years after moving back. Later in life we got to know each other better.

Just a Big Hearted Guy. I met Jerry Dunne when I started at Major Finance in 1970. He subsequently met and fell in love with Terry's sister, Kathy. They're catching up with Terry and me and have been married thirty-two years. Of all the people I've met over the years, Jerry is the one who stands out as being the kind of guy who literally would give you the shirt off his back.

Will Rogers. Will Rogers said, "I've never met a man I didn't like." I say, "I've never met a man who didn't like Tom Groft." Tom has been along with me for the ride, and we had a great and fun time traveling the road together. People who know Tom and his wife Nancy Lee are lucky.

A Saint. My mother and Jack at a celebration. When I think of my mother, I think of how difficult I was and how she dealt with it. I was much more of a handful than most adolescents and, in hindsight, feel bad that I put her through all the things I did. As much as I initially disliked Jack, he was a wonderful husband to my mom.

Not Just an Attorney.
Tom Hudson
contributed significantly
to my success. His
creative thought process
provided the roadmap
for several innovative
programs we introduced
over the years, and his
warm personality
provided endless good
times. He and his wife
Lily Grace have been
wonderful friends and
Terry and I value our
friendship.

Chapter 10

Opportunity Knocks

1986 to 1990

In early 1986, I received a telephone call from Ted Kozak, the headhunter. He was representing Chase Bank of Maryland, and they were looking for someone to run their newly acquired retail businesses. At the time, interstate banking wasn't permitted, and the only way to circumvent that restriction was to acquire entire banks or S & Ls under duress in other states. Maryland had undergone a savings and loan crisis in 1985, and Chase had purchased three troubled S & Ls. I explained to Ted that I was very happy with Loyola, that they treated me well, and that I wasn't interested. Ted was a great salesman, critical to being a successful headhunter, and that day he was in particularly good form. He discussed the possibilities of overseas assignments in the future, as Chase was a global organization. Working abroad was something I had always thought would be fun. We spoke several times over the next few weeks, and I finally agreed to a meeting.

I drove to Bethesda where the team from New York had set up headquarters. I met with several executives and finally with the president, Stan Burns. Stan was extremely charismatic and instantly likeable. He was a really charming guy. We talked at length and he described the challenges ahead, which were abundant and somewhat daunting. These organizations failed because they had been poorly managed. Chase found many problems: incompetence, poor underwriting, millions of dollars of distressed assets ranging from hotels to water treatment plants, fraud and embezzlement, the extent of which was greater than their due diligence had originally uncovered. Maryland had provided coverage for many of the obvious losses but not for all.

Stan brought in workout experts from New York to handle the troubled assets and hired others to build the commercial lending business. He needed someone with consumer lending expertise to build new businesses and manage the acquired residential mortgage business and its secondary marketing operations while the distressed assets of the "old bank" were liquidated.

I always enjoyed challenges, and these days Loyola was running on automatic pilot. Many people might relax and decide they had accomplished all they had set out to do and jump on the gravy train. Not me. I'd find that boring. I thought about the upcoming initial public offering (IPO) at Loyola and knew I'd be walking away from a potential windfall. But I also knew that I could help turn around the mess Chase had acquired and contribute to building the new bank. On balance, I decided the challenge would be more rewarding at Chase. They offered me a nice pay hike, a company car, and Chase Manhattan stock options to help with my decision process.

The next day I went to see Jim and Joe and broke the news. They didn't have any idea that I might leave. In hindsight I see why they felt that way. I was part of the family. They served me lunch daily, gave me a company car, a good salary, and autonomy to operate as I saw fit. All those things appealed to a guy like me. The one thing they could no longer give me was the excitement of a challenge, and that's what I craved.

I started with Chase in January 1986 working in Rockville, Maryland. Rockville was a seventy-five-minute commute each way. It didn't matter what time I left home or work, it was always an hour and fifteen minutes or longer if there was an accident. I had some exposure to the first mortgage business but my new position represented a steep learning curve. A fellow from Friendship Savings and Loan (one of the acquired) named Dan Pastros had a strong mortgage background. He helped me tremendously, especially with the ins and outs of secondary marketing. There was no consumer loan department. That was for me to build.

Building the Team

Shortly after leaving Loyola, the telephone started to ring from my old management team at Loyola asking if there was room for them at Chase. I hired Harry Schmidt, Doug Perkins, and Tom Groft in my first thirty days. I remember Tom asking me if this was it. Was I going to stay with Chase for a long time? I responded, "Chase is my life."

A few weeks later, I received a telephone call from Joe Mosmiller. He ranted, raved, and sputtered something about suing Chase and me. A couple of days later we received a threatening letter from Loyola's attorneys saying the same thing. Chase flew in lawyers from New York who held individual interviews with Harry, Doug, Tom, and me. We all told them the same thing: the truth. I hadn't solicited any of them. They called asking if I had a position for them. The lawyers concluded Loyola was blowing smoke, but there wasn't any fire. They responded to Loyola's attorneys that we hadn't done anything wrong, and basically, told them to go to hell. I subsequently received a few more calls from members of the old gang and hired them as well. We now had most of the team together again.

Chase was a different place, but our approach was a rerun of what we had done at Loyola. We originated car loans, boat loans, home equity lines of credit, unsecured lines of credit, second mortgages, and now first mortgages and secondary marketing functions. We developed new contracts and forms just as we had at Loyola. I called Tom Hudson again, and he got cracking. We needed support people and went through the interviewing process identifying the right people. In all, it took a couple of months before we were fully up and running.

We called dealers or we went to see them in person. We told them to lose the old phone number. That was the easy part. Dealers didn't really care what financial institutions they sent their business to, but they did care deeply about relationships and understanding with whom they were doing business. We had spent years developing these relationships and they were deep.

We decided to go with SSBA again for our data processing. It was the fastest and least expensive way to go. I knew the players in Dallas, and they were extremely responsive to our needs. I had been asked to serve on their board of directors while at Loyola and remained on the board, which added some clout.

While at Loyola and again with Chase, I worked with a great group of people. They were driven, did whatever it took to succeed, and knew how to have a hell of a good time. They were professionals, and we all respected each other tremendously.

After I experienced the dreaded hour-plus commute for the better part of a year, Chase decided to move its headquarters from Montgomery County to Baltimore City, my old stomping grounds. We rented three floors in the W.R. Grace building on

Baltimore Street across the street from Maryland National's main office, about ten blocks from my old office at Loyola. I was housed on the top floor with the other executives. The mortgage business was on a floor below, and we moved the entire consumer loan operation to office space in a building we owned in Timonium, a Baltimore suburb.

This arrangement was foreign to me, as I enjoyed being in the thick of things where the action was. Sitting on an executive floor was convenient for meetings and great for exposure to visitors from New York, but it was pretty quiet. I wound up keeping my office there but spending most of my time in Timonium.

Bill Van Blarcom made the move from Loyola to head up marketing for the consumer business. Bill really was a wizard who could think out of the box, and generally he came up with terrific ideas. In addition to the businesses mentioned above, the branches were also added to my division. This was something new since I knew literally nothing about branch banking or the banking most people think of when you mention the word "bank"—that is—where people make deposits or cash checks at a teller's window. I did know that I never had a great deal of respect for the branch's ability to generate business, regardless of incentive plans, contests, and the like.

The fellow who ran the branches was from one of the acquired S & Ls, and he was the type who never broke a sweat. He was a nice guy, but he didn't do anything to drive the business or lead the people. We had several discussions, and I determined that he simply didn't have the get up and go. Tom

Hudson had given me a large framed picture of cowboys driving a herd of cattle that I hung on the wall behind my desk. The caption read, "You either make dust or you eat dust." This guy wasn't making dust. I terminated him and was faced with finding a replacement. Bill jumped up and said he could run the branches in addition to his marketing duties. I'd always been impressed with Bill's creativity and mistakenly gave him the additional responsibility and a pay raise. His performance as a manager was abysmal. Subsequently, we had a meeting in which I told him he had two choices. He could run marketing only and have a salary adjustment to reflect his reduced duties, or he could have a severance package. Egos being what they are, he selected the package.

I felt bad, but I really didn't have a choice. Bill was a freelance type of guy who marched to the beat of a different drum. His creativity was excellent, but his management abilities were unremarkable. I wished him well, and we parted company. He was the only member of the team that we lost.

Doug Perkins was a talented person who made excellent credit decisions. He was great at developing people and had a wild sense of humor. One year he had a birthday coming up, and we hired a stripper to surprise him at his office. We called his wife Bobbie and told her of our plans. On his special day, the stripper arrived downstairs at the appointed time, and we provided her with information from a declined automobile application. The receptionist called Doug and told him Miss So-and-So was in the lobby and wanted to discuss her application. She was a very attractive girl outfitted in a low-cut dress with a high hemline.

Doug escorted her into his office and we all (including his wife) hovered outside. The stripper gave an Academy Award-winning performance continually getting up from the chair and trying to sit on Doug's lap, while saying, "I really need this car and I'll do *ANYTHING* to have it." At one point she sat on his adding machine, and the paper kept spinning out of the spindle. Doug continually asked her to sit down, and so it went until we all came into his office. Thank God he didn't weaken, or he might have wound up in divorce court.

I started a practice at Loyola that I continued while at Chase. Every fall at budget time, I'd rent an inn or penthouse condo, and the management team would arrive on a Thursday evening. We would plan the budgets on Friday until five, party until whenever, repeat the same drill on Saturday, and return home on Sunday. It was an efficient way to complete the budgets and a great team building exercise. We worked hard, played hard, and finished the budgets in record time.

Stan Burns

Stan and I took frequent day trips on Amtrak to Chase Plaza in New York. We left on the 7 a.m. train in Baltimore and typically arrived back around 8 p.m. Stan reported to Tim McGinnis, who had been the country manager in Japan for a number of years. He knew little about the consumer business, but he did know quite a bit about commercial lending. I got along well with Tim, but Stan had total disregard for him, and it showed.

In an effort to bury the knife, Stan and his wife Christa held a dinner for Tim and his wife, Terry and me, and another couple from work at his home in Potomac, Maryland. Tim held everyone captive as he regaled his days in Japan, and it soon became obvious that Tim was quite the raconteur. At the end of the evening, Terry said how impressed she was with his broad level of knowledge on several fronts. I explained that Tim was so good at storytelling, it was difficult to discern what was factual and what was not. Nonetheless, his tales were interesting.

Our most memorable trip to New York occurred in October 1987. Stan and Christa owned a brownstone in Brooklyn Heights that they were renting while living in Maryland. Stan wanted to check on it. Afterward we sat on the promenade eating a sandwich while looking across the Hudson admiring the skyline. When we arrived back in Manhattan, we met pure bedlam. The stock market was crashing, and people everywhere seemed to be walking around in a daze reminiscent of scenes from 1929.

In November of that year, Stan and Christa invited Terry and me to dinner in Baltimore. They moved from Potomac and we met at their beautiful stately brick home for appetizers before heading to the restaurant. They said they had found a terrific oriental restaurant in a Holiday Inn in Towson. I hate oriental food, and eating in a Holiday Inn wasn't particularly appealing to me, but they seemed very excited about it, so I stayed mum and decided to grin and bear it.

We took two cars and headed for the restaurant. Stan led us down a long hall and opened the door. It turned out it wasn't an oriental restaurant but a large room full of people there for a surprise fortieth birthday party for me. I was stunned and very surprised. Normally I can detect a surprise event, but this one was pulled off with perfection. There were well over a hundred people attending, and many took the microphone to roast me. Most of the speeches were memorable, but Bill Sisler's really stood out. Bill and Elaine were married within a month of Terry's and my wedding. During the years he attended Johns Hopkins for his master's and doctorate degrees we spent a lot of time together. Bill waxed poetically and presented me with a trophy of a bull. Embossed on the brass plate was "Forty Years and Full of It." Touching. Tom Hudson had a lot to say, most of which was embarrassing but true. Frog was there along with all the gang from work and several neighbors, and car and boat dealers also attended. I deeply appreciated the party and all who attended. It was a great night.

On another night out with Stan and Christa, we went to hear Dick Gessner play the piano and sing in Annapolis. Stan was a reformed smoker, but Terry and I were still puffing away. The more Stan drank and sang, the more he smoked. We encouraged them to spend the night, but they wouldn't hear of it. The last we saw of Stan he was pulling out of our driveway in his Mercedes with a cigarette hanging out of his mouth.

Stan and Tim were on very different wavelengths. Their dislike for each other was obvious, and at times, boiled over. As we continued our trips to New York, the strain became more apparent. Then one day Tim was transferred somewhere else, and Bill Balderson was appointed to head up the regional banks. Bill was a gentleman, but he was nobody's fool. He was a genteel man but also demanding in a subtle manner. I thought he and Stan would hit it off, but, for whatever reason, they didn't. I don't know if Stan poisoned the well in New York, or if Tim badmouthed him, but the end was in sight for Stan. It wasn't long before Stan announced he was resigning from Chase. I felt terrible.

When Bill came to Baltimore he introduced himself to everyone. He was likeable and, unlike Tim, he knew the business. He had been chairman of Lincoln First Bank headquartered in Rochester, New York, with regional offices in western and upstate New York prior to being acquired by Chase Manhattan. Bill said he wanted to talk to me about taking over as president of Chase Bank of Maryland. We had several meetings, and I felt positive. Then one day he called and said he was flying to Baltimore, and he wanted to meet me for breakfast the following morning. We met at the hotel where he was staying, and he lowered the boom. He said he was very impressed with me but that a person who used to work at Lincoln First had contacted him, and he thought he would be a better fit. He asked me not to be rash and to please stay. I told him I needed to think about it and that I would get back to him.

The new president was Kevin Brynes. He had been a commercial lender who left Lincoln to take a flyer with a startup S & L in Florida that failed. He was a nice enough guy who went out of his way to be friendly. I told him that I didn't have any grudge against him and that I was happy for him, but that didn't assuage my disappointment in not getting the nod. He asked me to stay, and I told him I'd commit to three months and see how it went. After a couple of months, I recognized we could coexist and discarded thoughts about moving on.

It wasn't long before Stan called and said he had a concept he wanted to discuss with me. There was another troubled savings and loan association in Baltimore that Stan thought we should consider purchasing. Baltimore Federal Savings and Loan had been in existence for more than one hundred years. It had a branch network similar to that of Loyola Federal, and it had more than a billion dollars in assets. We met and decided we'd dig in to see if buying it made sense. Stan and I signed a confidentiality agreement and were given access to the company's financial records. The more we dug in the more optimistic Stan was. I had the opposite reaction, as I noticed many disturbing issues. After a few months of looking at the deal, I concluded it didn't work for me, and I told Stan so. He wanted to keep trying to piece it together. Ultimately, a year or so later, Household Bank purchased the assets and Baltimore Savings and Loan ceased to exist. I never looked back. The deal was simply too full of pitfalls to pursue.

News on the Home Front

Meanwhile, Terry and I loved our new house and everything about Annapolis. Terry had been with St. Mary's as the high school secretary for ten years. She enjoyed being with the kids and most of the teachers and faculty. The notable exception was her boss, the recently named new principal. She had one way of doing things, and Terry had another. Finally, Terry had enough, resigned, and took another job with a fellow named Vince Ambrosetti, who had two different interests. One was his mortgage company that originated residential mortgages, and the other was his interest in being a religious singer. Quite a combination. Terry liked Vince but found working for him to be difficult. After six months we decided she could, and should, retire.

I had the idea of buying a small powerboat. I thought it would be enjoyable and easy for us to go out for an hour or so in the evenings and have a couple of drinks and hors d'oeuvres on the water. Terry suggested we build a swimming pool. After a few months Terry asked how my search for a boat was going, to which I responded I hadn't had time to look. Her response was poignant. She said, "If you don't have time to look for a boat, what are you going to do with it if you buy one?" As much as I hated to admit it, she was right. Shortly thereafter we hired a local company to build a swimming pool. It was an irregularly shaped gunite pool carved into the slope of the backyard. It was as much a landscape feature as a functional swimming pool. We had many parties poolside, and we used it a lot more than we would have used a boat. Building it was a good decision for which I take no credit.

Terry, Michelle, and I spent time discussing colleges. We agreed that a large university would not work since Michelle had become used to a small environment, and then we discussed geographic locations. Michelle wanted to stay on the East Coast within driving distance from home. We started screening potential schools and visiting those that were of interest. One of the schools we visited was St. Joseph's in Emmitsburg, Maryland, on a weekend that was billed as an open house for parents and prospective students. The campus was small, a couple of hours from home, co-educational, and seemed like it might be a good fit. We toured on our own and couldn't help but notice the number of beer bottles in the bushes and in the corridors of the dorms. I thought if this was the best foot they could put forward, St. Joe's wasn't for us. We moved on.

Eventually we drove to see Elon College in North Carolina near Greensboro and the Raleigh-Durham-Chapel Hill triangle. It was love at first sight. Both Michelle and I liked everything about it, and she subsequently applied for admission. She was accepted, and in September 1988 we packed her belongings, spent a fortune at Target for school items, and moved her into her dorm. I was very happy for her but very sad for myself. All of a sudden, I realized why. It hit me like a ton of bricks! Michelle was leaving home, probably never to return, and I had spent scant time with her for the past eighteen years. I kept finding reasons for not leaving the dorm room until Terry finally said we had to leave. I made it out the door to the car before I broke down and sobbed.

College Bound

Back in Maryland, I gave a lot of thought as to why I hadn't been selected for the bank president position. I determined that it might have been due to my abysmal education record. It could be that my thoughts were diverted in that direction with Michelle beginning college. I hated the thought of sitting in a classroom just as much as I did when in high school. The prospect of attending classes at night to obtain an undergraduate degree was distasteful and unrealistic.

I had heard of executive MBA programs where students worked Monday through Thursday and had class all day Friday one week, and then worked Monday through Friday and attended classes all day Saturday the following week. Loyola College (another Jesuit institution) in Baltimore had an executive MBA program structured in that way, and I decided to make an appointment with the dean of admissions. It was 1989, twenty-five years since I last sporadically attended regularly scheduled classes. I had taken a few classes at Johns Hopkins, an executive leadership program at the University of Virginia Darden School of Business, and a banking course at Northwestern University. This, however, would be a whole new ball game.

The dean and I had a cordial meeting in which I described my educational background resplendent with the two tosses from high school and my GED accomplishment. I also described my work background. We talked for about an hour and a half, and at the end of the discussion he said the class had an enrollment of forty students, of which they would consider two provisional members. Provisional in my case meant admission without an undergraduate degree. The stipulation was that I had to take the Graduate Management Admissions Test (GMAT) and score well to be accepted. I spoke with Kevin Brynes and Bill Balderson, and they agreed that I could attend the program, and they also agreed to have Chase pick up the tab.

I bought two study books that were designed to prepare students for taking the GMAT. Both were the size of a large city telephone book; they contained sample questions and solutions throughout. When I first paged through the books, I felt overwhelmed. Yet as I dedicated more time and began to study the contents, I found the topics not to be so daunting. I discovered I needed to sharpen my study habits. I had become so used to scanning memos and documents that I found I had to slow down to absorb information. I don't know if I ever really developed study habits during my intermittent stints in high school, but even if I did, it had been a long time ago, and I needed to start over.

I spent hours and hours studying the books and working on the sample problems and questions until I felt I was as prepared as I was ever going to be. The test was given at Loyola. I showed up on the appointed date and at the appointed time with three new sharpened pencils with erasers. I felt like a first grader showing up at school with my pencil bag. There were a few hundred young people taking the exam along with a handful of oldies like me. I dove in and thought I did reasonably well. Several weeks later I received a letter from Loyola accepting me into the program.

School Days

The first day of my new educational experience was interesting, as I had never spent time on a college campus except for attending a few classes here and there, taking swimming lessons as a child at the University of Buffalo, and as a parent traveling with Michelle to look at colleges. The students met each other, and all the professors outlined the structure of their courses and classes and their expectations. Then we jumped right into class work.

My job at the bank didn't change; nonetheless, I added one day a week at school and another twenty-five hours of study in addition to trying to be home with the family once in a while. After a couple of months, I found the groove, but the pace was grueling. Statistics frustrated me the most. I could solve many of the problems in my head, but the professor wanted to see the methodical steps taken to arrive at an answer. I worked long and hard at statistics and even hired a tutor, whom I met twice a week for two hours each session. The day of finals came, and I did miserably on the exam. The next week when the test scores were handed out, I discovered I was given a B. "Given" is the correct word, as I sure as hell didn't score a B. I later met with the professor, thanked him, and said I was surprised at the grade. He agreed that I did poorly on the exam, but he said he had never had a student who tried so hard. The B was clearly a gift. Years later I was at Loyola College interviewing graduating students for inclusion in a Management Development Plan at MBNA, and I ran into the professor. He remembered me. The real test score apparently was a memorable one.

Moving On Up

Bill Balderson's boss was a vice chairman of Chase Manhattan named Don Boudreau, commonly referred to as "Neutron Don" due to his reputation for cutting expenses and staff. Don came to Baltimore to meet the senior staff and have a business dinner with us. This was the first time I met Don, and despite his reputation as being a tough guy, I liked him. He told me he wanted to meet with me privately before dinner, and we found a vacant conference room. Don was complimentary about my accomplishments in Maryland and offered me a position overseeing the consumer lending operations at the regional banks, which included Arizona, Florida, Maryland, Chase Lincoln First Bank in upstate New York, and Chase Manhattan Bank in New York City. It was a big job. Don said I'd have to relocate to either New York City or Rochester, but that was my choice. He went on to say he understood I needed to discuss the opportunity with my wife but that he wanted to meet for breakfast the following morning and hear my decision.

I sat through dinner oblivious to my surroundings. All I could think about was the job opportunity. I couldn't wait for the evening to end so I could discuss it with Terry. I arrived home late, and she was in bed. I woke her and told her of my discussion with Don. She was still half asleep, said I should do what I thought was right, and she returned to "Slumberville." We discussed it further with clearer heads early the next morning. I still felt that a "request" was really a "demand," and a refusal would be a hit to my career. Terry agreed.

I met with Don and we cut the deal. The bank would pay for the relocation, including the purchase of our house in Annapolis. I would relocate to Rochester. It really didn't matter where we lived, as I'd be in the air most of the time. Joanna was a senior at St. Mary's where she had attended since first grade, and we didn't want to deal with a transfer in the middle of her final year. I explained this to Don. He agreed and said the bank would pay to fly me home every weekend until Joanna's graduation. He also threw in a very nice increase in pay. Done deal.

Moving would mean an end to my studies at Loyola. I thought I would transfer my credits and pick up where I left off somewhere else. Realistically, between traveling and my additional work responsibilities, continuing with an executive MBA program proved to be impossible. It was an interesting experience and a challenge, but I determined it wasn't something I needed for my career. I never completed studies for my degree, but who knows? I might some day just for the hell of it.

Chapter 11

The Big Apple
1990 to 1991

A couple of weeks later I flew to Rochester, leaving my old company car behind and picking up a new one upon arrival. The bank paid for my temporary residence and all my living expenses. I lived at the Stratthallen Hotel in a one-bedroom apartment on fashionable East Avenue. The hotel had a restaurant and bar on the top floor, which was convenient on cold wintry nights. It was November 1990 and already cold.

I could have lived in New York, which on the surface would probably appeal to most people. However, I'd been in New York enough to realize it was a great place to visit, but it could be a difficult place to live. I soon had an office at Chase Plaza and spent two or three days there a week, enjoying my status as a visitor rather than as a resident. Typically I'd fly into La Guardia, climb into a waiting limo to the Downtown Athletic Club where I'd drop off my belongings, and walk the few blocks to work. I told people I loved New York to which they'd respond, "You don't know New York." Then they would comment about how much easier it was for me to come to work via airplane and limo versus Path trains and subways. They had a point. Rochester was the right choice.

I spent most of my time between New York and Rochester. Several hours a week I was on the phone with or visiting the other regional banks. The majority of activity was in New York State. Chase had a significant presence in Garden City on Long Island, employing about 150 people in the home equity department. I went there one day a week. Chase Lincoln had about half that number of employees doing the same thing in Rochester. Rent on Community Drive in Garden City was sixty dollars a square foot. Rent in Rochester was twelve dollars a square foot. I closed the office in Garden City and consolidated the operation in Rochester. It was a no-brainer. However, the difficult part was dealing with the Garden City employees. I offered jobs in Rochester without relocation coverage, so that obviously wasn't appealing to many. In the end, we were able to place about half of the people in other positions at Chase, while the other half retired or took severance payments. I had terminated employees for cause, but I had never laid people off. It was difficult.

I developed an excellent relationship with "Neutron Don" Boudreau. I thrived on autonomy, and he gave me a lot of it. About once a month I'd set up an appointment and meet with him in his office on the executive floor where the president, chairman, and other vice chairmen were situated. It was always a treat to go there. I'd get off the elevator and enter through two bulletproof glass doors with an armed guard standing inside.

Don and I typically met for a half hour, and I always started the conversation the same way. I'd ask if there was anything I was doing that he didn't want me to do, or if there was anything I wasn't doing that he wanted me to do. That got us right to the point and kept the meetings on track. Periodically Tom Labreoque, the chairman and CEO, or Art Ryan, the president, would duck in and join the conversation. It was exciting to spend time with the most senior executives as it provided exposure to them. Tom reminded me of a person who was "pressed for success," always perfectly groomed without a wrinkle in his shirt or suit. I thought he must have had a dry cleaner in his office with a steam presser. Art was the more gregarious of the two, the kind of guy with whom you would want to have a beer, which I did a few times.

On a few occasions one of my daughters, Michelle or Joanna, would alternate taking the train to New York, to spend the weekend sightseeing, going to shows, and visiting restaurants with me. We always had a great time, and it forced me to learn about New York, as I'd be the tour guide. One of the best trips was in December when Joanna came to town and we tripped on the Christmas Spectacular at Radio City Music Hall. We couldn't get two seats together, but I could see her from where I was sitting, and I felt comfortable with that. Whenever the girls visited, we always went to the Bruno's Pen and Pencil in Midtown, which was one of my very favorite restaurants. Unfortunately, after several years serving excellent meals by the same tuxedoed waiters, the restaurant closed. Alas. Those were memorable times.

Rochester's economic status was different from what I had known as a child. Home to behemoth corporations such as Xerox, Bausch and Lomb, and Kodak, Rochester was thought of as an intellectual Mecca, while Buffalo was regarded as a blue-collar city. It was said that as goes Kodak, so goes Rochester, and Kodak in those days was in financial difficulty. I remember the first time I flew into the Rochester airport. There was a kiosk with post cards and one of them was plain glossy black with the words "Rochester at Night." It was true. There wasn't much going on there in the evening.

A Change of Address

After a few months, the Stratthallen became old, and I decided I needed a change of scenery. At my request, the bank rented a one-bedroom apartment in a recently rehabilitated warehouse on the Genesee River and furnished it with rented furniture. Conveniently, the Water Street restaurant was downstairs.

I spent my spare time looking for a new home, but I didn't find anything I thought we would like. Terry flew to Rochester a few times, and we agree we needed to expand our search. We decided to purchase land and build. Everyone spoke of the village of Pittsford as if it were Maui. We were told we simply *had* to live in Pittsford. Instead, we decided to buy land in Victor.

We bought about five acres in a community named Hiawatha Hills (hated the name but loved the property) and identified an excellent builder named Dominic Caroselli. He introduced us to an architect, and with that, we were on our way to building our new home. Construction was steady, but things moved along slower than I would have liked. Summertime was upon us; it was apparent the house wouldn't be completed anytime soon. I decided to find another temporary place that would accommodate Terry, Joanna, and me after Joanna graduated from St. Mary's. I found a beautiful spot named Bristol Harbor on Canandaigua Lake, and the bank rented a two-bedroom condo on a hill overlooking the lake for us to live in.

Joanna and I spent time looking at colleges. She thought she wanted to be a veterinarian. I had a business trip scheduled for Denver, so we flew there together and looked at the University of

Colorado. She gave further thought to her career choice, determined she wasn't sure what she wanted to do and decided she would start in a liberal arts curriculum and go from there. After weighing her options, she decided to join Michelle at Elon. Although she would be leaving Annapolis for North Carolina in the fall, she was not looking forward to living in New York for the summer. She arrived with Terry but was homesick, missing her friends. It was a difficult summer for her. Meanwhile, Michelle stayed in North Carolina and found a job at Cracker Barrel.

In the fall, we drove Joanna to Elon, and (wouldn't you know it) I had the same experience as I had with Michelle. The fact that I hadn't been around to help raise the children and didn't spend enough time with them was a terrible reality.

Charlie Beckons

Charlie Cawley called me from what was now called MBNA America Bank. MBNA was once the credit card division of Maryland National Bank. It had been formed as a new bank in Delaware a few years earlier to take advantage of that state's favorable interest rates and fee structure. Maryland National subsequently fell victim to the failing commercial real estate market and spun off the credit card division to provide capital. MBNA was now an independent bank listed on the New York Stock Exchange. During the phone call Charlie said he wanted to talk to me about an opportunity. I explained I was quite happy with Chase. He said I should come and hear what he had in mind. It piqued my curiosity, and I agreed to go to Delaware for an informational meeting.

At the same time, there were two banks in Connecticut that were in trouble. The FDIC worked with Chase to be the acquirer. I was called to New York where a strategy meeting was held regarding the takeover. It was to be a surprise takeover to avoid a run on deposits, and I was to head up one of the teams. To prepare for this action, one hundred people drove from New York to Bridgeport to spend the night. The first thing in the morning the FDIC posted signs on the doors that the banks had been taken over and that Chase Manhattan was the acquirer. It was raining like crazy, and I went from bank to bank and from branch to branch to meet employees and to learn more about their business practices. We had financial data, but it was helpful and necessary to understand how the banks operated.

Charlie had lined up a private jet to meet me in Connecticut to fly to Wilmington. At about six the following morning, I left the hotel via taxi to the small regional airport. A private jet was waiting for me, along with two pilots, a box of doughnuts, and several bottles of orange juice. We arrived in Wilmington after a short flight, and a limo pulled up to the jet, where I climbed in for the short drive to the bank. Charlie had orchestrated a welcoming committee with everyone I knew lined up on both sides of the sidewalk leading to the front door. It reminded me of the Knights of Columbus without the swords. Charlie was ever the showman.

Charlie guided me on a tour through the building into each department where representatives explained what they did and how they fit into the organization. Then we went back to his office and had lunch while he reviewed the bank's short- and long-range plans. It was impressive. Charlie had a crystal clear vision of where the company was going and exactly how he would lead it there. He asked me to consider leading a group of diverse businesses called the Individual Bank, consisting of commercial credit cards, the merchant business, insurance, deposits, and unsecured lending. We had a heart-to-heart conversation, and I said maybe the best thing was not to rejoin and just remain friends since we had a tough time working together. I had a high level of admiration for Charlie and his business acumen, but I wasn't sure I wanted to climb back into that saddle again.

He ignored my comment and continued outlining his plans, and then changed the discussion to compensation. I was making an excellent salary augmented by stock options and grants. Charlie wrote a number on a piece of paper, folded it, and slid it across the table. I opened it. It was a very generous offer, but I kept a poker face and said I thought it was a good offer but our house was virtually finished in New York, we had been moving around a lot, and I thought we'd stay where we were. He then asked what it would take. I took his paper and wrote "+ 25%" and slid it back across the table. I also said I had become accustomed to operating autonomously and expected to continue to do so. The last detail was MBNA would have to buy the house in Victor and sell it at their expense. He agreed to all the conditions and even went so far as to say he would never set foot in the building from which I would be operating. He asked if I wanted that in writing. I responded no, but that a handshake would suffice. We shook hands.

The salary increase was impressive and persuasive, but the real determining factor was the opportunity to work with Charlie again. He was tough, and he was demanding, but he had a leadership quality that was inspirational and magnetic.

I flew to the Rochester airport aboard the private jet and drove home to tell Terry. By coincidence my mother and Jack were visiting. When Terry opened the door to the condo, she took one look at me and said, "We're moving, aren't we?" I said yes. My mother thought I was crazy as she often did when I made moves.

I loved my job at Chase. I loved New York City, the autonomy Don gave me, the opportunity and excitement of working at a world-class bank, and the stature I gained while being there. The problem was I loved a new challenge even more; that is, once again, the opportunity to create something new, to make it grow, and to build it into a powerhouse. Certainly Chase offered me those opportunities, but MBNA was more of a giant marketing company than a bank; also, it didn't have the layers of bureaucracy that could stifle creativity. Charlie had been the innovator who created affinity and co-branded credit cards. The bank had several thousand relationships, including major universities, medical associations (such as the American Medical Association and the American Dental Association), and professional sports teams. Charlie pioneered the concept starting with his alma mater Georgetown University and grew the business rapidly, leaving very little room for competitors to catch up. I knew I made the right decision even though it was a tough one.

I called Don on Monday morning and told him of my decision to leave. He asked me to keep it to myself and said he would fly to Rochester to meet with me. That evening, we had dinner at the Rochester Country Club and the meeting started cordially. Don said he was going to recommend a promotion to which I responded, if I was worthy of a promotion, why did it take an event like this to make it happen? The tone of the conversation began to deteriorate and I finally said that if I stayed, I was concerned the bank would feel like it owned me— that it would cut my heart out and put it in the vault. I went on to say I'd like to remain friends and that we should enjoy our "Last Supper." We finished dinner and Don left. That was the last time we spoke. I left Chase for my new job three weeks later.

Chapter 12

MBNA
America Bank
1991 to 1995

For the next two weekends, Terry and I flew to Philadelphia, where representatives from MBNA picked us up and drove us to Wilmington, Delaware, to look for a new house. We stayed in a penthouse apartment in Wilmington that was owned by the bank, and we were supplied with a Buick Roadmaster to get around. Charlie was an avid car enthusiast and collector, so when Buick produced a new model named after the old Roadmaster, he bought several to be used as company cars.

Wendy Bunch was the bank's realtor of choice and she took us all over Wilmington to look at houses. Charlie and several of the bank executives lived in a section named Westover Hills, and Wendy thought that would be the ideal place for us to live. We looked at everything that was for sale in addition to houses Wendy thought might be available for the right price. The attitude about Westover Hills reminded me of the attitude regarding Pittsford in Rochester. We expanded our search sans Wendy.

We found a very nice small community in Chadds Ford, Pennsylvania, named Cross Creek. There were about sixteen lots of two or three acres each situated on a ridge. There were a few homes built and occupied and two that were spec houses under construction. We became very attracted to one of the homes constructed by John Thompson, which was about ninety percent completed. We called Wendy, who promptly replied that Charlie wanted his executives to live in Delaware. I called Charlie on a Sunday afternoon and explained that we found a house we liked in Chadds Ford, to which he responded that Chadds Ford was close enough.

We made an offer with conditions listing the makes and models of kitchen appliances, lightin'' fixtures, and carpet. John was somewhat surprised about the specificity of the conditions until he learned we had very recently nearly completed another house in New York. We came together on the price and conditions and set completion and settlement dates.

Goodbye New York, Hello Pennsylvania

We returned to Canandaigua to pack our clothes, pick up our black Great Dane, and make the drive to Delaware, where we stayed in a Marriott Courtyard. Our quarters were comfortable enough with a living area, small kitchen, and a loft bedroom. The big plus was they permitted dogs. This is where we lived for the next six weeks while the house was being completed. Each day I'd leave for work and Terry would leave to explore the area. We had to post a sign on the door that the dog was inside. Our dog was named Babe. She never barked and would never hurt anyone or anything but she was an intimidating animal.

In November 1991, we moved to 114 Montana Drive in Chadds Ford, Pennsylvania. It was a two-story house with four bedrooms, three full baths, two powder rooms, and a three-car garage constructed with cedar, stone, and stucco with a cedar shake roof. It was the most beautiful house we had ever lived in. We went about decorating and furnishing it, which was a never-ending job but an enjoyable one. The house was situated on a sloping lot with a walkout basement having several windows with views of the ridge. After a few years we finished the basement space, adding a large sitting area, another bathroom, kitchenette, computer area, wet bar, cherry bookcases, and a marble encased fireplace. It was a beautiful addition and a great party room.

Life at MBNA

I arrived at work on my first day at seven in the morning and nobody was in the building. I went to my office and there was a hand mirror on the desk with a note saying something about projecting your image. I thought back to years earlier while with Maryland National when Charlie and I made a trip to a telemarketing firm in Boston and met with a fellow whose last name was Feldman who owned a company named RSVP. He had a hand mirror on his desk and explained it was important to see yourself while projecting a message to prospective customers. I think that stuck with Charlie and he imported the idea to MBNA.

Shortly after I arrived, I met my secretary as well as others who stopped by to introduce themselves. In the interview process Charlie hadn't mentioned that I was taking over from a fellow who couldn't cut it and was no longer with the company. I had been led to believe that my job was the result of a reshuffle that created a new division. No matter. The challenge would be even greater.

The environment at MBNA was very different from that of any other bank or, for that matter, any organization to which I had been exposed. Over every door in every building was the expression "THINK OF YOURSELF AS A CUSTOMER."

Throughout every building in every location, expressions on walls, such as "COMPLACENCY IS DEVASTATING," were commonplace. Charlie had created an ethos, an unshakeable standard, to which he held everyone. He was determined: we would be the very best in our business and we would excel in everything we did. That was not negotiable. It was dogma from which we could not deviate. For a person like me who didn't like a lot of oversight, who enjoyed freedom to make decisions, take risks, and willingly assume the consequences, this was a very rigid place. But, for some reason, I liked it. Undoubtedly, it was the charisma of Charlie Cawley that made it exciting and that allowed me to operate in an environment that would have been objectionable in the past. The fact that Charlie promised me independence was certainly helpful.

I asked my secretary to schedule meetings with my direct reports. It's amazing how much you can learn in twelve hours by listening and asking probing questions. I discovered we had several strengths, but also we had several areas requiring focus. MBNA was primarily a credit card bank, and the ancillary businesses had, in many cases, been ignored. Even worse, the businesses had been the home to several substandard employees. As tough as Charlie was, he had an allergic reaction to firing people. Over the years I adopted the same allergy, determining that if I had to fire someone, it was because I made a bad decision in hiring or I hadn't provided the opportunity for someone to succeed. Surely there were occasions where termination of employment was warranted and necessary, but by adopting the above theory, I experienced it as a rare event.

During those first days I pored over monthly reports from the previous six months, digesting the financial data and identifying where my energy would be directed over the next few months. The division was self-contained with credit, operations, marketing, and later, collections. We relied on centralized personnel, payroll, and data processing. The organizational structure was sound, but we had a lot of work to do to grow the businesses.

Al Lerner

Shortly after I arrived, I received a call from Charlie's secretary asking me to come to his office to meet Al Lerner, who was the chairman of the board of MBNA Corporation. I found Al to be a fascinating fellow with exceptional business acumen. He had been on the board of Equitable Trust Company in Baltimore when Maryland National acquired Equitable, after which he was made a board member of Maryland National. When Maryland National experienced the real estate portfolio woes, Al structured the spin-off of the credit card division now known as MBNA. He invested $100 million dollars of his money in MBNA and was the principal stockholder.

Al was a U.S. Marine pilot in the 1950s after attending Columbia University. Following his stint with the marines, he was a furniture salesman and later became involved with insurance, real estate, and banking. In the late 1990s, he bought the Cleveland Browns football team. As successful as Al was, I found him to be a humble man with a brilliant mind, a person who could quickly analyze any business situation and determine the best course of action. He was very rarely wrong. I remember having dinner in London with him and his wife Norma, where Norma related his decision process about whether or not to buy the Browns. She told him, "If it's something you want to do and you can afford it, you should do it." I often remind myself of that comment. I think it was good advice.

The Fast Track

I had been hired as an executive vice president. A few months after I came on board, Charlie arranged for several of us to travel to Baltimore on one of the company buses to see a football game. On the way, Charlie made a few announcements. He explained that he decided to form a senior operating committee (SOC) and the ten or so of us on the bus were to be on that committee. He also created the new title of senior executive vice president, which we were all promoted to. The best part was he had created a SERP (Senior Executive Retirement Plan), which we became part of effective immediately. The SERP provided generous insurance benefits as well as a significant retirement benefit over and above the company's existing retirement plan. There were several other benefits, all of which were meaningful.

Charlie had a philosophy about compensation, which translated into salaries that far exceeded those of other banks, even money center institutions. He felt that if he challenged people to surpass what they thought was possible and paid them exceptionally well, they would never consider leaving, and he was right. His own level of compensation was very high but neither he nor Al was stingy about sharing the wealth. MBNA was a hugely successful, dynamic company, and we were compensated well for our efforts. Of course there is no free lunch. We worked long hours in a hard-charging, intense environment earning our salaries. The normal workweek was sixty hours or so, and the stress level was always high. I used to joke that I made a good living, but if I calculated my earnings on an hourly basis, it stopped looking so great.

Shaping the Businesses

One of the businesses under my control was the merchant business. This was a tough business in which to make money since the spreads were razor thin, and only huge volume and a high level of automation could make the difference. We were losing money in that business. I looked at it from every angle and determined the only way to turn a profit would be to make a considerable technology investment and to move the business to a much less expensive building with a much lower salary scale. Absent those moves, I thought we should exit the business. Conversely, the credit card business was a high volume business with a need for a high level of automation, but the spreads were multiples of those of the merchant business. I met with Charlie and Al to discuss selling the business. Charlie's initial response was precisely as I expected it would be. He made a few remarks about my inability to turn it around. However, after I reviewed all the financial data and the prognosis for the future, we collectively decided to sell it. We subsequently found a potential buyer, named Innova, located in Atlanta, Georgia. After several trips there and months of negotiations, we finally struck a deal and inked the contract.

I formed a second mortgage subsidiary, and we began offering conventional seconds and home equity lines of credit in multiple states. It was a struggle in the beginning. Each state required separate documents to conform to their laws, necessitating that we set up closing offices all across the country. The amount of time dedicated to getting the business up and running was considerable, but it was worth the effort.

We had a formidable deposit business without any branches other than two in Delaware. We established relationships with the same affinity groups that offered our cards, and we offered slightly higher rates to their members, which we were able to do since we didn't have to support a branch network. We used the money to help with the funding of our credit card business and matched maturities with other loan products.

The commercial card business was making a few bucks, but it was nowhere near where it could be. This was a tough business, one that had the interest rate margins, but it was very people intensive and had a history of audit problems. We cleaned up the audit issues and built the business but never really broke out into the big time with it.

The insurance business was a solid moneymaker, and we drove it into a significant contributor of profits. Our consumer lending business was doing okay, and we managed to grow it by introducing an unsecured revolving line of credit product that proved to be quite popular.

We thought it would be a good idea to offer mutual funds to our customers, and a few people took the SEC test to become registered agents. We interviewed several fund companies and contracted with a handful. One issue kept coming up: customers wanted us to give them advice about where to invest their money, something we decided we shouldn't do. After a year of lackluster results, I met with Charlie and Al. Al observed that people don't expect to lose money dealing with a bank, and, unfortunately, there was a high probability of losing money when investing in stocks. We decided that offering mutual funds wasn't such a great idea after all and closed the business. That was the beauty of working in a company like MBNA. We were willing to try new businesses and give them time to make money. We also knew when we had a dog, and, if we did, we weren't hesitant about exiting those businesses.

I enjoyed the diversity of leading several very different businesses, each with its own expense budget and profit and loss expectations. I had this experience at Loyola, Chase, and now MBNA and knew I'd never be content running only one line of business.

The Girls Go to Work

Meanwhile, our daughters were both in college. Michelle graduated from Elon in 1991 and enrolled at Widener University outside Philadelphia for her master's in social work. Joanna stayed at Elon for her freshman year but subsequently transferred to complete her undergraduate work at Widener as well. Once Michelle graduated, she sought work in her field and realized the salaries paid were barely above minimum wage. She loved the work but couldn't afford to live on the wages being paid.

MBNA had established a comprehensive yearlong management development program enrolling about twenty new college graduates into each class. I suggested to Michelle that she apply, and she did. The rule was if an executive's child applied, that the executive would not be involved in determining the acceptance of the applicant. Michelle didn't need my vote, as the other members of the selection committee were unanimous in their decision for her to join the upcoming class.

As grueling as the ordinary pace was, the management development program was intentionally designed to be a highly stressful experience. The class rotated through each division of the bank over the twelve months, with each candidate regularly being asked to give presentations to senior management. Michelle excelled in the program, and I was extremely proud of her accomplishments.

After graduation from Widener, Joanna also decided to apply for the program and was accepted. For a guy who stumbled into banking, I never thought we'd become a banking family. Joanna also took to the company and to the business and distinguished herself among her peers. I was a proud father.

The MBNA Culture

MBNA was often referred to as "Mothers, Brothers, Nephews, Aunts" due to its history of hiring family members. Initially I wondered if nepotism was such a good idea, but after seeing my daughters in the company, I realized there was increased pressure on relatives to perform well, since the expectation level was higher for both the executives and their relatives. It might have been a bit wacky, but it worked.

Each summer Charlie held an executive conference in Camden, Maine, at the Samoset Resort. Attendance was mandatory for the executives and their spouses. As with everything else at the company, it was fun but stressful. We were assigned rooms and met for all meals. During the day, group meetings took place while spouses took various tours or trips. We had group activities, such as sailing trips or driving one of the many antique cars the company owned. The food was out of this world, especially the lobsters—big enough to need collars and leashes! Evenings were filled with entertainment and bands.

Each year there was a different theme. For a couple of years George H.W. Bush and his wife Barbara spoke and stayed for cocktails in the evenings. It was quite a thrill to meet them. Honored guests also included General Colin Powell; General Norman Schwarzkopf; Rudy Giuliani; George Tenet, director of the CIA; Robert Mueller, director of the FBI; and other political luminaries. One year we had historian David McCullough and other authors. The following year, sports greats Whitey Ford; Arnold Palmer; Nancy Lopez; Tommy Lasorda, coach of the Dodgers; and Pat Riley, coach of the New York Knicks, were featured guests. No expense was spared, and, as always, Charlie put on a first-class show.

MBNA had expanded its locations and had telemarketing centers in Maine, Georgia, Florida, and Ohio. The headquarters moved from Newark to downtown Wilmington, and we became the largest employer in the state, surpassing longtime first place holder DuPont. The exterior of each building was beautifully landscaped, and both the interior and exterior were spotless. Charlie saw to every detail from the massive task of running the bank down to the lowest level of minutia.

MBNA was by far the largest charitable benefactor in Delaware and very generous in all the states where we had a presence. Charlie was as bighearted as he was demanding. He could be gruff and tough, but there was also the soft side of him, which, in the heat of the moment, was sometimes difficult to find.

We decided to expand overseas. In 1993, we formed MBNA International Bank, headquartered in Chester, England, with a sales office on Jermyn Street in London. The first president of the new bank was Tom McGinley, whom I'd known since my days at Maryland National. Tom relocated and set about hiring senior staff and, in turn, the support staff. The business plan was a mirror image of the United States, and various people jetted back and forth to set up procedures and processes. Soon after, we marketed and began issuing the first credit cards.

The United Kingdom had seen American banks come and go. The Brits had witnessed several unsuccessful attempts to grab market share from stalwarts such as Barclays, Lloyds, or Royal Bank of Scotland. As a result, naturally they assumed our attempt would be a repeat performance. They expected MBNA to go the way of its predecessors. They were wrong. Tom assembled a talented and strong management team, and business took off.

Each month we'd have senior operating committee (SOC) meetings. I always enjoyed hearing Tom McGinley's report. One of the reasons I joined Chase Manhattan years earlier was because it offered the possibility of an overseas assignment. I thought I might still get a crack at it.

August 1994 brought our silver anniversary, and we decided to renew our wedding vows at our house in Chadds Ford. Father Bob flew into town to officiate, and many relatives and friends attended. You may recall Terry's decision to ask for the smaller ring when we became engaged. At this event I surprised Terry with a new diamond ring. She surprised me with a singer who was out of sight on the balcony overlooking the family room who sang the theme from *A Man and A Woman*. We had a wonderful time.

We loved our home in Chadds Ford. We missed our pool from Annapolis, but the hilly terrain prohibited installing one. One evening, I received a telephone call from Stephen Mottola, who was at MBNA but who, also, was a realtor and a guy who had his finger on the pulse around town. He swore me to secrecy and told me there was a very special house quietly going on the market. It was the home of Joe Biden, the senator from Delaware (and currently—2013—the vice president of the United States). I arranged a meeting time and met Joe at his house. I had met him several times before, and we knew each other. Joe showed me through the house, and although it needed a lot of work, it was a stunning place. Two features were especially eye catching: the grand staircase that separated half way up into a set of stairs on each side of the foyer, and the ballroom with beautiful wood paneling. There were about five acres and a swimming pool that probably needed to be replaced. The tour took about three hours. Actually the tour could have ended in a half-hour, but Joe was known for his propensity for gab, and that day was no exception. I left telling him I'd think about it and discuss it with Terry.

The bank had recently hired a seasoned international professional named Fred Enlow who took on the responsibility for MBNA International and other international opportunities as they became identified. A couple of days after looking at Joe's house, Fred called me to his office and said he and Charlie wanted to know if I would consider moving to the United Kingdom to take over as CEO at MBNA International. What a question!

Terry and I discussed the idea, considering all the angles. We talked about purchasing Joe's house if we stayed and the complexities associated with relocating to England for three years. Since our first trip to Europe for our fifteenth anniversary, we had journeyed back across the pond many times, but we had never visited England. I knew the weather was rotten and that its cuisine was not well regarded, but this was the opportunity I had hoped for.

Taking a Look at the United Kingdom

The U.K. had strict rules requiring quarantine of dogs for six months, but that roadblock didn't exist because our beloved Babe had passed away a few months earlier. Terry owned a horse, and I said that I would make flying him over a condition of accepting the assignment. Terry was very apprehensive about leaving the girls but understood how important it was to me and agreed that we would take a flight there and see if we could adapt. I knew that the "request" was really more of a "demand," and Terry knew my philosophy about rejecting a request to move. So deep down, we both knew we would be going. However, we didn't openly discuss it as a fait accompli.

About a week after the overture, Fred, Bruce Hammonds (another vice chairman), Terry, and I took off in one of the corporate jets to JFK in New York. There we boarded the Concorde to London. Upon arrival, we boarded a British Air flight to Manchester where a chauffeur named Barry greeted us and whisked us away in a Rolls Royce to Chester.

We drove to the Grosvenor Hotel in the center of town where we slept for a few hours. I met Bruce and Fred for lunch, and afterward we jumped back into the Rolls for the mile trip to the bank. Tom met us and led a tour through the bank, followed by a long discussion about the operations. We met the group for dinner and stayed a couple of more days before flying back to Delaware.

All this happened just before Thanksgiving in 1995. As was customary, we were hosting a large crowd. We made it through the dinner, but it was difficult to socialize when all we were thinking about was the overseas opportunity.

After many conversations, we decided we should accept the assignment. Terry wanted to wrap up some loose ends at home, and I knew I'd be thoroughly occupied with my new position for a few months, so we agreed that I would go first and she would follow shortly thereafter. I flew back to London and made my way to Chester. Although we were apart, I spoke with her daily, and I knew I could fly back on a minute's notice.

MBNA
International Bank
1995 to 1997

Our New Home

The bank had purchased and renovated a large house on the banks of the River Dee overlooking the city in an area named Curzon Park North. It had a large kitchen, living and dining rooms, a family room, an office, and a powder room on the first floor. Off the spacious entry foyer was an elegant staircase leading to three ample suite bedrooms on the second floor. From the second floor, there was an additional stairway that led to a tower room on the upper floor. Most likely the third floor room inspired the name of the Tower House. It also had a small one-car attached garage and an in-ground swimming pool that seemed to be an amenity inconsistent with the weather.

Another unusual aspect of the Tower House was that I came to believe it was haunted. I never believed in ghosts (and still have serious doubts), but on several occasions, I'd close the doors to all the bedrooms at night, but when I awoke the following morning, one or another door would be wide open. I decided that when Terry came over, I wouldn't mention it.

I immersed myself in work and learned about every aspect of the bank. We had the credit card division with credit and collection departments, data processing, finance, marketing, deposits, consumer lending, insurance, personnel, auditing, legal, and all the usual disciplines necessary to run a bank. When I arrived, we had about 400 employees. In addition, we had a sales office on Jermyn Street in the beautiful and stylish St. James area of the City of Westminster in London that housed about forty people whose role it was to call on potential affinity groups to offer our credit cards.

Reunited

I came home for Christmas and a few other times before Terry traveled to Chester to be with me. It was February 1996 and her sister Kathy joined her for the trip. I missed her tremendously and was thrilled we'd be together again. A day after they arrived, Chester was enveloped in a huge snowstorm; a record setter. I walked the twenty minutes to work, and upon arrival I saw every type of farm equipment imaginable trying to clear the driveway and the parking lots. It was a three-ring circus with one bulldozer moving snow into an area followed by another moving it back. I called upon my skills honed in Buffalo and took charge directing the snow clearing operation. I didn't realize it at the time, but I was somewhat of a hero to those who were watching from inside.

After a few days, Terry's sister Kathy returned to Virginia, and we were on our own. It was winter in England and a bit dreary (or "dull" as the BBC referred to it), but we were excited to be together and looked forward to exploring our new surroundings. We went to the Lakes District a few times and stayed in small inns. Windermere was a favorite, and the drive took only a couple of hours from Chester. The inns were like an old pair of sneakers—comfy and familiar. Rooms weren't spectacular but adequate. The full English breakfast resplendent with blood pudding, bacon, tomatoes, mushrooms, and eggs was outstanding (skip the blood pudding), and dinners were an intimate affair with outstanding cuisine.

I received the *Wall Street Journal*, the *Financial Times*, the *Herald Tribune*, the *American Banker*, and *USA Today*, which I soon renamed *USA Yesterday,* at the office daily. When I traveled to the United States for monthly meetings, I'd read *USA Today,* and the next day when I returned to the U.K., the same stories would be in that day's edition. The best section was the world weather. Taking that information into consideration, along with the BBC reports, we'd decide where we would go for weekend mini-vacations. During the dank days of winter, it was important for us to find the sun, and we depended on these two sources to steer us in that direction.

Every few weeks I'd take off a half-day on Friday and a half-day on Monday and off we'd go to Paris, Venice, Rome, Florence, Montreaux, Madrid, Munich, Bellagio and the lakes district of Northern Italy, and many other places we'd likely find sun. It was a magical time.

Wonderful Wendel

Terry's horse Wendel flew across the pond via KLM along with Terry's trainer. They landed in London and, after clearing customs, boarded a lorry to Chester. We rented a stall in a stable located on a magnificent estate named Chomolomly Garden Park where the parkland included mixed woodland and plantations, lakes, gardens, and farmland. The Foden family rented a parcel of land on the estate, and their daughter ran an equestrian training program.

We had owned several horses prior to buying Wendel, but he was a very special horse. His registered name was Eliten, but, as with most horses, he had a nickname, and for some reason, the name Wendel fit him perfectly. We didn't select the name, but we kept it.

Wendel was a real trooper. He was a Sweedish Warmblood that we bought from people in Florida and he lived in Maryland not far from our home in Chadds Ford after we acquired him. Now he was in the U.K. and adapting well. One of the qualities that made Wendel so special was he had a way of knowing if you needed a little lovin'. He'd wrap his long neck around yours with his head draped over your shoulder and just stand there as if he were hugging you.

On one day when it was raining particularly hard, Terry called her trainer to say she was going to cancel her lesson. The trainer asked if she was feeling all right. Terry said she was fine but was canceling because it was raining so hard. The trainer's response was if they canceled lessons every time it rained, there would seldom be any lessons. She had a point. Often thereafter I'd look out the window of my corner office to see the rain pouring down and blowing sideways and remark to others that my wife was most likely riding her horse in that terrible weather. She was doing just that on a daily basis.

Oudie the Wonder Dog

Terry told me that she'd like to have a dog, to which I responded that we lived in a company house, I traveled a lot, we liked to take trips, and owning a dog was impractical. A few weeks later we drove to Liverpool to "just look" at Bichon Frisé puppies at a champion breeder's home. A few weeks later, after she was weaned, we picked up Oudie.

I told Terry that Oudie was her dog and that I'd be embarrassed walking a dog of such small stature. After about a week, she endeared herself to me and suddenly became my dog.

We seldom had dinner at home, preferring the pubs or small restaurants around Chester. Oudie quickly became familiar with the proprietors, since taking dogs into restaurants is a common practice in the U.K. Oudie was our regular dining companion. On a weekend trip to the Yorkshire Dales, we stayed at a magnificent hotel named the Devonshire Arms Country House, where following dinner, we were invited to bring Oudie into the Doggie Lounge. There, surrounded by oil paintings of dogs, we joined several others lounging in large leather chairs who were enjoying a roaring fire in the stone fireplace, while, like Oudie, their dogs relaxed beside them on oriental rugs.

During our time in England, Oudie had two experiences as exciting as her excursions dining out. You will recall that I thought the Tower House was haunted. The house had an elaborate security system that was connected to the guard station at the bank. One night, I was awakened by Oudie's growls and saw several lights on the alarm control board blinking—a signal that someone was moving in several different rooms. I looked throughout the house and didn't find anyone or any sign of entry. I was forced to admit to Terry that I had experienced similar phenomena, and we mutually came to the conclusion that ghosts were a possibility. We decided that as long as the ghosts didn't disturb us that we could coexist.

Oudie's second night of excitement came when a bat flew into our bedroom window. I truly hate bats. It's not that I've even had a negative experience, but they are scary creatures. The dog went out of her mind—running and jumping—trying to catch the erratically flying mammal. Terry and I made a quick decision. We grabbed Oudie, and the three of us ran out of the room slamming the door behind us. I was in favor of simply moving into another bedroom for the night, but Terry wanted the bat out of the house. I was determined that I wasn't going to wrestle with that creature, so I came up with a solution. I called security at the bank and asked if anyone wanted to get a bat out of our bedroom. Within five minutes, two burly guards appeared at our front door. Since Terry and I were in our nightclothes, we quickly put on our Burberrys, which must have been quite a sight. We looked like two flashers with the coats bundled around us with our bare legs visible below the bottom of the coats.

The guards had torches (flashlights) and a tennis racket with them, and we provided a bed sheet. They cautiously climbed the stairs, rushed into the bedroom, and slammed the door behind them. What ensued was a lot of commotion—crashing of lamps and tipping of chairs and tables. After about five minutes the guards appeared triumphantly with the bat entangled in the sheet. I thanked them, gave them a tip, and asked that we keep "our little secret" between ourselves. The next morning I went to the bank as usual and nearly everyone I encountered asked about the bat. So much for keeping a secret!

Chester, England

Chester, one of the best-preserved Roman walled cities in Britain, is located in Cheshire County, situated on the River Dee in close proximity to Wales.

A considerable amount of land in Chester is owned by the Duke of Westminster, who owns an estate, Eaton Hall, near the village of Eccleston. Grosvenor is the Duke's family name, which explains such features as Grosvenor Bridge, the Grosvenor Hotel, and Grosvenor Park.

The more interesting landmarks in the city are the city walls, the Rows, and the black-and-white architecture. The walls encircle the bounds of the entire city, measuring approximately two miles with only a short break in the structure. There is a footpath on top of the walls crossing roads by bridges over Eastgate, Northgate, St. Martin's Gate, Watergate, Bridgegate, and Newgate, affording excellent views of the city. It's a bustling town with many stores, shops, restaurants, hotels, and inns, with the foremost being the Grosvenor Hotel, and the most prominent buildings being the city hall and the cathedral. Along the walls at Eastgate, which was the original entrance into the city, is the Eastgate Clock, built in 1899 to celebrate the diamond jubilee of Queen Victoria two years earlier. Between our house and the city was a small hamlet named Handbridge that had a butcher shop, a bakery, a green grocer, and a florist where I would frequently ride my bike to do minor shopping.

The "Rows" are white and black buildings with shops on the lower level and additional shops above, reached by steps. They are unique. The pictures most frequently taken by tourists include the Rows, the Eastgate Clock, and the Chester Cathedral.

Although Chester is a friendly town, it's frequently loaded with tourists and with tourists come pickpockets. Terry had two unpleasant experiences. The first occurred when she was in the post office addressing letters when someone walked in and walked out with her purse. The bank was about a mile away, and by the time I arrived after receiving her telephone call, the police were already there. Shortly thereafter, she was in a shoe store in town when a couple came in and tried to take her purse. The shop owner yelled at them, and they ran out. The police came (the same officer) and upon hearing the story advised Terry to "dress down" when in town.

The London Office

As mentioned earlier, MBNA also had a sales office in London on Jermyn Street that I'd visit frequently. We were on the fifth floor of a small office building that was nestled between some of the finest shops in London. Next door was the Floris soap shop, and two doors down was Paxton and Whitfield, the oldest cheese shop in Britain. Across the street was Burlington Arcade with its many fine stores selling very expensive jewelry, clothing, and even pens. Penfield's was always an interesting store to "just look" at vintage and modern pens, and they had several hundred in stock. Two blocks away was the famous department store, Fortnum and Mason, and across the street from there was the Ritz Hotel. Old Bond Street where the really exclusive shops were was two blocks away.

Typically I'd stay at the Dukes Hotel or the Stafford or Browns, all within walking distance of the office. I probably stayed at twenty different fine hotels in London, but my favorite hotel was the Landmark located in Marylebone. While the area isn't as classy as St. James, the hotel is exquisite.

It was always fun to be in London and I enjoyed it immensely.

The Niceties of Life

When we moved to the Tower House, we retained the weekly cleaning lady whom Tom McGinley had hired. Her name was Jackie. She had a full-time position at the Grosvenor Hotel but also found time to help with the Tower House. She was a delight. In addition to helping with the house, she was a great dog sitter. Oudie enjoyed being with us and enjoyed Jackie's weekly visits, but she especially enjoyed her vacations at Jackie's apartment when we traveled.

The local florist kept the arrangements fresh at the bank on a weekly basis. We had an expansive entry foyer at the Tower House that held a large round table with a beautiful cut glass vase. The same florist came to the Tower House every Monday and performed the same magic at our house. We also had gardeners, and as spring approached, they transformed the front gardens into a showplace of spectacular colors.

As a young boy growing up in Buffalo, I thought if I ever had a chauffeur I would have "arrived." I don't know why that stuck with me since I don't think I ever saw anyone being chauffeured. Now I had Barry along with my choice of two Bentleys and a Rolls Royce. At the time, it seemed to me that a chauffeur should have three qualities. First, he should be an excellent driver. Second, he should have an excellent sense of direction. Third, he should be discreet. Barry possessed none of the above. Consequently, I used Barry's services sparingly and preferred to drive myself.

Not only did Barry lack the basic skills mentioned above, it seemed almost every time I asked him to drive me somewhere, something went wrong. Once I was invited to the Chester Cathedral for lunch with the dean, the Reverend Stephen Smalley. The cathedral was in the middle of the city, parking was often a challenge, and it was raining like crazy, so I asked Barry to take me there and wait for me. I enjoyed a meal with the dean and another elder of the church and was intrigued by the architecture and history of the building. The cathedral was constructed between 1093 and the sixteenth century, with additions made each century up to the present time. Much of the interior is in Norman style and the elaborately carved canopies of the choir stalls are stunning with their intricate designs. Over lunch, as I expected, the conversation quickly turned to money, and I committed the bank to a modest amount, explaining we were a new organization. I said as we grew and became more profitable, we'd consider a larger donation. They were gracious and understanding and walked me to the door where Barry had the exhaust pipe of the Bentley snuggled against the doorknob. If ever I wished we owned a rent-a-wreck—or, for that matter, any rusted out, banged up car for transportation—it was then.

Another disaster with Barry was the time Terry and I were invited to a garden party with the Queen at Buckingham Palace. I had been in the States for a meeting and arrived back in Chester that morning. The dress code was tails and top hat.

I owned a couple of tuxedos but tails and top hat were not part of my wardrobe. I arranged to rent the outfit from Moss Brothers, Ltd., and to pick it up on Regent Street in London the afternoon of the event.

Normally Terry and I would take the train to London, but due to the timeline, I asked Barry to drive us. I fell asleep in the back seat and awoke to the car rocking and rolling from side to side. I opened my eyes to see the countryside but not the motorway. I asked Barry where the hell we were, and he said he really didn't know. We were lost and running late. Finally we found the motorway and sped into town. Traffic was snarled as usual, and once we were within five or six blocks, I decided to run to Regent Street leaving instructions for him to meet me at the store.

I was tempted not to try the outfit on but thought better of it and took the time to do so. Everything fit, I ran outside and to my surprise, Barry was there. We checked into our hotel, took a quick shower, dressed, climbed back into the car for the short trip to the palace, and made it—amazingly—on time, with no thanks to Barry.

The Queen, The Rich, The Famous

We checked in with the guards, showed them our identification and the invitation, and we were invited to join a few hundred others in the garden. We kept going from open space to covered space along the way, and I was reminded to remove the "lid," my top hat, every time we entered a covered space. The gardens were beautiful with flowers in full bloom, the orchestra playing, and guests enjoying themselves while munching on scones with clotted cream and other delicious delicacies.

Eventually the Queen joined us with her entourage following. Every hundred feet or so, a guard would select particular guests from the lines on either side of her pathway and invite them to speak with the Queen. We weren't selected, but it was still a thrill.

The event lasted a few hours, and when it was over, we exited through the building into the front space where hordes of tourists were lining the iron fence. There was a rather large group of Japanese tourists who were yelling, "Hold it, hold it!" and clicking away as fast as they could. I placed my right hand in my jacket pocket Charles-like while Terry gave them the Queen's wave. I imagine our photos are still on many mantles in Tokyo.

Our social calendar was exciting and full. One of our affinity groups was the Prince's Trust, and Prince Charles held a board meeting at MBNA soon after I arrived. His helicopter landed, and we took him on a tour of the bank prior to his meeting. People have asked me what he was like. The answer is simple. He was charming. He was born into royalty and raised to be charming, and he did so with aplomb.

We were frequent guests at Eaton Hall, the ancestral home of the Duke and Duchess of Westminster that was located about ten minutes from our house. Their home was a fabulous castle with equally impressive grounds.

The governor of the Bank of England is the United Kingdom's version of the chairman of the Federal Reserve Bank in the United States. Periodically the governor holds luncheons with industry leaders in various parts of the country to hear their impressions of how things are going. I was invited to Governor Eddie George's luncheon in Cheshire County along with another nine people. It was there I met the chairman of Marks and Spencer and Lord Pilkington, famous for glassmaking. Terry and I were subsequently invited to the lord's home for a Sunday dinner.

We were invited to a reception held by Prime Minister John Major at 10 Downing Street in early 1997, but I had to decline as I had committed to be in the States for meetings. However, we did have the opportunity to meet the new Prime Minister Tony Blair and his wife Cherie over lunch that summer in Chester.

I attended a dinner at the British Consulate's home in New York along with other business leaders on St. Patrick's Day in 1997. It was a great dinner, great company, and a great venue, but a poor date selection. Traffic in New York is always a challenge, but March 17 proved to be especially difficult.

Terry and I had several lunches with the Lord Mayor of Chester and his wife. The food was always very good and the wine wasn't bad either.

We attended a chamber music recital at the Archbishop of Canterbury's residence and had a wonderful time.

We were invited to a Fourth of July party at U.S. Ambassador William J. Crowe's residence, but had committed to go to the opera at Glyndebourne with a partner from Goldman Sachs and his wife. We didn't know much about opera and wished we could attend the Oklahoma-themed party at the ambassador's home, but we were committed. Surprisingly, it turned out Glyndebourne was quite a treat. The grounds were beautiful, the company superb, and the performance outstanding.

Terry had met Lord Anthony and Lady Diana Barbour through her equine activities, and we became good friends. They lived outside the city of Chester in a large castle surrounded by hundreds of acres and beautiful gardens. The first time we were invited to their home for dinner, we brought a bouquet of flowers thinking that would be appropriate. We rang the doorbell, and when the butler answered, we saw a huge arrangement on a table in the foyer similar to the one in the Tower House but about four times the size. Nonetheless, our flowers were warmly received.

Dinner was an interesting affair with an oblong table set for about forty guests. It was one very long table. We were seated apart from each other and quickly met our dinner partners who were intriguing people. After appetizers and the main courses were served, we were asked to turn over our place cards, which showed a different name. We then rose and found our new seat and met our new dinner partners for desert. It was a nice way to meet more people and a trick I'll use if we ever seat forty people at a table. Once dinner was over, Diana made the announcement to adjourn. I stood and Anthony discretely signaled for me to sit. "Adjourn," meant the ladies were leaving the table so the men could have port and cigars while solving the troubles of the world. The ladies left and regrouped in the master bedroom where they chatted and sampled various perfumes while the men held lively conversation. It soon became apparent that many of the men were business titans and some were "names" associated with Lloyds of London. A "name" is a silent investor with Lloyds.

It was a most interesting group. All in all, both Terry and I enjoyed the evening immensely.

On another evening we were invited to the Barbour's to hear a presentation from the British Sporting Art Trust. It was an educational evening, and I'm proud to say I became a lifetime member of the trust.

Each summer we hosted the MBNA Board of Directors for a meeting in London. Upon arrival chauffeurs picked up the board members and their spouses and took them to the Ritz where suites were reserved. The next morning we held the board meeting in an elegant conference room in the hotel, and that evening we had dinner at the Spencer House, resplendent with music, exquisite food, and white glove service.

We had many parties at the Tower House. Typically, we hired a harpist or a neighbor with a keyboard and situated them in the foyer for background music. Even though the house had undergone a major renovation a few years earlier, I thought it still needed work. Specifically, the ceiling height on the wing with the family room was too low, and the room was isolated from the rest of the house. Also, the swimming pool was of no earthly use given the climate. I obtained estimates for the work, called the States, and was given a $250,000 budget. The results were magnificent. Installing new steel supports, we raised the family room ceiling. We renovated the French doors across the back of the room and created an oval opening to allow access from the dining room. We had the pool removed and replaced it with a large fountain surrounded by circular stone benches. It made entertaining all the more fun.

The Tower House Hotel

My arrangement with the bank entailed specific details: the bank would maintain our house and grounds in Chadds Ford, pay to fly Terry's horse roundtrip, provide and maintain housing in the Tower House, provide the use of a company car, and pay for ten roundtrip business class tickets from the States to the U.K. annually. I wasn't sure if Terry would be commuting or if we would fly friends and relatives, but the ten tickets would accommodate either situation. As it turned out, Terry never returned to the States for a visit, and we used the tickets to fly friends to see us. Additionally, many who were in a financial position to do so made the trip on their own dime. We soon felt like we were the proprietors of a bed and breakfast. People just kept coming. The kids came over a couple of times to surprise Terry, which was wonderful. Uncle Dick and Aunt Jean, Terry's younger brother Marty and his family, my brother, and Terry's mother and her husband were among the throngs.

Mom and Les decided they would take a flight over and sail back on the QE2. I had hundreds of thousands of miles accumulated from my monthly flights to the States from British Airways; I upgraded them to the Concorde for their trip over. Barry was dispatched along with Terry to pick them up at the airport, and they arrived safe and sound at the Tower House. After a nap, they went with Barry for the short trip downtown, where Mom slipped getting out of the car. They hustled her off to the hospital where suspicions were confirmed and she was outfitted with a cast. We moved them from one of the bedrooms on the second floor and set up a new bedroom in the family room. All this would have been difficult for anyone of any age, but it was especially challenging for a person in her eighties, and it made for a long month of company. At the end of their stay, we drove them to Southampton in record time and waved goodbye as the porters made their way with Mom in a wheelchair and Les walking alongside to board the ship.

Number One Visa Credit Card Issuer

Work was terrific. We were growing in a controlled, but rapid, pace. The original 400 employees had grown to more 1200, and the asset growth was on a tear. The longtime U.K. giant in terms of Visa assets was Barclays. In 1997, we left them in the dust and surpassed one billion pounds in loans, or about $1.6 billion U.S. dollars. We held the most outrageous "One Billion Pound" party ever for all the employees and their guests. It was over the top, well attended, and appreciated by all. The following week the president of Visa Europe came to the bank and presented us with an award. It was made all the more sweet as he was formerly in charge of the credit card program at Barclays, and, to his credit, was effusive with his remarks.

Money's Not Everything

Charlie loved to fiddle with things, always trying to fine-tune them to perfection. On one of my trips stateside in the autumn of 1997, Bruce Hammonds called me to his office. We exchanged the usual pleasantries, but I could tell he had something to say, and after a while he got to the point. Charlie wanted to install a woman from the States who was a contemporary of mine as chairman of MBNA International with me reporting to her. Bruce knew we didn't get along very well, and I reminded him of it. We had some terse words, but Bruce said Charlie had made up his mind. Apparently Charlie knew this wouldn't set well with me. Bruce said I'd be paid $500,000 net of taxes if I stayed in the U.K. until the end of 1998. This amount was over and above my annual salary, bonus and stock options, and grants. I told him I'd think about it and see if it could work.

My new "boss" arrived with flair and immediately met with all my direct reports and their direct reports. Shortly thereafter she went about changing things without consulting with me. Each day was more intense than the day before, and finally, I had enough. It was apparent we wouldn't be able to work together. I turned fifty on November 18 and decided to give myself a special birthday present. I called Bruce and explained there was only room for one sheriff in town and that Terry and I wanted to return to the States. We discussed it, but I remained steadfast. A half million dollars is a lot of money to walk away from, but it was worth it. I couldn't be bought. And even though I had a few thoughts about sleeping on a park bench and eating cat food in my golden years, I had made my decision. It may seem that I was brazen or foolhardy, but the opposite is true. I tell this story to illustrate that principles are principles. Money shouldn't change that.

We had grown the bank to two and a half billion dollars in assets; we had taken the bank from a loss position in 1995 to an income of $45 million in 1997. We had hired an additional thousand people. Best of all, we had one hell of a good time doing it. No regrets.

Packing Our Bags, Horse, and Dog

We spoke with Tracy Foden, where Terry kept Wendel, and unexpectedly, the conversation became quite animated. She and her boyfriend had recently built an extension onto their barn and apparently assumed our monthly rent would be continuing for some time. We never entered into an agreement, and I thought it was understood that we were free to change boarding facilities or move the horse as we saw fit. To make a long story short, they refused to release our horse unless we paid them for six months of board costs. I met with the boyfriend at a pub to try to work out an arrangement and came close to fists. Terry and I were over a barrel. Ultimately we paid the money to release Wendel for his flight back to the United States.

MBNA had opened an office in Dublin on Saint Stephen's Green months earlier, and I traveled there several times. Terry is of Irish decent (Theresa Mary Bridget Dwyer—previously O'Dwyer) and had never been to the old sod, so we planned our last trip. We bought Christmas items for friends and family living in the States, enjoyed a few pints, and sang along with Irish singers. It was our last hurrah before heading back home.

We stayed at a new luxury hotel near the office named the Merrion Hall Hotel, which was formed by renovating four Georgian mansions and creating a hotel with beautiful woodwork and detail. We went shopping and brought back our purchases to the room, whereupon we retired to the pub downstairs for a refreshment and dinner. Just as we were walking down the hall back to our room, a person was exiting the room and ran when he saw us. I entered and called security. It was at this time there were frequent bombings by the IRA, and since none of our belongings was missing, our minds gravitated toward the possibility there might be a bomb in the room. The security people went through the room meticulously and didn't discover anything unusual. The manager offered to move us to a different room, but Terry wanted them to move us to a different hotel, which they did. By this time, it was about midnight, and the assistant manager of the Merrion drove us to a nice hotel nearby where we were situated in a suite. We no sooner turned out the lights when we heard a man's voice crying out, "Let me in, pleeeease!" I opened our door and saw a fellow sitting on the floor outside a room down the hall crying and obviously drunk. I yelled, "Either let him in or shut up!" It worked. There was silence. All in all, it was a memorable trip.

A couple of weeks later, the shippers packed our belongings, we packed our suitcases, and Terry, Oudie, and I left Chester. Barry drove us to London where we spent our last night. The next day we headed to Heathrow for our flight home. We had a wonderful run in the United Kingdom—an experience of a lifetime—but it was time to move on. We arrived home in time for Christmas 1997.

Chapter 14

Bank One—
First USA
1998 to 2000

Back in the United States
December 1997

When we walked into the house, there was a wonderful fragrance of pine. The kids had bought an enormous Christmas tree, erected it, and decorated it in the family room. It was a great "Welcome Home." The house appeared to be in good shape, and we planned Christmas dinner with the family. On Christmas morning, we discovered that the oven had stopped working and that we had a generous leak coming from the dishwasher. Even though in our absence the bank had employed regular cleaning, our lack of use created problems for the appliances. We salvaged dinner by taking the turkey and side dishes to the kids' homes in Wilmington. Then we carted everything back to ours. It was a frustrating day, but it was great to be with family for the holiday.

Monday morning came, and I showed up for work not knowing where to go. I met with Bruce, and he told me I was to work in the business card area helping Len Kidwell. I knew I'd be put in the penalty box, but this—pardon the expression—was a severe kick in the ass. Business card was one of several businesses that reported to me before I left for the U.K. Fortunately, Len and I were good friends, as we had worked together at Major Finance, and I recruited him to MBNA, so that wasn't an issue. Nevertheless, it was a serious blow to my ego. My "office" was a conference room. No real office, no secretary, no administrative assistants, no direct reports, and no businesses to run. Apparently, Charlie was really ripped.

This arrangement went on for several weeks until I thought I'd done my penance long enough. A joke's a joke. I tried to make an appointment to see Charlie but couldn't get past his secretary. Patience was never one of my strong suits and neither was languishing while waiting for the standoff to end.

My next-door neighbor asked me how things were going, and I told her not so well. Her husband had previously been an executive for PepsiCo, and was now an entrepreneur. While at PepsiCo he worked with a fellow in human resources who was now working for First USA, the credit card subsidiary of Bank One, and the archrival of MBNA. His wife was also entrepreneurial and had a background in executive recruiting. She asked if I'd like to meet the fellow from First USA, and I agreed to do so.

I was a bit nervous—not about the interview—but because First USA's headquarters was five blocks from MBNA's, and to be seen entering First USA would present serious problems. First USA understood this and arranged for me to enter the building via a private parking lot under the bank and provided me with a magnetic card for fast entry. MBNA and First USA were intensely fierce competitors in every way, and everyone in town knew it.

I went through a series of interviews with senior executives for several hours. Late in the day, Dan Barr, the head of human resources, asked me if I'd be willing to take a psychological test. He explained they had a proprietary test that had been designed especially for them that they asked every potential employee to take. I didn't have any objection, and although I thought it a bit odd, I took it.

A few days later, Dan called to schedule another round of interviews. This time I met with Randy Chistofferson, the president; Dick Vague, chairman and Dick's boss from Ohio; and Rich Lehman, who was a vice chairman of Bank One. This series of meetings took a few hours, and I thought they went well. First USA didn't have any international businesses, and they asked me a myriad of questions about my U.K. experience. There were certain things I felt were confidential, and I told them so, which may have won some admiration. They were interviewing me for the position to head up their international expansion.

While I wasn't particularly happy with MBNA, I knew I'd get out of the doghouse sooner or later, so there really wasn't any pressure, and I rather enjoyed the interview experience. We parted company at the end of the day with no commitment, but I had a good feeling that one would be forthcoming. Three days later, Dan called me and asked me to come meet with Dick Vague again. We set an appointment for the following day.

Dick and I chatted for about an hour when he asked particulars regarding my compensation package at MBNA. I was in the driver's seat and explained my salary, history of stock options, and, most importantly, stock grants that would come due in the future. He knew I wouldn't walk away from the grants, and First USA would have to buy them out to make me whole. He wrote down all the information and two days later, Dan called again and made the offer. The valuation of the grants was complex, and they were using a methodology called the Black Scholes model, which I wasn't familiar with. I did a quick study of Black Scholes and interpreted parts of it differently.

After three more days of back and forth, we struck the deal. We agreed on the salary, stock grant valuation, and buyout, among other benefits, and I accepted the position of president of Bank One International.

The next day I called Bruce Hammonds and made an appointment to see him. I always got along well with Bruce, so I opened the meeting by saying, "I'm going to make the situation easy," and went on to tell him I'd accepted a position with First USA. He was inquisitive about the position and asked if it was final. He knew as well as I did that once you resign, that is final, and there is no looking back. I reconfirmed that.

No other senior executive of MBNA had ever resigned, and my doing so meant I had closed the door forever. Charlie didn't take kindly to anyone who was not one hundred percent in his corner. My going to First USA would only serve to strengthen his resentment.

I told Bruce I'd drop off my company car, but he said to use it until I had a car from First USA, which I will always remember as a kind gesture. I gave three weeks' notice, but I knew it would be over that afternoon, and it was. Bruce called a meeting with my peers, and they wished me well. I walked out the door, handed in my security badge, and felt sad to be leaving.

Bank One—First USA

During my interview process at First USA, the most obvious difference I noticed between them and MBNA was the dress code. MBNA was suits—not sport coats—suits, starched shirts, ties, and shined shoes. First USA was in a constant state of "dress down," with the most dressed down person being Dick Vague. His attire took the expression to a new level. Of particular interest were the flip-flops, which he wore on most days, along with tattered golf shirts and wrinkled pants or shorts in the warmer weather. He was certainly different from Charlie in every way.

Dick was from Texas. He was about six foot three with a large frame. He loved to play basketball and had a half court in his house. Randy was more refined with an MBA from Harvard. To see them together created images of The Odd Couple. This was in the spring of 1998 and Internet companies were all the rage with alternative management styles and a different approach to environs, hours, hierarchy, and business as usual. Dick was a devotee of the movement and a strong advocate of the nonconformance espoused by those companies.

I was given a comfortable corner office and a secretary. That was the initial staff of Bank One International. A week later I hired a sharp young guy named Jeff Courtney, who had been an administrative assistant for a man named Rick Struthers at MBNA before defecting to First USA. I also hired Bill Van Blarcom (again) from MBNA, Helen Williams from MBNA International in the U.K., and Sue Wildman, who was working at First USA. The five of us were the startup team.

Obviously, I knew the marketplace in the U.K., and it was only natural that I would want to open a bank there. I had been involved with studies of other countries while at MBNA; therefore, I was currently knowledgeable about the demographics, competition, regulatory landscape, workforce, compensation, and the potential to be successful. I quickly concluded the two best countries to start new banks were the

U.K. and Canada. The next step was to meet with the regulators and to decide where in these countries we should locate.

Initially I flew to the U.K. since that was where I had the most familiarity. I arranged a meeting with the Bank of England and met with the same regulators I knew from MBNA. The Bank of England had a practice of meeting with banks every few months. While with MBNA, I'd attend these meetings with our CFO to discuss the bank's financial statements, any audits that had occurred since the last meeting, and our financial forecast. These were always collegial meetings over tea and cookies, and I came to know the regulators quite well. On this occasion we had a constructive and friendly meeting where they laid out their requirements for the new bank, including capital ratios they expected to be maintained. I reviewed our five-year plans and went into great detail about our strategies and how we intended to execute them.

Next we visited several cities in England, ranging from Birmingham to York, and then we went on to Wales and Ireland. After several weeks of meetings with mayors, councilmen, economic development people, realtors, and local businesses, I narrowed the search to Cardiff, Wales, and Dublin, Ireland, although York in England was a close third. The next move was to have more meetings with the economic development people to determine tax breaks and other financial incentives to locate in their city.

York had a thriving insurance industry and was doing well economically. Dublin was on a tear and aggressively seeking business growth, while Cardiff had experienced some economic declines and was anxious to have us. The process went on for about a month with me making trips back and forth from the States several times during that period. I finally settled on Cardiff, Wales, for our operations center and London for our affinity sales office. Cardiff made a generous offer to bring us there, although not as generous as Dublin. In the final analysis, I felt the recruiting would be healthier in Cardiff, as Dublin was teaming with new companies. Also, Ireland was a small market, and I thought we should stay on the opposite side of the English Channel.

We leased commercial space in a new corporate center on Cardiff Bay and additional space a couple of miles away for the operations center. I had several meetings with Total Systems from Columbus, Georgia, and I negotiated an agreement with them to outsource our data processing. I was familiar with Total Systems, as I'd used them to process our business card accounts at MBNA America. I knew their senior management quite well, and I trusted that they would do whatever it took to do an excellent job for us. I would have also considered SSBA but they had recently been purchased by MBNA, which was now their exclusive client. I retained the accounting firm of Coopers and Lybrand in Cardiff to help sort out the various accounting issues, and they were excellent in every way.

During the same period, I was doing the exact same thing in Canada. The geographic proximity and my use of corporate jets made the trips much easier. I used one of the jets for a week in late spring to look for appropriate cities according to the same criteria I used for the U.K. I traveled as far north as Nova Scotia in my search. I met with the same type of people as I met across the pond. I had several meetings with the Bank of Canada's Office of the Superintendent of Financial Institutions, where I presented five-year pro forma business plans for their review and approval. As with the U.K., I also provided details about how we intended to be successful. Unlike the U.K., I didn't know the officials in Canada, and they didn't know me, but the meetings were cordial, instructive, and constructive.

In Canada, I decided on the capitol, Ottawa, for the operations center and Toronto for the sales office. I lined up space in anticipation of approval from the regulators.

Time Out for Wedding Bells

While I was traveling, Terry had been busy finalizing wedding plans with Michelle. I didn't realize how much planning went into a wedding. The wedding gown, bridesmaids' dresses, invitations, flowers, limos, food, drinks, music, staff, cake, etc., etc. Fortunately, as with our own wedding, the majority of the work was performed by Terry and, this time, Michelle. The wedding was in June 1998, with the ceremony at a large older church in Wilmington, Delaware. It was a particularly warm day for June, and the church was so hot it seemed to be smoldering. Adding to the perspiration from the temperature was my nervousness about walking down the aisle and keeping my composure. About a month before, we attended the wedding of my friend Len Kidwell's daughter and he performed admirably. I asked him how he did it. His advice was, "Get in the zone... not so deep in the zone that you don't recall the wedding but in the zone." When I saw Michelle in her beautiful gown, I thought what a beautiful girl she was and how lucky we were to have such a terrific daughter. I don't think I entered "the zone," but maybe I did (just a little). She looked radiant and I was proud to be walking down the aisle with her. Adding to my happiness, Terry was the perfect mother of the bride, beaming and looking beautiful. The reception was held at the Greenville Country Club. It was a beautiful day, a great wedding, and a fun reception. The amount of effort that Michelle and Terry put into planning was clearly evident. Afterward, Michelle and John went to the South Pacific for their honeymoon and settled nearby in Delaware.

Back to Business

In August 1998, I received the approvals from both regulators enabling First USA to proceed, and we started interviewing people in both countries for management positions. We also interviewed support people. Our goals were to hire one hundred people for the initial startup in each country and an additional five hundred over the next six to nine months. We retained search firms for the executive level people and advertised for support staff. In both countries, we had a terrific pool of people to choose from, and we were fortunate to be able to hire top-notch management teams.

We bought all new office furniture and equipment. We had local law firms draft the disclosures and other legal documents; we had signage made, business cards ordered, telephones and computers connected, and hundreds of other tasks completed down to the smallest detail. Everything was locally obtained, as nothing was transportable from the States. We experienced pure bedlam with very little sleep, but I found it an extremely enjoyable time.

We commenced operations in November and began marketing for credit cards in both countries with Canada following the U.K. by two weeks. We were provided with extensive press coverage in the host countries as well as the States. It was a hoot!

Business took off like a rocket. I knew our only real competition in both countries was MBNA, and I knew how they operated. We slugged it out for various top-named affinity groups, sharpening the pencil to eke out victories. In a couple of instances, we entered agreements knowing they would be loss leaders (companies with high visibility, but unlikely to produce a high level of earnings), but names like Wimbledon, United Manchester, and the Canada AAA carried a lot of name recognition to tout to other prospects.

Tennis Is More Than Just a Sport

Wimbledon is an interesting story. We had tried to sign them at MBNA but couldn't get through the front door. In the spring of 1999, I called the organization and spoke with their president, who suggested I speak with Mark McCormack from International Management Group (IMG). I had heard of IMG, and I knew it to be the premier sports management organization with emphasis on golf and tennis. I found out Mark lived in Isleworth near Orlando, Florida, and called him at his home. Someone else answered, I asked to speak to Mr. McCormack, and after I explained who I was and the nature of my call, he picked up the phone. We spoke for a few minutes, and he suggested we meet at his home in a couple of weeks. We set a date for lunch.

I flew to Florida on a corporate jet with Bill Van Blarcom, donning a sport coat and tie. Before the visit, I read about Mark and discovered he had published several books. I bought a copy of *What They Don't Teach You at Harvard Business School*, and took it along with me.

We pulled up to his most impressive mansion and rang the doorbell. An attractive young lady answered and invited us in. From the top of the staircase, a man wearing a warm-up suit called down saying he'd join us in ten minutes. We were served a cold drink and waited a few minutes until Mark showed up. I use the familial term Mark, since he insisted we call him by his first name. What a delightful guy. We were served lunch by two very attractive girls (the one who answered the door and an equally beautiful lady) and got right down to business. Mark explained Wimbledon could sign a contract with literally any provider of any service but historically shunned the practice with only a few exceptions. We discussed issuing a Wimbledon credit card and the prestige it would carry along with fees they could earn. We had a businesslike conversation, and Mark said he would consider what we discussed and get back to me. I asked him to autograph his book, which he did, and he asked if we'd like a tour of his grounds, which we did.

Just outside the rear door was a beautiful swimming pool along with a cabana. There was another young attractive lady sunning herself on a chaise that Mark introduced as his wife, Betsy. I thought she was about thirty years old. Mark was then close to seventy, and I thought, *Good for you!* There was another woman holding a baby, who Mark introduced as his and Betsy's.

We walked on decking along a large lake where Mark mentioned that the boat docked there belonged to golfer Tiger Woods, a neighbor, and one of his many clients. We learned Isleworth was home to many sports icons. Next he took us to the trophy room, which held numerous trophies belonging to Betsy, who we discovered was a two-time Australian Doubles Champion and a Wimbledon Doubles Finalist. Mark, his wife, and their home were most impressive.

A couple of weeks later, Mark called and told me I should meet with him and the president of Wimbledon in London later that month. We met and within two hours reached agreement. To the best of my knowledge, Mark didn't receive any compensation for the deal. After our meeting, Mark invited me to join him for the Wimbledon Championship in June. That day I had lunch in his beautiful tent with Mark by my side and enjoyed champagne and strawberries afterwards.

We went to the stands to his reserved seats at center court and watched the games. Along the way, every player we came near said hello to Mark. I didn't know anything about tennis but followed the volleys and applauded when Mark did. It was a memorable experience and an honor to meet and spend time with such an accomplished person.

A Dream's End

Meanwhile, I was taking alternating flights between Cardiff, London, Ottawa, and Toronto every couple of weeks. As I mentioned, Canada was easy. The United Kingdom was more exhausting, but it was an exciting time.

At that time, Bank One was the sixth largest bank in the United States. Its size was created by a series of acquisitions. One of the largest was First Chicago NBD, acquired in 1998. The bank had an impressive market share in the Midwest and a huge branch network. But I observed a major flaw: when Bank One made an acquisition, it didn't take time to fully absorb the new bank into its processes and procedures. Nor—and this was important—did they merge the acquired bank's data processing onto a single platform. The result was a corporation with a disjointed group of individual banks. The First Chicago acquisition process was extremely difficult in terms of culture, and that generated problematic issues.

John McCoy was the chairman of Bank One and the successor to his father and grandfather, who held the position before him. I met John on several occasions and found him to be easy going, but I didn't get a feel for his abilities to lead a bank as diverse and large as Bank One had become. I simply wasn't around him enough to know his strengths and weaknesses.

We rapidly built the assets in Canada and the United Kingdom. In just over a year, we started to turn a profit in both organizations. We had 600 employees and $500 million in assets between the two banks. The growth and quality of the assets were impressive.

Meanwhile, as busy as I was with the bank, the winter of 1998 and spring of 1999 were also busy times for our family. Terry and Joanna were planning Joanna's wedding to Michael. As with our wedding and Michelle's, I was content to be involved when needed but knew the girls could manage the process much better on their own. Joanna and Michael were married in April at St. Mary's in Annapolis, with their reception on the harbor at the Marriott Hotel. Both Michelle and Joanna were born and raised in Annapolis and both attended St. Mary's School. Having the wedding there brought back special memories of their childhood. The wedding and the reception were wonderful, lasting into the wee hours of the night. As with Michelle, I managed to make it down the aisle smiling but frankly, it wasn't easy. It's not an easy thing to let your "little girl" go. As father of the bride, I danced with Joanna to the tune of "My Girl" made famous by the Temptations. It was a really fun event.

Back at work following the wedding festivities, I began to notice disturbing economic events. The credit card business in the United States was mature and didn't offer the low-hanging fruit available overseas. The competitive landscape in the United States drove the business, meaning banks took on more and more risk, and with it, more and more losses. In August 1999, Bank One issued an earnings warning resulting from several missteps and, most notably, mistakes at First USA in the States. John McCoy, Dick Vague, and Rich Lehman left the bank. John Boardman, who was a senior executive at Bank One in Chicago, was temporarily put in charge of First USA.

John was an attorney by profession. His specialty was mergers and acquisitions. John called me to his office and told me the company needed capital, and he wanted to sell "my" two banks. My reaction was that would be a big mistake. After all, there were growth opportunities overseas, and the initial heavy lifting had been accomplished. Now was the time to start counting the money. He listened, but I could tell he wasn't hearing me. Naturally he would expect me to defend what I had created, and naturally I had a strong bias. The decision had been made, and he was carrying out orders from Chicago. He asked if I'd be willing to relocate to the corporate headquarters, and I gave a two-word (and rather coarse) response that ended with "you." It wasn't well received, but I didn't intend it to be. I told him I thought it might be a good time for me to retire, as there wasn't any position at Bank One in the States that interested me. After a cooling off period, he asked if I'd stay until we could sell the banks. I agreed, not for Bank One's sake, but rather for the sake of all the people I'd hired overseas. I felt I had a responsibility to each one of them to try to sell the banks with them included in the deal.

John brought in a fellow from the bank who had helped him in the past with acquisitions to head up the search for potential buyers. I was pretty much cut out of the process; nevertheless, I was expected to keep peace overseas. When we dramatically slowed down marketing, the people knew something was going on. Ultimately I explained to John that we owed it to the people to level with them or we would run the risk of a mass exodus of talent, and that would make the sale more difficult. He agreed, and I flew to the four overseas sites to break the news to the executive teams. After a few months, both banks were sold to competitors for a profit.

Retirement at Age 52

In June 2000, after spending twenty-eight months at Bank One, I decided I'd had enough. I retired at the age of fifty-two. I didn't know if we had enough money to retire, but I was pretty sure we did.

I was used to working long hours, evaluating and taking risks, and traveling extensively for business and pleasure. Also, I had an exercise routine that involved an hour or two, six days a week, which I had begun seven years earlier. Now I was retired.

I recall on the first morning of my retirement waking up at five o'clock and nudging Terry. She opened one eye, and I exuberantly asked her what she wanted to do that day. She answered, "I don't know what you're going to do. I'm going back to sleep," and rolled over.

During this period Terry and I occasionally drove the two hours to Lewes, Delaware, to visit my mother and stepfather. They had retired to a comfortable small home there in a planned community. The home they purchased, however, had a drawback: it was situated in the middle of very large mature trees that blocked virtually all sunlight. From time to time, these large old trees came roaring down to the ground.

My mother mentioned a new nearby community named Plantations, and on one visit, we drove there to take a look. The primary difference between where they were living and the

Plantations (aside from the lack of sunlight and falling trees) was that most of the residents at the Plantations were there year-round. My mother craved being with people and around a lot of activity. I used to joke that her ideal house location would be located in a median strip on a major highway. The area was very pretty, and it featured an expansive man-made lake. I decided I'd build them a new home there, and after some coaxing, they agreed. I would be happier if they were happier, and I thought a house would be a reasonable investment.

Plantations had three models to choose from, and we selected one that I modified, enlarging the master bedroom and the sunroom overlooking the lake. The project required someone to stay on top of it, and I had the time and experience to do so. The construction was slow but steady. Jack had emphysema, and his quality of life was deteriorating. I was in a hurry for them to move in and enjoy the house before the inevitable happened. The house was finally completed and my sister Patrice took charge of the packing and moving the five miles from their old house to their new one.

After the completion of the Lewes house, I kept occupied doing some painting and gardening around our house. At the same time, we decided to add a screened porch off the family room, which kept me busy supervising the project.

Michelle and John had been transferred by MBNA to Cleveland, where in July she gave birth to our first grandchild, Tyler. We traveled there for the event, but after the first day, I felt very ill with a fever and chills. All I wanted to do was get back to Pennsylvania to see my doctor. Terry drove me to the airport, where we exchanged my ticket, and I flew to Philadelphia. I went to the doctors' office and discovered I had Lyme disease. I went home to bed where I stayed with Oudie, my faithful pup, by my side while I took the medication the doctor prescribed. After a few days I was able to get up and about, but it took several months before I was completely back to normal.

In autumn of that year, we invited Father Bob Beiter, who had married us, to join us for a trip to Italy. We had been traveling to Europe on a regular basis, but it was fun to go with someone who had never had the experience. Bob's brother had died in an airplane accident years earlier, and he dreaded flying. However we got "Roberto" (as we called him) on the plane anyway. We had a ball on our journey throughout Tuscany. He was a great guy to travel with.

I had purchased a condo in Bonita Springs, Florida, a few years earlier for my mother and stepfather to use in the winter. It was a second-story villa with a one-car garage, two bedrooms, two baths, a study, kitchen, dining area, living room, and a lanai with a scenic view of a lake. We used it for ourselves a total of four or five weeks over the years, but it was open for use by relatives and friends. We never rented it. That fall and again in the spring, I went there for a few days with Peter Mills from my Chase days, and we played golf. I was getting more and more bored with retirement and missed the excitement of doing deals and running businesses. In the spring of 2001, I decided to do something about it and called Charlie at MBNA.

Shortly after I left MBNA, I'd heard from a mutual friend and a confidant of Charlie's that he had admitted his experiment with dual leadership in Chester was a mistake. A few months after I left, the woman he sent was brought back to the States and replaced by Bill Daiger, formerly the president of Maryland National Bank. Also, soon after joining Bank One, Bruce Hammonds called to tell me they were sending a check for $250,000, representing half of the forfeited retention bonus. I certainly didn't expect it, but the gift supported what I had heard about Charlie's decision. Although I thought he might not take my call, I had nothing to lose.

To my surprise, Charlie spoke with me, and we had a cordial conversation. I was frank, told him about my level of boredom, and asked if there might be some consulting work available. He asked if I wanted to return full time, and I explained I just wanted to do some consulting. He asked me to call Bruce Hammonds when I returned north.

Chapter 15

Back in the Saddle Again
2000 to 2002

A few days later I followed up with a call to Bruce, and we set a date to meet. At the meeting we discussed how a consulting contract might work, and agreed I would work *a maximum* of ten days a month with a set fee per month. I still had COBRA health insurance from Bank One, so that wasn't an issue. Besides, both Terry and I were quite healthy.

I had various assignments but none were particularly fulfilling. I found it difficult to merely make recommendations rather than making decisions and implementing them. The maximum of ten days a month started to stretch to eleven, then twelve, and so forth. I ran into Charlie at a dinner party, and he asked if I'd think about coming back full time. I responded that I might just as well, since the ten-day deal wasn't working.

Terry and I went back to Florida for a few days. Then Bruce called me. He said they would like for me to work in the co-branding department with a peer named Bill Morrison. The arrangement was fine with me. The next day he called and said they had reconsidered where I'd best fit in, and that I'd be working in the individual bank. The person who had taken over my old position, Jack Hewes, was a guy with a lot of experience and a great sense of humor but also a guy who had his own team. I doubted that I would be a part of it. Then, too, it would be difficult for me to work in an area I had previously run. After the call ended, I turned to Terry, told her of the reporting structure, and predicted it wouldn't work.

A combination of factors brought me to that conclusion. First, I'd be running a few businesses in a division, which was a small job; second, I'd be reporting to a guy I got along with personally but had reservations about working for; and third, perhaps the biggest obstacle, I was used to starting and running banks with a high level of autonomy. In short, regardless of whom I would be reporting to, I would find it a struggle.

Heartache

I ended the consulting contract in mid December and planned to start back full time with MBNA in January after taking off for a couple of weeks. I was in high gear with my workout routine and felt great. On the morning of December 22, 2001, I headed to the YMCA in Kennett Square for my daily habit and had an aggressive work out with cardio and weights, after which I showered and drove the fifteen minutes home. Terry wasn't there. Suddenly I felt nauseous, broke out in a cold sweat, and felt pains in my chest. I had undergone a stress test a few days earlier and passed with flying colors, but the symptoms certainly caught my attention, and I called 911. A short time later the ambulance arrived. I struggled off the sofa to let the medics in and quickly returned to the sofa. Our neighbors across the street were Howard and Marsha Borin. Howard was a pediatrician, and Marsha was an attorney. A couple of minutes after the ambulance arrived, Howard opened the door to see what was going on. The medics were putting me on a gurney preparing me for the trip to Wilmington Hospital. Howard intervened and instructed them to take me to Christiana Hospital in Newark, saying he would call ahead, and they'd be waiting for me.

I called Michelle and she arrived just as we were leaving our house. She followed me to the hospital and contacted Terry.

Thank God for Howard. When we arrived I was whisked to the cardiac center where I was given an EKG. The medics had administered medication on the way and the pain had subsided. The EKG was normal. I was put in a waiting area with drapes dividing each bed with Terry and Michelle at my side. I'm a very poor patient, and since the EKG was normal and the pain had subsided, I wanted to leave. Terry and the nurses insisted I remain for a while. After about a half-hour, the pain started again, only this time it was much more severe. I was wheeled into a private examining room where I blacked out. I don't remember what happened next, but later I found out the nurses brought in the crash cart and applied electric paddles to my chest for defibrillation. I regained consciousness, and I was told I was going to surgery.

I was given a local anesthesia and recall asking the doctor if I was going to die. He said not on his watch, and I'd be okay. Then he performed catheterization and installed a stent. I spent the night in intensive care, was moved to a regular room the next day, and discharged on Christmas Eve. It was my best Christmas present ever, even better than my first pair of ice skates. I was happy to be alive.

Back to Work

I started back at MBNA on a full-time basis in January. It was a big adjustment being in the back seat, and I didn't enjoy it. Obviously, my boss, Jack, wasn't enjoying our relationship either. We simply didn't get along. I don't know if it was the heart attack or the job, but I lost the fire in the belly I had always had. Jack seemed to go out of his way to exclude me from any decision-making processes, and I resented it. I was running four businesses—business card (again), aircraft financing, a new business-to-business initiative (that didn't make any business sense whatsoever), and one interesting venture soliciting delinquent customers for second mortgages. Resulting loans from these solicitations were purchased at a premium by Household Finance and later Countrywide Mortgage Company in Plano, Texas. The profit and loss statement for the mortgage referral business showed a loss, but when the avoided credit losses were factored in, it was a homerun. Nonetheless, as this was the only exciting and interesting business that I was running, I was bored. As time went on, Jack and I became more and more distant and combative, and I wasn't having any fun. To add to the frustration, we had severe differences of opinion on how to run the businesses.

Despite the discouraging situation at work, on the home front we had very pleasant news. We had another blessed event in October 2002 when Michelle and John had their second child, Joelle. She was, and is, beautiful with a vibrant sense of imagination and an unbreakable spirit. She's a delight.

Parting Company

For the thirty-three years I was involved in financial services, I loved virtually every day of work. It was my hobby, and I thought about it twenty-four hours a day. But now, for the first time in my working years, I wasn't happy.

In November I had a meeting with Jack and his boss. It didn't take long to determine that our reporting relationship wasn't workable, and we discussed alternatives. Since it was a rarity for senior officers to leave the bank (I was the only one to ever have done so voluntarily), the bank was heavy with senior management and there really weren't any opportunities to take on other responsibilities.

After months of back and forth, we agreed that I would retire from full-time employment at the bank and once again have a management consulting role. I signed an agreement that would last for five years. It was a reasonable solution to the problem and one that was satisfactory to me. I had been driving a Lexus LS430 as a company car, which had about 3,000 miles on it, and, although it wasn't part of the agreement, the bank gave it to me as a gift. It was a nice gesture and one I appreciated.

Things like that happen at senior levels. Only one person wins. I'm sure Jack thought he won, but I had to admit I was terribly unhappy in that work situation. I would have liked to have left the work community in a more graceful way but it was the best outcome given the circumstances. Sometimes, you just have to move on.

Chapter 16
Moving Forward
2003 to 2004

This time I was convinced it was the right time to slow down. It was February 2003, I was fifty-five years old, and I was tired. I had spent every waking hour working or thinking about work. It was time to dedicate time to Terry, the kids, the grandchildren, and to share time with charitable endeavors. It was time to move forward with our lives. It was just time.

We boarded our horse and had our small British dog, Oudie. We were mobile and free to travel, so we decided to go to our condo in Florida for a couple of months. My stepfather had passed away, and my mother wasn't going to head south, but we convinced her to make the trip and stay with us for a while. After a couple of weeks, I began to think that perhaps living in Florida would be a nice change from cold and snowy winters, instead, enjoying the sun and palm trees. We met Roxanne Jeske, a realtor with Premier Properties, which was a large realty firm in southwest Florida, and we started looking at houses. After visiting scores of houses, we finally found a spec home in a community named Quail West in Naples that we quickly became enamored with. It turned out to be too quickly.

Quail West was similar to many communities in Southwest Florida with two significant differences. The lots were larger than most, and the homes were all single-family dwellings. Amenities included two championship golf courses, a 70,000-square-foot clubhouse, and six tennis courts. Like most, the community was gated with twenty-four hour coverage by guards, most of whom were retired police officers. The landscaping was magnificent, and homes ranged in size from 4,000 to 12,000 thousand square feet. There were roughly 550 building sites, of which about one-third were developed with homes. The residents were successful retirees with only a handful still working. The majority of the residents used these houses as second or third homes.

The House from Hell

The house that caught our eye was a Mediterranean-style home with stucco exterior and tiled roof. It was a one-story plan with soaring ceilings twenty or twenty-five feet in height and had been professionally decorated and furnished. There was an outdoor kitchen on the lanai and a unique swimming pool with a waterfall and hot tub. All in all, it was a beautiful place.

The housing prices in the Naples area were two to three times those of Pennsylvania, and the market was red hot. We signed a contract to purchase the house in March and left a fifteen percent deposit with a six-month closing date, contingent on a satisfactory home inspection.

About a month later, we had visitors and took them to see our new house. When we arrived, we saw part of a wall ripped out in the living room with workers doing repair work. They said they were working on some water damage. I didn't like the looks of it, but their story was plausible, and I let it go. Soon thereafter, we had a home inspection that came back with a long list of deficiencies. We discussed the list with the inspector, our agent, and the builders who asked for an extension of the closing date so they could complete the repairs. I met with our attorney, and she advised me there was no danger in signing the extension.

The work dragged on and on, and I decided to cancel the purchase agreement. I called the builders and told them of my decision. They said fine, but I would forfeit the deposit money. I called our attorney again, and after two meetings and two weeks, I was told that since I signed the extension, I would in fact lose the deposit if I walked. This was a different story from what I was told prior to signing the extension. I was mad as hell, but I was struck.

Here We Go Again

We returned to our home in Pennsylvania. On Terry's birthday, August 5, 2003, I started having chest pains similar to those of my heart attack a couple of years earlier, although not as severe. I asked Terry to drive me to Christiana Hospital and when we arrived, they started with an EKG that didn't show any abnormalities. I met with the doctor and reminded him the same thing happed the last time, and I knew what I felt. He gave me the choice of going home or going into surgery the following morning. I chose the latter and that resulted in another stent. I went home the following day and made an appointment with the cardiologist. I told him this was getting a little old and apparently the medication he had prescribed after the last episode wasn't effective. He responded that I was a "ticking time bomb" and sooner or later one of these events would take my life. I left his office depressed but determined to find a solution.

I called a doctor who had been employed with MBNA and was now associated with the University of Pennsylvania Hospital. I had become acquainted with Dr. Kevin Dolan and held him in high regard. I relayed my conversation with the cardiologist and asked him, if this were his mother or child, whom he would refer them to. I told him not to consider expense or geographic location. I was looking for anyone anywhere in the world who could help me. He said he'd do the research and get back to me.

A couple of weeks later, he called and said he narrowed it down to two doctors, one of whom was in California, and the other in Philadelphia at the University Hospital. I chose Dr. Daniel Rader of the University of Pennsylvania Hospital, and it was one of the best decisions of my life, although even with Kevin's connections, it took me three months to secure an appointment.

Dr. Rader was a widely recognized lipid expert. I conveyed the conversation I had with my cardiologist, and Dr. Rader said he thought my cardiologist had used a poor choice of words. Dr. Rader prescribed a regimen of medication that I remain on today, and I've been free of heart problems since. I'm careful about my diet and exercise daily, but then, I had been careful before meeting him. The medication made the difference, and I'm forever grateful to Dr. Rader and to Dr. Dolan for his research that led me to him.

While our house in Chadds Ford was listed for sale, I took trips to Florida periodically to check on the progress of the work. The day before one of these trips, my sister called to tell me my mother had been visiting them in Virginia, fell, broke her hip, was in the hospital, and scheduled for surgery the next morning. I told her I'd cancel my trip and drive to Virginia that evening, but she said everything was under control. Mom, she said, was resting comfortably, and she would undergo a long recovery period. She suggested I take the trip and be available to help during Mom's recuperation. After giving it some thought, I agreed.

The next morning on April 16, 2004, I drove to the Philadelphia airport to board a flight to Ft. Myers, Florida. I had my cell phone with me but turned it off while going through security. Once through security, I stopped for breakfast and turned my phone on to check for messages. There were two. The first was my sister saying our mother was through with the surgery and that everything went well. The second was from her husband, John, saying something terrible happened, and my mother had passed away. I called and found out that the surgery was successful, but my mother had suffered an aneurysm to her brain and died. I couldn't believe what I was hearing, but it was true. My mother was gone.

I returned home and waited to hear from my sister regarding funeral arrangements. I was in shock over the whole chain of events. A couple of days later, my mother was cremated according to her wishes, and her ashes buried next to Jack's in the VA cemetery in Millsboro, Delaware.

Several days after the services were over, I flew to Florida. The repairs were substantially completed and the inspector went through the entire house again finding two or three incidental items. Several months had passed since we contracted to purchase the house. We finally scheduled the closing for June 1, 2004. In the meantime, we had activity on our Chadds Ford home and sold it shortly after closing in Florida. We thought things would finally get back to normal.

Hurricanes

Whoa! Not just yet. The 2004 hurricane season in Florida produced the record number of major hurricanes since 1964, including six that reached Category 3 or above. Hurricane Charlie was the second most costly hurricane in U.S. history, brushing past Naples but clobbering Punta Gorda and Port Charlotte, located forty-five minutes from our house. That was followed by Category 5 Hurricane Ivan, which surpassed Charlie in terms of losses caused by its damage. I began to wonder if we were going have a peaceful retirement in beautiful sunny southwest Florida.

We stayed in our house for Charlie but left for Orlando the day before Ivan made landfall. During Charlie the wind howled and windows shook, but the only damage we sustained was a fallen large live oak tree in the backyard and miscellaneous debris from fallen foliage. I called the landscaping company and they came with a crane to erect the oak and charged me $1,000 for their work. They fortified it by securing it on three sides with two-by-fours. On our return from Orlando, I spent a second $1,000 to put the same tree up again, securing it with three two-by-sixes. During a later storm, the tree came down again. This time I called the landscaping company and asked them to take the damn thing away and replace it with a couple of palm trees. The lesson learned is you can't beat Mother Nature. I'm an optimist, but I was beginning to have serious doubts about our move to Florida.

During all the stormy weather in Florida, we had a bright ray of sunshine from Delaware when Joanna and Michael brought Bridget into the world after a difficult pregnancy. Bridget was a stunning baby girl and has grown to be an exciting young lady. When she and Joelle get together, look out!

Back in Florida, the residents of Quail West were most welcoming. We moved there in "off season," and things were relatively quiet. The Quail West club was the gathering place on Tuesday nights, and we stopped in a couple of weeks after our move. It was refreshing how many people came to us, introduced themselves, invited us to join them for dinner, and made us feel very much at home. We made lasting friends with people like Lee and Patsy Rattigan, Tom and Jan Kreher, Jim and Barbara Burkett, Jim and Eileen Johnson, and many others. They certainly helped with our transition.

Naples and Bonita Springs had an array of excellent restaurants, and since we liked to go out for dinner regularly, the different venues were exciting. There was the buzz of obvious wealth everywhere. It was not the level of wealth of Monaco, Dubai, or places of that caliber, but it was real wealth nonetheless. The shops, the restaurants, the cars, the boats, and the mansions all spoke of success. It was a very different place from anywhere we'd lived before, and it was fun.

Jamaica Outreach

I now had time to devote to becoming involved in charitable causes. I'd always had a place in my heart for those less fortunate but rarely had the time to become seriously involved or make a commitment. One Sunday while attending mass at St. John the Evangelist, the priest mentioned an upcoming mission trip to their sister parish in Kingston,

Jamaica. The information was in the bulletin and requested parties to call Ann Kerns.

I called and Ann explained that a few years earlier, one of the parishioners suggested to the pastor, Father Tom Glackin, that we share our wealth with a poor parish somewhere. Father Glackin was known for his delegation skills and told the parishioner to find a good match and come back to see him. After searching various places, it was determined St. Pius X, located in the slums of Kingston, would be perfect. Father Tom flew there and met with the pastor, Father Burchell McPherson. They hit it off and agreed to the partnership.

Ann said the trip was to last four days, about twenty-five people would go, the expenses were paid individually, and when we arrived, there would be a multitude of jobs. I signed on for the trip and attended an orientation meeting a week later for those who had never gone before.

The day arrived and we met before sunrise at the church parking lot to take a chartered bus to Ft. Lauderdale, where we would board an Air Jamaica flight for Kingston. Before leaving Naples, everyone stuffed their suitcases with drugs, medical equipment, church supplies, and everything our friends in Kingston had requested us to bring. Upon arrival we went through customs and didn't declare anything. It was an interesting experience to smuggle prescription drugs into a foreign country, and that added to the excitement. No one was caught, and we exited the airport to meet the chartered bus that would take us to St. Pius. Waiting outside was Father Burchell, a man with a shaved head standing about six feet four with broad shoulders and an even broader smile. He was a giant of a man with a warm disposition and instantly likeable. We went directly to the grounds of the church, where an elementary school was also located as well as the medical clinic and food pantry, both of which we stocked.

Mrs. Bradshaw was the secretary. She was very thin, weighing no more than ninety pounds. I soon learned that behind that small frame was a dynamo to be reckoned with. She ruled the roost and, after Father Burchell, was clearly in charge. We also met Boxer (so named for his previous profession) who was the go-to man, a man with a great sense of humor and a willingness to help anyone in any way he could. He lived next door in White Wing, which was a collection of hovels with a central shower and a bathroom located in the middle of the fifty or so shacks.

The children at the school were dressed in uniforms, and all were inquisitive about their visitors. The buildings housed students from first to sixth grade. They approached us and rubbed their hands across our white skin. White people were nowhere to be found near this neighborhood. We were a novelty.

We stayed in a historic building about a half-hour away that had served in many capacities including a hospital. Franciscan nuns now owned the building and grounds and rented rooms to mission groups and charitable groups to help cover expenses. The rooms had cement floors and two or three cots and a bathroom. Some of the rooms had small balconies overlooking beautiful gardens. There was a central kitchen area that was the morning and evening gathering place.

Ann Kerns could really pack them away, you might say, and a couple of years later changed her email address to "beer lady," which is what the Jamaicans called her. Her husband Al was an oncologist and no slouch, and although I usually kept up with them beer for beer, it was sometimes a challenge. Others on the first trip included Joe and Trudy Gagnier and Jeanne Stamant.

Joe was about ten years my senior and became a role model. He was in excellent physical shape and had a very strong work ethic. He and I spent most of the trip painting walls, buildings, and pillars. Jeanne was very organized, very dedicated, and a very nice person. Everyone in the group was congenial, and we remain friends to this day.

All day we worked hard with a lunch break usually prepared by teenage students enrolled in a cooking class on the grounds. Sister Sophia would oversee their activities and make sure we were well fed.

On Sunday, we attended mass in the small church. The choir was absolutely amazing. Music was an area that brought youths together in this troubled neighborhood. The sermon was lengthy, and the church was hot, but nobody noticed. The ceremony took an hour and a half with lots of singing and swaying affirmations of "Amen" during the homily. It was an entirely uplifting experience. Here I sat with people who owned literally nothing, but their faith and outlook were joyous. They were truly inspirational.

I remained involved with the Jamaica Outreach Program for six years, serving on their board for five and traveling to Kingston numerous times. Our outreach expanded to providing several hundred houses, building daycare centers, building a dental clinic to augment the medical clinic, having optical missions provide screening and eyeglasses, bringing doctors two or three times a year to perform cataract surgeries, and establishing a relationship with a second parish. The organization continues today, raising hundreds of thousands of dollars each year to help the impoverished in Kingston. It was a heart-touching experience where I met many wonderful and caring people from both the United States and Jamaica. Sometimes people commented on what a terrific thing I was doing. The reality is I received much more from the people of St. Pius X than I could ever give them.

The Joy of Helping Others

While involved with Jamaica, I was asked to serve on the board of the Immokalee Foundation. Immokalee is located about thirty miles east of Naples. It is home to thousands of Mexicans, Guatemalans, and Haitians who harvest crops, primarily tomatoes. The foundation focused on the youth and offered four-year scholarships to deserving students as well as numerous other programs to advance students in ways to help lift them from poverty. I served for two years and enjoyed the work tremendously.

Father Glackin and I became good friends. He was an extremely intelligent priest who was loved by all who knew him. Even those he regularly beat on the golf course (including me) loved him. I met many people through Father Glackin, but two are especially memorable. The first was Bob Valentine. Bob was a principal in a construction company in Naples. He is a good golfer, an even better handicapper for horse races, and, best of all, a great guy. He and his wife Kathy and Terry and I shared many memorable times together. The second person was Bob Garbinsky along with his wife Barbara. Bob Valentine and Bob Garbinsky were best of friends, and we were happy to have known both of them.

Father Glackin had been at St. John's for about twenty years. He was directly involved in raising money years earlier to build St. John the Evangelist Church and, years later, an even bigger mission church nearby named St. Agnes. He decided it would be appropriate to establish a parish council and asked me to be president. I balked since I didn't have any idea how to establish or run such an organization. I quickly experienced his persuasive powers and before I knew what happened, I was the president of the new parish council. I maintained that position for two years.

Terry and I worked as volunteers for the soup kitchen at the Guadalupe Center in Immokalee once or twice a month as needed. The center fed about one hundred people, five days a week. We met people from all walks of life who were polite and thankful.

Chapter 17

Time for a
Change of Scenery

Naples was a beautiful place, but after a few years, we began to feel like we were in a rut. The pastime for most residents was golf. Many people would golf several days each and every week. The other pastime was the cocktail hour, which seemed to creep in a little earlier each year. I found I was soon involved in both activities.

Golf was never my game. I took lessons and practiced regularly, which was easy since the course was literally just beyond our backyard. I reached a point where I could pretty consistently shoot in the low to mid nineties, which meant I could play with even scratch golfers, since I wasn't an embarrassment. However, the likelihood of my dramatically improving my game was remote. I have often remarked that golf is the one activity in my life where I was content with mediocrity. I enjoyed the camaraderie and the outdoors much more than the sport.

I did have one moment of glory on the links on May 1, 2008, when I shot a hole-in-one on the second hole of the Preserve Course at Quail West. Fortunately, Father Glackin was with me. When we finished the game, I announced my feat at the pro shop. The pro looked at me with a jaundiced eye, but I had an excellent witness. I was awarded a plaque and $1,000 gift certificate from the pro shop. I still have jackets, hats, shirts, and belts with the Quail West logo.

In 2005, we were invited to the wedding of a friend of Terry's named Stacy Parvey. The wedding was to be held in Ocala, Florida, and we accepted. Terry had met Stacy years earlier when she attended equestrian camp at Hilltop Farm in Maryland.

Since then, Stacy had become a proficient dressage rider and had developed quite a following. The groom was Olaf Larsson—a talent in his own right—who worked for Chester Weber, a world-renowned carriage driver.

The wedding was a unique affair with the bride arriving to the outdoor ceremony site in a horse-drawn carriage. The reception was terrific; we met several people and had a wonderful time. Seated at our table were Aileen and Sean Daly. Terry had met Aileen through Hilltop Farm in Maryland years earlier, and we had fun reacquainting. Aileen had previously lived in Naples but had relocated to Aiken, South Carolina. She was exuberant in describing Aiken and suggested we fly there to take a look. We agreed and said we would in the near future.

In the spring of 2006, we decided to see what Aiken was all about. We took a flight to Augusta, Georgia, via Charlotte, North Carolina, and drove the forty-five minutes to Aiken, South Carolina. Aileen had recommended a realtor, and we booked a room at the historic Willcox Hotel. When we arrived, we were led to a beautiful suite. I said there must have been a mistake, but we found out that Aileen was a friend of the manager and had arranged for us to be upgraded. What a treat.

Aiken, South Carolina

Aiken is a one-of-a-kind town. Among its unique characteristics is an area known as Hitchcock Woods. It is the largest urban forest in the United States with about 2,100 acres containing seventy miles of sandy trails for walking or horseback riding. Also within its city limits, Aiken sports the Aiken

Training Track, which serves to give young thoroughbreds experience for the racetrack.

The city of Aiken offers beautiful tree-lined streets and dirt roads surrounded by stately historic residences. It boasts a lively downtown scene, and it is home to the University of South Carolina, Aiken, which has some 5,000 students. More than forty polo fields dot the Aiken County landscape; and Palmetto Golf Course, one of the oldest in the country, is within its city limits. It offers every equine discipline and has a fascinating history as the winter colony of many of the wealthiest families in twentieth-century America.

We toured for two days looking at several "Winter Colony" homes. These houses ranged from 6,000 to 12,000 square feet in size; they were built in the 1930s; and they were architecturally interesting. The Winter Colony people built these homes for their use while visiting Aiken during winters. The downside was that most of them needed considerable renovation. We also looked at new construction and several homes that were for sale. The housing prices were startling in a pleasant way. I suppose we had become accustomed to housing costs in Naples; maybe we had lost perspective on what was realistic. Imagine our delight when we discovered that the cost to build a new home in Aiken was about a third of that in southwest Florida!

We were intrigued by this small town and knew we'd come back for another look. Over the next month, we discussed living in Florida, compared it to South Carolina, and we knew we were ready for a change of scenery. We decided to keep looking for a house in Aiken and to put our home in Naples on the market, expecting to sell it within six months.

I asked the realtor in Aiken to send me all multiple listings for houses within the parameters I set. Many of the homes were located in Woodside Plantation, a massive planned golf course community. Although Woodside was a beautiful place, we had had enough of living in a planned community and ruled that out. We traveled back to Aiken again in March, joined by our friends Bob and Charlene Edwards, and continued the search. After looking at just about every house on the market, we concluded we should refocus our search and look for land to build on.

Finally!

We started our search for the elusive "perfect" property. That entailed several more trips to Aiken. Finally, in January 2007, we found what we were looking for. We drove down a dirt road about a half-mile from the pavement and saw a beautiful twenty-four-acre parcel of land with a soft incline leading to a plateau on top. The property had just been harvested of its pine trees, and it was covered with scraps of forest, making it very difficult to walk on. But we persevered, and I knew this was it. Terry questioned how we could convert this mess into a horse farm, but I knew this was the right place for us. We learned that coniferous trees don't create a root structure that lasts beyond the time stumps are uprooted as opposed to deciduous trees that do.

With that, I contacted the Ledford brothers who were in the business of clearing land, and obtained a bid to pluck every single stump out of the ground and burn them. I took their bid into consideration, and we made an offer on the property; the owners countered, we countered, and they accepted. We closed on the property a month later, and Doug and Darrell began work on the stump project. It took several months, but eventually they completed the work, estimating they had pulled up and burned between 8,000 and 10,000 pine tree stumps.

Following the clearing, we hired a fellow named Ronnie Cook who was well known in the area as an expert hay man. We decided to sprig the entire property with Tifton 44, a hybrid Bermuda grass. It was in the middle of summer, and before they could sprig, they wanted to run their Rotavator, a machine with rotating blades that break up soil, over our land to loosen the soil and pull up any remaining roots. Due to the draught, that was delayed until it rained. A few weeks later after we received much needed rain, they cranked up their equipment, gathered the remaining debris, and sprigged about twenty of the twenty-four acres. The remaining four were cleared but remained sparsely wooded.

I hired a draftsman in Aiken who had been recommended to me as capable of drafting the design for our house. I spend considerable time and money defining what we wanted to build and even flew his assistant to Naples to show her some design ideas. After several months and $10,000, I realized what we wanted was beyond his capability.

We interviewed several builders in Aiken and narrowed the search down to one. Steve Kisner had been building houses in Aiken for twenty-five years. We walked through several homes he had built, and between the quality of his work and his personality, we decided he was "the horse for the course."

We told Steve of our false start with the draftsman, and he recommended a fellow in Martinez, Georgia. We met with him several times and reviewed several drafts, but again, he didn't produce what we were looking for.

Finally, the light bulb came on. The house we bought in Chadds Ford was a beautiful design and one that was an award winner. The architect was a lady in Philadelphia named Ann Capron. I searched the Internet, and after looking under various names, found the firm of McIntyre-Capron. I called and discovered that Ann had retired, but there were other architects in the firm. I made an appointment to meet with Murray Spencer. Terry and I flew to Philadelphia for a visit with the kids, and we met with Murray. After an hour, I was convinced we were on the right track.

I hired Doug and Darrell to drive by every couple of weeks and call me with a report on how the grass was coming along. With each report, I received more encouraging news. About six weeks after we sprigged, I decided to fly to Aiken to see for myself and was surprised to find a bumper crop of weeds across the entire property. I called Doug, and he and Ronnie met me there. Doug had been riding by, but hadn't walked over the grass. From the car everything looked nice and green. My concerns were put aside after Ronnie told me this was normal in the germination process and he'd spray 2-4-D, an inexpensive herbicide that would get rid of the weeds but would not affect the new grass. He sprayed, and on my next visit, we had a handsome crop of grass.

A Dead Florida Real Estate Market

When we bought our house in Naples, the market was on fire with demand far outpacing supply. The opposite was true now. We initially thought we would list the house, and it would be sold just like every other time we'd put a house on the market. We had numerous showings and some second showings and many open houses. The thing we didn't have was an offer. The market had a glut of homes, interest rates were falling, and people were convinced prices and rates would fall further. Inertia hit and everything was at a standstill. Then the stock market crashed in September 2008, bringing the economy to a screeching halt. I called our architect in Philadelphia and told him to stop working on the plans, to put them in the freezer, and that if and when we ever sold our Florida home, we'd resurrect them.

We were on vacation in Italy that September and news of the unraveling of financial markets was everywhere. Each day the news got worse. We returned from Rome on October 6 and the market was in a free fall. It kept dropping and dropping until it leveled out after about a fifty percent drop. The dire situation hit home: we had the Naples property on the market where there were hundreds of homes for sale and the world was in financial shock. It wasn't a particularly good time to be selling property.

As time went on, we became more and more discouraged. We began to think we'd never fulfill the dream of owning our farm.

Bite the Bullet and Sell!

We went on a vacation to Italy and Southern France in May 2009. Shortly after our return, out of the blue we received an offer on the house. Terry called me, said we had an offer and that I should call our realtor. The realtor told me the offer, and my first reaction was it wasn't an offer, it was an insult. The offer was an amount about twenty percent less than what we had paid for the house five years earlier. The plus side was the offer was a cash deal with no contingencies other than a home inspection and the buyer wanted to close in thirty days. I'd made money on deals and I'd lost money on deals, but if I agreed to this deal, it would be the most money I ever lost on a single transaction.

Terry felt we should take the offer, saying if we didn't, we may well wind up being too old to run a farm. It reminded me of that time I wanted to buy a boat while living in Annapolis. Three months later Terry asked me if I'd found a boat I liked. I told her I hadn't had time to look. She then said if I didn't have time to look, what would I do with a boat if I owned one? She was right then and she was right now. Prices of homes kept falling, the stock market was anemic, and unemployment was rising. Hell, we were in a recession. I lost sleep thinking about the rotten offer and finally agreed with Terry. I held my nose, closed my eyes, and signed the contract.

Next I called our realtor in Aiken and asked her to look for a house that we could rent during construction. My second call was to our architect, Murray Spencer in Philadelphia, telling him to take the plans out of the freezer and to work on completing them. My last call was to Steve Kisner to tell him we would be in Aiken in a month, that the plans were being finalized, and we were ready to move forward with building our new house.

On several trips to Aiken, we met with various barn builders and had decided on a fellow named Mark Hopkins from Box Springs, Georgia (I love the name of the town). He had built a magnificent barn nearby for new acquaintances, and the quality of his workmanship and materials were outstanding.

Knowing we'd be in temporary housing for about a year, I decided to pack our belongings myself and catalog each box so we would have a fighting chance of finding items if needed while in storage. This was a monumental task, and I wound up with some 200 boxes. Terry spoke with Aileen Daly, who agreed to board our two horses, and I flew to Aiken to look at rental houses. The availability of rental houses was limited, which made the process easy. I decided on a small two-story home in a community named Houndslake North. I met with the owners and signed a ninety-day lease.

Step One of a Four-Step Dance

As part of the lease agreement, the owners were to clean out the two-car garage, which was so packed with stuff they were embarrassed to show it to me. We had a new Corvette, and I wanted it and my favorite car—the Porsche—kept in the garage.

Moving day finally arrived. The movers loaded the boxes onto their truck, and Terry, Oudie, and I moved out of our house and stayed at the Hilton Hotel in Naples. We had the Lexus and Porsche packed to the gills with breakable and valuable items.

We arranged to ship the Corvette. The next morning we left after breakfast and traveled as far as St. Mary's, Georgia, just beyond Jacksonville, Florida, where we spent the night and continued the following morning, arriving in Aiken in the early afternoon. When we arrived at the rental house, the owners were loading a U-Haul with the contents of the garage. Once the truck was full, they decided they weren't moving any more items, leaving only one bay available for one car. Not a good way to start, Terry and I agreed, but we were over a barrel.

We kept the Corvette in the garage and the other two cars in the driveway. The neighborhood had towering trees and the leaves and debris created havoc with my sports car. The Corvette rode low to the ground, and there were several intersections in town where the bottom of the front bumper scraped the ground. We decided to sell the red Corvette, listed it online at Auto Trader, and sold it to a fellow from Texas, who flew up, wired money, and drove it away. We replaced it with a Ford F150 truck. This wasn't nearly the culture shock I experienced in 1970 when I sold my Corvette and replaced it with the Fiat station wagon. We still had the Porsche, and we would need the truck for the farm.

Once we settled into the house, we realized how absolutely filthy it was. We cleaned and cleaned to make it livable. All in all, it wasn't a good experience, culminating in our having to call the pest control company to fumigate for fleas, which Oudie had apparently contracted from their dog. The ninety days were coming up, and their realtor called to see if we wished to extend the lease. After I stopped laughing, I went through the litany of issues we'd experienced and simply said, "No."

Step Two of a Four-Step Dance

Once again we were hunting for a rental and once again we found slim pickings. We located a house in a community backing up to Hitchcock Woods. Obviously, the owners had numerous animals, which even a blind Ray Charles could readily see by looking at the carpets. The house was attractive other than the animal artwork on the rugs. We signed a six-month lease with the stipulation that all carpets would be professionally cleaned and that Aiken Pest Control would fumigate to ensure that any crawling critters met their demise.

Oudie was old and growing senile. We had watched her slow down for years but her decline was accelerating. She had cataracts, was almost totally blind, and she was having difficulty hearing. We knew the end was in sight, but after fifteen years, it was difficult to say goodbye. We went to Delaware and Pennsylvania for Christmas and boarded Oudie with instructions to groom her before we picked her up. We made arrangements with our veterinarian to put her down, and after we picked her up, we took her there. We had both become very attached to that little dog that I didn't want any part of when we bought her in England. She was, and is, deeply missed. Dogs ask for so little and give so much.

Meanwhile, our architect was completing the final design for our house, and I was in contact with him. I've always been a frustrated architect and worked on the design for hundreds of hours. I enjoyed it, and working with Murray was a delight. Once the plans were complete, it was time to find out how much the construction would cost. After several discussions with Steve

Kisner, we signed a contract, and he applied for the building permit.

We were having the same discussions with Mark Hopkins regarding the barn and apartment. I had already hired a fellow named Matthew Yoder to construct a forty-by-sixty-foot storage barn, Michael Johnson to install four-board fencing around the perimeter of the property and the paddocks, and Kevin Warner to install an Olympic-size dressage-riding ring. I loved having all the balls in the air.

Step Three of a Four-Step Dance

We extended our lease for a few months while the barn and apartment were being completed, and, finally, after a year of nomadic existence, we moved into the apartment adjacent to the barn and across the field from the house. Subsequently we moved the horses to our farm.

The apartment was very comfortable, but I wondered if we would enjoy it since we hadn't lived in so small a place since our apartment in Annapolis just after we married. I rationalized that we would be there for about six months, as the house also had already been under construction for six months, and it was due to be completed in March 2011. After a few nights, my fears were allayed. We loved living in the apartment, and as the house construction progressed, I sometimes asked out loud why we were building such a big house.

Step Four of a Four-Step Dance

Spring arrived, and with it, the completion of the house. We loved everything about it. Both the house and the barn were everything we could wish for, and we were thrilled. As beautiful as the house was, it took us three weeks before we finally moved in. We had become so attached to the apartment that we weren't in a hurry.

Life in Aiken

After all the construction projects, our dream of owning a small farm finally came true. It wasn't easy to accomplish—buying land, living in two rental houses as well as the barn apartment, and taking a beating on the sale of our house in Naples—but we did it. I've often said you can put a square peg in a round hole if you're determined and have a sledgehammer. We gained a sense of accomplishment and joyful anticipation about our future in Aiken.

Now that we are settled in, we feel that we belong here. No more trips to the storage building to retrieve an obscure item. You'll remember when I packed the 200-plus boxes, I numbered them and itemized their contents. When the movers arrived, I instructed them to load even numbered boxes on one side of the storage unit and odd numbered boxes on the other to make it easier to locate items. After a half-hour, I went inside, and both even and odd numbered boxes were intermingled. I subsequently discovered the fellows unloading couldn't read. So much for that plan.

We've found everyone we've met to be interesting and welcoming. The president of the Aiken Chamber of Commerce has an expression that says it all, "If you're lucky enough to live in Aiken, you're lucky enough."

We joined a social dinner club named the Green Boundary Club, where I serve on the board. Terry is on the board of the Aiken Community Medical Clinic, and we're social members of the Edisto River Hunt. Additionally, Terry gives dressage lessons and stays connected to many people in the horse community.

Aiken is a very social town with people having dinner parties regularly. The Aiken Triple Crown is held here each spring with three events over consecutive weekends. The first is the Horse Trials where young horses race for short distances. The second is the Aiken Steeplechase, and the third is Polo. Thousands of people attend each event.

There are the annual Lobster Races, St. Patrick's Day parties, the Christmas Parade with Santa riding in a horse-drawn sleigh, the Katydid carriage driving weekend, the Blessing of the Hounds in Hitchcock Woods on Thanksgiving, hunt breakfasts, hunt dinners, Dining Around Aiken Weekend, and the list goes on and on. I can't imagine anyone being bored in Aiken.

We love living in the country. We are thirteen miles and eighteen minutes from downtown. It used to take us that long to drive five miles in Naples. The pace in Aiken is laid back, where one seldom hears someone honking their horn if the person in front of them doesn't gun it when the traffic signal turns green.

With the help of a local farmer named Fred Plunkett, I have learned how to operate a tractor and various farm implements, and I am comfortable handling the horses even on the windiest of days. I work outside during the spring, summer, and fall, most of the day spreading fertilizer or herbicides, weed whacking, cutting grass, repairing fences, or just puttering around. Terry has become adept at operating the tractor and the cutter, and between the two of us, we make short work of the grass. Three years ago she bought me a chain saw for my birthday, and this past year it was a 200-gallon sprayer for the tractor. True love!

We replaced Oudie with Lotta, an eighty-pound female German shepherd that had the good fortune to be born on 1-1-11. Terry's two horses are retired and aging gracefully. Like her beloved horses, Terry takes aging in stride, while I struggle with it.

Good Times and Bad

My life has been exciting, never boring, and I have been fortunate to have my wife by my side every step of the way. I sometimes wonder if, when she spoke our marriage vows forty-four years ago, saying, "In good times and in bad," she knew what she was getting herself into.

When my father died at age forty-four, I assumed my life would be similarly short. Perhaps that belief was what drove me to try to do as much as possible as quickly as I could. I've been an impatient person for most of my life, and I've been intolerant of people who say, "I can't do it," or "I haven't had a chance." I believe America is the most extraordinary and remarkable country in the world and that those of us who have the good fortune to live here have both opportunities and obligations. I also believe that success—no matter how you measure it—is available for everyone who wants it badly enough and works hard enough to get it.

It's been a good journey all in all, and I have enjoyed sharing it in these pages. To sum up, I will leave you with five axioms that have served me well over the years:

1. There's a difference between trying and doing.

2. If you strive to do all the right things all the time, things will work out.

3. Tell the truth—it's easier to remember.

4. Winston Churchill's famous quote—"Never, never, never give up."

5. Enjoy your life.

So I bring this story to an end. Reviewing my life, I think of Buffalo where it began—a city with its ups and downs. As with my hometown, I've been up and I've been down.

Up is better.

Coda

I've been told that writing a book is like having a baby. It takes about nine months. During these months I've indulged in something I have rarely done—I've looked back. Now, it's time to look to the present. For the benefit of the reader, I thought I would bring you up to date on several of the people within these pages...

Our first daughter, Michelle Blewett, is a single mother living in Lincoln University, Pennsylvania, with her two children, Tyler, who is thirteen, and Joelle, who is ten. Additionally, she has a special relationship with Rob, a surveyor, a farmer, a jack of all trades, and, most important, a person with a terrific positive influence on Michelle and the children's lives. Michelle has continued in the banking business and has a successful career with Bank of America. Tyler plays on basketball and football teams and is a walking sports encyclopedia. As for Joelle, we would be very surprised if she doesn't wind up as an artist or performing on Broadway. Both children are honor students.

Our second daughter, Joanna Schmuff, lives in Wilmington, Delaware, and is married to Michael. She, too, continues in banking with a successful career at Barclays Bank. When they were married, Michael was employed at MBNA America bank. He followed his dream, took helicopter lessons, and is now a medevac helicopter pilot. He also flies fixed-wing airplanes as a hobby and loves extreme sports such as wake boarding. Bridget is nine, precocious, and like her cousin, is most likely heading for an acting career. Bridget is also an honor student.

Richard Blewett, my uncle, still lives in Buffalo and still practices law. An interesting fact is he's never lived more than forty miles from the house he was born in. He is now eighty-seven years old and in excellent health.

Jean Blewett, my aunt, developed cancer and passed away in 2007. She was my mother for three years and a wonderful person. I'm forever grateful to her for her love and understanding.

Timothy E. Blewett, Sr., "Poppy," lived to be eighty-eight year old and passed away in 1969. He provided valuable life lessons and taught me how to do many things.

Anna Blewett, "Grammy," lived to age ninety-four (ninety-three if you were to ask her) and passed away in 1979. She was the kindest person in the world, always there for me and generous with her affection. She is missed.

Tim Blewett, my brother, lives with his wife, Florence, in New Albany, Ohio. Tim graduated from Canisius College and had a successful career at MacDonald's Corporation. Although retired, he nonetheless likes to stay active and works part-time at Trader Joe's. Florence works for Home Depot as a kitchen designer. They have three children, Brendan, Caitlin, and Evan. Brendan is active in the music industry, while Caitlin is an advertising executive in London, and Evan is completing his law degree at DePaul University.

Patrice Wolff, my sister, lives with her husband, John, in Spotsylvania, Virginia. John is an executive at the American Bankers Association in Washington, D.C. Patrice graduated from Catholic University and went on to graduate from nursing school. They have three children, Jennifer, Tracy, and Kelly. Jennifer is a medical doctor, married, and has two children. Tracy is married, has one child, and is a successful sales manager for NV Homes. Kelly is recently married and works for Ryan Homes.

Tom Groft, my longtime good friend and business associate, is retired and returned to his hometown of Westminster, Maryland. He and his wife Nancy Lee also have a summer home in Ocean City, Maryland, or, as Marylanders say, a "place by the shore, Hon."

Al Lerner, former chairman of the board of MBNA Corporation, was diagnosed with brain cancer in 2001 and passed away in 2002.

Charlie Cawley, former president, CEO, and chairman of MBNA bank, lives with his wife Julie in Camden, Maine. Of all the people I've met in my life, Charlie is probably the most interesting. It's rare that one can look at a company and recognize the overwhelming impact one individual had in its success. That was certainly the case with MBNA and Charlie. He is a colorful guy, determined, intense, generous, and likeable. I was fortunate to have had the opportunity to work with him.

Tom Hudson, partner in the law firm Hudson Cook, LLP, has been a great friend since 1974. He and I have enjoyed many good times and his legal advice has been invaluable. In many ways, Tom was inspirational in my taking on this endeavor, as I was impressed by a book he wrote about his early years growing up in Acworth, Georgia. He and his wife Lily Grace live in Gambrills, Maryland, part of the year and on Pawleys Island, South Carolina, the remaining time.

Stan Burns, former president of Chase Bank of Maryland, died unexpectedly at the age of fifty-five of a sudden cardiac event in April 1992. After negotiating the acquisition of three troubled savings and loan associations for Chase Manhattan, Stan went on to become an author, consultant, and served on various boards. He was truly a gentleman and a good friend.

Father John G. Sturm, former prefect of discipline at Canisius High School, died at the age of ninety-five in 2012. I credit Father Sturm for trying to keep me on the straight and narrow during my two years at Canisius. After serving as prefect of discipline for eighteen years (from 1952 until 1970), he said masses at St. Michael's church in Buffalo and was known for his colorful reflections on life and spirituality as well as his folksy homilies. Often he was referred to as "The Downtown Priest."

Father Robert G. Beiter, the priest who married us in 1969, has been our friend ever since. He retired five years ago at the age of seventy; he still lives in Buffalo and comes for a visit every year. In October 2013, he will celebrate fifty years as a priest, and we intend to be there to celebrate with him. We've enjoyed his great sense of humor, his friendship, and our two trips to Europe together.

Mark McCormack, founder and chairman of International Management Group, passed away in 2003 at the age of seventy-two from a cardiac event he suffered four months earlier. He is another example of a man who single-handedly built a powerhouse company. I'll always be grateful for the generous help he provided in the negotiations with Wimbledon.

Ray Nichols, former executive at Maryland National Bank, is still active with his entrepreneurial activities and lives in Annapolis, Maryland. Ray was a great person to work with, and I enjoyed the years we were associated. He is yet another self-made man who worked hard to build successful companies.

Ed Dyas, my friend who had the courage to invest in The Money Tree and also provide me with employment when I was desperate, is semi-retired and lives on the Severn River in Severna Park, Maryland. "Frog" has been a successful businessman, an entrepreneur, and a hell of a lot of fun to know.

Dick Gessner, one of the most talented entertainers I've had the pleasure to know, is retired and living in Ellenton, Florida. There was never a time when we went to hear Dick that we didn't have an absolutely great time. What a talent!

Father Thomas Glackin, a scholar, excellent golfer, and all-around good guy. Father Tom and I became great friends in Naples even though I never once beat him in a round of golf. His significant accomplishments in life have been an inspiration to many, many people, and I'm fortunate to have him as a friend. He's a great guy.

Harry "Car Czar" Schmidt, the best car credit guy ever, passed away in 2004 from a cardiac event. Harry was a true Baltimore native, with the thick accent and the slang expressions associated with the east side of Baltimore. He was as intense about work as he was about having fun. Harry was a good friend and a person I could always count on. I think of Harry often and miss him.

Doug Perkins, the person who withstood the temptations of a stripper on his birthday, passed away from brain cancer in 2004. Doug had a wild sense of humor and was always fun to be around. His work ethic was excellent, and, like Harry, he could always be counted on for anything we needed.

Bill Van Blarcom, a great marketing guy and good friend, passed away in 2004 from prostrate cancer. Bill was one of the most talented marketing people I've had the good fortune to know. We sure had a lot of fun together.

Bill and Elaine Sisler, our friends from Buffalo and later Baltimore, are living in Acton, Massachusetts. Bill is the president of the Harvard Press, and Elaine is very active in theatrical performances and spiritual dance. We had many, many great times together but haven't seen each other for about four years. We need to do that! By the way, I still have the bull trophy.

Len Kidwell, typically referred to as "Kid Lendwell," was a guy I met at Major Finance and kept in touch with while we moved from bank to bank. He went into commercial lending while I stayed in the consumer business. As soon as I had an opportunity that met his skills, I called him and brought him to MBNA. Len is now retired and working as a volunteer for SCORE. He and his wife Maryann live in Bethany Beach, Delaware. As with other members of "the team," we had many great and fun times together.

Jerry Dunne, who I first met at Major Finance and who later married my wife's sister, lives in Falls Church, Virginia. Jerry works at the U.S. Senate Credit Union, and his wife, Kathy, is a consultant for the mortgage business. Jerry has several qualities, but one stands out among the others: he's one of the most bighearted guys in the entire world.

Wendel, or Eliten, as he was more formally known. I mentioned in the book that he was a special horse and, therefore, he deserves one last accolade. I talked about his travels and his kindheartedness, but there is a postscript. Wendel retired and stayed at the farm of our good friends Scott and Susanne Hassler in Chesapeake City, Maryland, until he passed away. In his retirement years he was a companion for a blind horse. As with everything he ever did, he performed his duties admirably.